INSTRUCTOR'S GUIDE

for use with

NEW WORLDS
OF
LITERATURE

Writings from
America's Many Cultures

Second Edition

AUTHORS' NOTES

Carolina Hospital is a Cuban-American poet and essayist, and is an associate professor of English at Miami-Dade Community College, Kendall Campus, where she teaches writing and literature. In 1988, she published *Cuban American Writers: Los Atrevidos*, an anthology of Cuban-American writers in the United States. In addition to publishing in numerous magazines and newspapers and giving poetry readings, Hospital often lectures and gives workshops on the literature of Latinos in the United States.

Carlos Medina is an educator who has served as a consultant for the State of Florida Department of Education on curriculum and professional development. Currently, he teaches at Ransom-Everglades Preparatory School in Coconut Grove, Florida. He also writes children's fiction.

INSTRUCTOR'S GUIDE

for use with

NEW WORLDS
OF
LITERATURE

Writings from
America's Many Cultures

Second Edition

Carolina Hospital
Miami-Dade Community College, Kendall

Carlos Medina
Ransom-Everglades Preparatory School

W. W. Norton & Company
New York • London

ISBN 0-393-96355-1

W. W. Norton & Company, Inc., 500 Fifth Avenue, New York, NY 10110
W. W. Norton & Company Ltd., 10 Coptic Street, London WC1A 1PU

1 2 3 4 5 6 7 8 9 0

CONTENTS

USING THE INSTRUCTOR'S GUIDE

The purpose of the *Instructor's Guide* is to assist you, the instructor, in using *New Worlds of Literature*, Second Edition, in the classroom. We've organized the *Guide* into four sections, each with a specific application relevant to the anthology. These sections complement and expand upon the materials in the text in various ways.

The first part, entitled Reading and Writing with *New Worlds of Literature*, is an essay that addresses the teaching of multicultural literature and writing. In it we first explore attitudes and approaches that we hope will help the instructor in dealing with this culturally diverse body of literature in a classroom that may or may not be culturally diverse. We then discuss several approaches to teaching writing in an effective and meaningful way, and offer suggestions on how to weave the reading materials of the anthology into a course about writing. Another section of the introductory essay discusses the anthology selections in terms of their value for the students.

The second part is the Chapter-by-Chapter Guide to the anthology. It suggests possible interpretations for each work and offers additional questions and activities designed to enhance the analytical and creative skills of students. For each chapter, we have developed several components.

First, we discuss each chapter's theme, summarizing the main ideas of the thematic introductions in the anthology, adding further reflections on those ideas, and providing a Pre-Reading Activity. The themes lend themselves to personal reflections by students; it is useful if students give thought to each topic before they discuss the views of others. The Pre-Reading Activity section furnishes step-by-step suggestions for this process.

The Chapter-by-Chapter Guide continues with a discussion of each work, including the following:
- A brief biographical summary of each author.
- The genre, length of each work, and page number where it is found in the text.

- A discussion of the work that includes an historical context for the work where applicable, challenging topics to explore with the class, analysis of areas touched upon in the Study Questions at the end of each work, and a brief statement concerning the literary element for that chapter in the anthology. For example, "Setting" is discussed at the end of chapter 1; therefore, references have been made to the role of setting in each of the works in that chapter.
- Suggested Assignments, inquiries aimed at engaging students' interpretive and intuitive skills. The questions are designed to elicit responses in terms of justification, forced choice, categorization, value judgments, and role playing. The questions are open-ended and reflect on themes, ironies, contradictions, and possible interpretations of the work. We hope they will lead to an exciting intellectual discourse in the classroom.
- The Encounter Activity, designed to provide a creative, experiential, interactive activity that will stimulate the students to examine their own values and attitudes. These activities can serve as a springboard for a writing assignment or can be used to generate class discussion. The Encounter Activity challenges the creative as well as the analytical mind of the students.
- The Craft of Writing, with a two-fold purpose. First, it complements the discussion of the literary element in the Afterword of each chapter in the anthology. Second, it offers teaching strategies to help the students in using the Writing about the Reading segments of the anthology.
- A commentary on the Student Writing found at the end of each chapter in the anthology. The commentary offers suggestions on how to utilize the student writing sample within the context of the anthology and the classroom.

After the Chapter-by-Chapter Guide there is a summary of the Writing about Literature segment at the end of the anthology, which includes suggestions for how this segment might be used in class. Finally, the *Guide* offers sample syllabi for a fifteen-week and a ten-week writing course at the beginning or intermediate level.

Reading and Writing with
New Worlds of Literature

The editors of *New Worlds of Literature* have put together a selection of short stories, poems, plays, and essays on a range of subjects that reflect the interests and concerns of a diverse group of American writers. The anthology is suitable for an introductory course in the study of literature or as a reader for a course in composition; we assume that reading and writing play an important role in your class.

In their introduction to the anthology, the editors outline their rationale and objective in choosing contemporary literature by non-mainstream writers. As they state, their intent is not to replace Sophocles or Whitman, but to provide an option of quality literature that illustrates the true diversity of North American culture.

Their goal is to present literature that explores our own times and places, to present to students literature that is relevant to their lives. These texts will, in turn, provide a perspective through which to see and appreciate literature of the past; if students can relate to a universal theme presented in a contemporary context that is accessible to them, then they will be better able to transfer that perspective to texts with a similar theme written in a different historical context.

We would add that the literature in this anthology should be offered to students for two additional reasons. The first is that "it's about time." While these writers are contemporary, the issues, cultures, beliefs, and concerns they explore are not new and, in the Native-Americans, are even older than the first Europeans in the Americas. It is also true for African Americans, Mexican Americans, and Cuban Americans whose presence in this country can be traced back for centuries. Native Americans, African Americans, Hispanic Americans, and Asian Americans have been producing literature of high quality in this country for a long time. The question arises, then, of who was listening to these voices outside of their own cultural group? It's hard to tell, since the assumption has been, and in many cases continues to be, that American literature is that of white Euro-pean Americans—usually males. This we know is not true, nor has it been true for centuries. The diversity of writing in this anthology offers a balance that reflects a truer representation of the variety of cul-tures and beliefs that make up this country.

This country has always been a land of immigrants; this is nothing new. What is new is the attitude that diversity can be an asset, that assimilation or the "melting pot" theory is no longer seen by sociolo-gists as the only model for a healthy society. The increase of cultural diffusion in the United States offers a challenge to its citizens: to arrive at an understanding of one another without losing the cultural ele-ments that define each person. As more groups maintain the language and culture of their heritage, while adapting to American social and political institutions, a person's tolerance and willingness to accept diversity in the society will become critical assets in order to get along. The selections in this anthology can serve as a step for greater under-standing and empathy.

With these pieces, your students can explore stereotypes, preju-dices, expectations, misconceptions, and beliefs. They will encounter cultural, social, sexual, and religious worlds that are new to them, or perhaps familiar but not often depicted in the literature they read. They will relate to some of the works and be challenged by others. At the least, the selections will force them to see beyond their own super-ficial perceptions; at the most, they will enhance their cultural under-standing and empathy for the conditions and circumstances of others.

We take the liberty of suggesting that you explore your own ste-reotypes and expectations of what you will find in this anthology. As humans, we teachers are not immune from these limitations. We believe strongly that we cannot demand from our students what we are not willing to give. We must give the literature a chance to teach us and touch us in some way. Through the process of reading and writing about this literature, we may all discover how similar we ultimately are.

We believe that literature can enhance any writing course, and that the selections in the anthology work particularly well as sparks for writing. Literature introduces us to written voices that generally reveal much more than is possible from verbal communication. The written form allows for an emotional detachment that urges a clearer relation-ship and understanding of those very emotions. It also allows for the manifestation of ideas and attitudes in creative ways that encourages and stimulates new perspectives. The literature in this anthology will introduce student readers not only to new external worlds but also to new approaches to their own world of ideas and attitudes through the written form. The combination of reading and writing is a powerful one in promoting critical thinking, creativity, increased intellectual rigor, and awareness of others as well as of ourselves. We will continue this introduction by sharing certain strategies and approaches that have helped us to make the experience of reading and writing more meaningful, effective, and pleasurable for us and our students.

One of the first things we like to deal with in our courses is the unease with writing many students have. By the time we get our students, many are already predisposed to dislike the activity. They associate it with failure, an atmosphere of constant correction, or personal embarrassment. These attitudes are often based on the misconception that writing is something that should come naturally to them, and that if they have to labor at it they must not be good at it. For this reason, we emphasize writing as a process, one that begins with reading. Most instructors of writing emphasize process in writing—that is, working in stages and on multiple drafts. However, we like to add reading as an ongoing preliminary stage of writing that must take place before even a topic is chosen.

Since reading is a central part of our courses, even if we are emphasizing the skill of writing, we discuss how ideas come from other ideas, and that without constant reading to stimulate both our ideas and our language skills we cannot improve as writers. We want our students to understand the reasoning behind the activities they will be performing in class, so we spend time discussing the importance of reading in stimulating creativity, language, reasoning, and communication. We also emphasize how the readings in this anthology will be particularly provocative and stimulating.

After discussing the role reading plays in improving written skills, we move on to the three stages of the written part of the process. (Sometimes we first discuss what a process is by asking our students to provide examples of processes they encounter in their daily lives, such as cooking, changing a tire, and being in school. The goal here is to let them see that if writing is a process with stages, then these stages must be followed in order to generate an effective product.) From here, we review the three main stages of writing: preparation, drafting, and rewriting. Our objective is to discover how many of our students actually conceive of writing as consisting of stages demanding multiple drafts and to help them understand it as such. Many expect single final drafts; so, after highlighting what each stage involves, we ask students to pretend that they have three hours to complete an assignment.

Based on their present writing habits, we ask them to jot down how they would distribute their time according to the three stages.

The results of this exercise won't surprise you. We have discovered that most students who consider themselves ineffective writers, and who dislike writing, allot the most time to the drafting stage of the process. In some of our classes these students constitute the majority. We then share with them that, for most advanced writers, the drafting stage is usually not the most laborious, as in their case, but actually the quickest: a burst of energy that emerges only after effectively planning ideas and strategies. We try to get them to see that if they do not prepare sufficiently before beginning the writing, they will experience the same frustration and even failure as a runner who participates in a race unprepared. In the same vein, we tell them that if they have prepared well, they will enjoy the actual writing more and be more inclined to spend a good amount of time polishing "the diamond in the rough" in the final rewriting stage. Many students don't realize the need for rewriting; they believe correcting language or proofreading is sufficient, and we find it important to help students to learn to revise their own work.

We address students' unease with writing further by discussing expectations, theirs and ours. We believe realistic expectations have a lot to do with success; therefore, we acknowledge that the process of writing is not usually easy. It demands time, thinking, research, and sometimes even dealing with painful issues. We remind our students that, in the words of Georgia O'Keeffe, "it takes courage to be an artist." We also emphasize the rewards of discovery and accomplishment. We have observed that when our students begin the course with realistic expectations about reading and writing, they are happier and ultimately more effective. We recommend that you review with your students your personal expectations about their writing—that is, what you expect to find in their writing. For example, we look for progress and development in three areas: creativity, intellectual rigor, and commitment to the topic. For us, these are the ingredients of effective writing, and we let our students know that from the beginning.

You will probably find that, in addition to addressing students' need for help with writing, you will encounter resistance from a few of them. The selections deal with themes that your students should be able to relate to, but in ways that will probably challenge their attitudes about familiar topics such as culture, heritage, language, and home. We have written the Pre-Reading Activities and Student Encounter Activities in this manual to elicit personal observations and reflections from students and to involve them more personally in the selections. The more our students relate to a topic or a situation at an emotional and psychological as well as intellectual level, the more willing they are to break down barriers and to discard stereotypes. They also enjoy both their reading and writing a lot more.

You can balance the reading with the activities and the writing assignments at the end of each chapter. We suggest you encourage students to follow their own interests as much as possible. The editors have provided a large number of pieces, more than any teacher can use in one course. This allows you to pick and choose depending on your goals. From time to time, you may also want to let your students do the same. We like to assign some required readings and then allow students to choose from other possibilities in the chapter. It makes them feel more involved in their learning process.

We also recommend class discussion of the readings. If you are concerned about student participation, we suggest you use the Study Questions at the end of the selections in the anthology and the Suggested Assignments in this manual as a springboard for further discussion. We usually ask our students to keep a reading journal and to write an entry for each assigned selection. The student should summarize the main points of the selection and then note his or her personal reaction to it. The students then have to share their responses with the class, before we open up to a general discussion. (We alternate five or six different students reading their entries from class to class.) The journals usually improve class discussion considerably, plus they provide an informal medium for the students to practice their written communication skills.

We have provided two sample syllabi at the end of this manual that will demonstrate how we organize these suggested activities.

┌ I ┐

HOME

About the Theme "Home"

In the introduction to this chapter, the editors define home not only as a physical place but also as an emotional, spiritual, and cultural place. Home is defined differently by many people. It can be seen as a house, a neighborhood, a country, a culture, or even a feeling. All these views about home have one thing in common. They are familiar to the individual, whether they offer pleasant or unpleasant experiences and memories. Home is universal in this sense. Thus, by reading literature that explores the theme of home, students may gain awareness of the place they each call home. They will also gain insight, understanding, and empathy for what home is like for someone else, a place that will more likely be similar than different.

Pre-Reading Activity

We feel it is important that our students explore their own perceptions of home before reading the chapter. Through written assignments and oral discussions you can probe their views about home.

At home or in class, ask the students to free write for fifteen minutes their personal concept of home (memories, physical details, people, landscape, etc.). Discuss what they've written in class and group the writings according to categories, with the aim of finding similarities and differences. Brainstorm expressions that include the word "home" ("Home sweet home," "There is no place like home," "Run away from home," etc.). From these phrases, discern different meanings of home. Then have the students read the introductory theme "Home." Compare their explorations of home to those of the editors.

Michael Anthony

SANDRA STREET

Michael Anthony is one of the best-known Caribbean writers writing today. He was born in Trinidad in 1932, and except for six years abroad, he continues to live there. He is a novelist, short story writer, and historian who often writes about growing up in Trinidad.

Short story, 6 pages   p. 3

"Sandra Street" is a story about a childhood memory. The title establishes the setting as central to the story; indeed, the relationship of the two main characters, Steve and the teacher, Mr. Blades, revolves around a discussion of Sandra Street. We've found that opening with a discussion of setting and the use of detail can work well as a springboard to begin the discussion of the story. You can also use it to emphasize the importance of specific and concrete details in the students' own writing. The Study Questions also work well to generate responses from the students about the details in the story.

We found that a discussion of the narrator is also essential to understanding this story. You may want to point out differences between the narrator's voice, an adult voice, and the recollections of the young Steve who is looking for approval from the teacher. Discuss with the students some of the critical adjectives used to describe the teacher, such as "looking sharply at me," "his voice was now stern and acid," and "he said with bitterness." Mr. Blades comes from the other side of town and wants to awaken in Steve the sense of admiration for Sandra Street that he feels looking out at the quiet street bathed in light. He shows disappointment for what he perceives as Steve's apathy towards home.

For a more thematic discussion, explore with the students why Mr. Blades and Kenneth, who, after all, are outsiders, see Steve's home in a different light. Is Steve indeed ignorant of his surroundings? Or, being the insider, does he simply live his surroundings rather than observe them? The last scene of the story can be used as an example to discuss this question. While Steve is excited as he interacts with his environment—in this case the bananas—Mr. Blades is observing the street below with the awe of a spectator. We found that discussing the difference between the outsider's and the insider's version of a place can be helpful to the students. Some say only an outsider can describe a place.

You may want to ask the students to agree or disagree with this statement, a good question to generate discussion in your classroom.

After discussing setting and narrative point of view, you can analyze the student/teacher relationship. How does this relationship speak to us about rejection and approval? Is the teacher condescending in any way? How has the relationship shaped Steve's own perception of home?

Finally, you may want to discuss the role of the writer as a spectator, an observer who may idealize a place, especially if he is an outsider.

Suggested Assignments

Q.1. This story, in some ways, is about perceptions (and misperceptions), especially about a place called home. In the story, there are three ways of looking at Sandra Street. Describe how Steve, Mr. Blades, and Kenneth each perceives Sandra Street. Then compare/contrast these perceptions. In your opinion, who has the most "authentic" perception of Sandra Street? Support your opinion with examples from the text.

Q.2. The action revolves around two main characters, Steve and Mr. Blades. Search the story for examples of dialogue between the two. Categorize their verbal exchanges into harmonious/discordant. Based on your lists, decide whether the relationship between Mr. Blades and Steve is a positive or negative one. Be prepared to defend your decision.

Student Encounter Activity

Visit a travel agency and pick up travel brochures on Trinidad or other Caribbean islands. Study the descriptions and photographs used. Compare these descriptions to those of "Sandra Street." If you called one of these islands home, how would you feel about the perceptions outsiders are given of your home? Discuss your feelings using the photographs.

Amy Tan

A PAIR OF TICKETS

Amy Tan was born in 1952, in California, to Chinese immigrants. She visited China for the first time in 1987. Inspired by her visit, she began her career as a novelist.

Novel excerpt, 16 pages   p. 10

Amy Tan's story is an excerpt from her first novel, *The Joy Luck Club* (1989). The novel revolves around four Chinese women in San Francisco who, in 1949, begin to meet to play mah jong, a game similar to dominos, and tell stories of their past. They call these meetings the Joy Luck Club. "A Pair of Tickets" is narrated by the daughter of one of the members who has recently died. As a result of the mother's death, American-born Jing-mei/June May decides to travel to China for the first time.

This story deals with the search for home. Home in this story, however, is not restricted to the place one grew up in, since the narrator has never set foot in China. Instead, home holds a broader meaning that encompasses the familiarity that stems from shared values, customs, and ancestry. When June May visits China for the first time, she immediately feels at home, a surprise to her. By accepting her identity as Chinese, she accepts herself and discovers home within herself.

The setting is important here in that the character has to travel to embrace her culture. The shift of landscape allows her to understand her mother, her culture, and herself more fully. She has been struggling with her double identity as a Chinese American, always with a sense that she has disappointed her mother with her more Americanized traits. Note the details that support this: her perfect English, yet awkward Chinese, and her own words "wondering how disappointed my mother must have been." Yet her relatives in China desire to eat typical American food during her stay in an Americanized hotel in Guangzhou, embracing the Americanized traits that she is so self-conscious about. We see in the journey "home" that she has synthesized her two identities and thus become spiritually whole.

You may also want to discuss the narrative technique in the story. The narrator shifts back and forth in time between the journey in the present to the stories of the past. You can point out that these stories work like pieces of a puzzle allowing the main character to become whole in the present. Learning about the past, meeting her relatives and stepping on Chinese soil, grounds the main character and allows her to let go and blossom. The shift to the past emphasizes the importance of roots and a sense of tradition for establishing identity.

Finally, you may want to explore the exile experience and the significance of the first trip home, especially for a person born abroad. Ask the students to imagine such an experience and empathize with the impact of such an event in a person's life.

Suggested Assignments

Q.1. A person can have a sense of more than one home. This sense can be gratifying and expansive or stressful and destructive. In this story, the main character has two names, June May and Jing-mei, and two homes, the United States and China. A key element to "home" is a private sense of familiarity with it. Compare how the main character views being Chinese from the United States to how she views being American from China. Based on this comparison, discuss how June May feels about herself and her "home."

Q.2. Are the concerns and experiences of the main character, a Chinese American, unique or can they be found in people with other backgrounds? Do these concerns and experiences exist solely within an ethnic realm or do they exist within economic, racial, and gender realms as well? Discuss the rationale for your answers.

Student Encounter Activity

Find someone whom you feel has two "homes," in any sense of the word. Interview them and try to understand how they cope with this experience of duality. Share your findings with the class.

Richard Dokey

SÁNCHEZ

Richard Dokey is a native of Stockton, California, where he still resides and teaches philosophy at San Joachin Delta Community College. He has published novels, a play, and a collection of short stories. Before he began to teach, he worked as a laborer on a railroad, in a shipyard, in a bottling company, and in an ink factory.

Short story, 11 pages   p. 26

This story revolves around Juan Sánchez, a Mexican immigrant in California. As a young man, he seeks a gentler, idyllic place to raise his family, fearing the harshness of his homeland which took the lives of his parents. He rejects his home in Mexico to seek a cleaner place in the mountains across the border. With La Belleza, he tries to establish an idyllic homestead, setting down roots there: buying a home, selling baskets and carvings, and working the migration routes. However, the birth of his son, Jesús, causes the death of La Belleza and a great loss.

Nevertheless, Juan stays in the mountains hoping his son will acquire his own love for the simplicity and beauty of the mountains. In the end, the son is seduced by the materialism and commercialism of urban life in the United States. The father realizes this and returns to Mexico, feeling futile in the mountains. Many years after his wife's death, he finally realizes home is where he was born and thus he returns. You may want to discuss the purpose of this return.

Setting serves as the backdrop for this story. Explore the setting with students by asking them to contrast the details of the three settings provided: the rural Mexican town, the mountain cabin, and the urban town with the cannery. Discuss how the physical differences influence the attitudes and behaviors of the characters.

In discussing character development, you may want to analyze the differences in attitudes between the father and his son. In some ways, they are very different; however, you may ask the students to explore whether the son is not driven by the same motivations as his own father was, as a young man.

You can also discuss leitmotifs running throughout the story, such as the repetitive references to holes, empty lots, and wrecker balls in the beginning scene.

Finally, ask the students to discuss what attitudes are revealed about Mexicans and their culture in the story.

Suggested Assignments

Q.1. This story has an abundance of descriptive details. The author uses description to convey many ideas about the physical places, the emotions, and the values of the characters, and also to give the reader a sense of the present. Scan the story, looking for descriptive passages and match them with the particular idea you think the author is attempting to convey. Is the author successful in his use of description? Could there be too much use of description? Be specific with your examples in presenting your opinions.

Q.2. Analyze the differences and similarities between the father and the son. Are they as different as they appear to be? Could history be repeating itself? Use the text to support your answer.

Student Encounter Activity

Take a walk around town. Choose a physical structure that reflects how you feel at that very moment in your life. Describe the structure in detail, using the description to communicate a certain idea or attitude you wish to convey.

Vanessa Howard

ESCAPE THE GHETTOS OF NEW YORK

Vanessa Howard is an African-American poet who wrote this poem when she was a teenager growing up in New York in the sixties.

Poem, 1 page   p. 37

This poem, written by a teenager, reflects a strong sense of irony about a place. You can discuss the voice of the poem in terms of where the voice lies. Is it intimate with the subject? Does it expose its feelings? In spite of the simplicity of the language and imagery, the irony provides depth to the poem and a sense of detachment from the events and the people. Discuss with your students why this may be so. Ask them to explore whether the poet indeed sees alcohol and drugs as paradise.

Note the choice of details to define the setting and discuss how they reveal the poet's attitude towards home. In contrast to other stories and poems in this chapter, home evokes negative sentiments here.

Also, try discussing how the modern structure of the poem, with its rupture in syntax between verses and stanzas, reinforces the theme of the poem. The students may be familiar with only more traditional poems with structured rhyme patterns. It would be worthwhile to discuss the shifts in modern poetic perspective as they reflect modern culture.

Suggested Assignments

Q.1. Is this description of urban life still relevant today? Would you consider this poem too tame for today?

Q.2. How does the poet feel about her home? Is there hope in the poem? Imagine the poet as an older woman now. Do you think she has escaped?

Luis Cabalquinto

HOMETOWN

Luis Cabalquinto was born in the Philippines. He studied both in the Philippines and in the United States and now divides his time between the two. He is the author of three recent collections of poetry.

Poem, 1 page   p. 38

For us, this poem's strength lies in the simplicity and clarity of images that evoke strong feelings about a place we cannot possess. Try discussing with the students the difference between this type of imagistic poem and a narrative poem, helping them to imagine and appreciate the details that paint a picture of a place and the sense of satisfaction and fulfillment it evokes.

Note the duality in the poet. Even though he feels a desire to remain at this place, he must also deal with his other self from the city. Discuss the tension between these two environments, urban and rural, and how it can create angst. The poet is pulled by the food, sounds, and sights of this place, but he is also aware of his other self.

This poem can be used to discuss the students' own sense of home and feelings of nostalgia. For some, it may be too soon to experience nostalgia for a place they have yet to leave. Ask them to contrast their sentiments with those of the poet.

Suggested Assignments

Q.1. There is a sense of nostalgia for home in this poem, expressed directly and indirectly. Find the different expressions of nostalgia and list them. Then decide whether the speaker is effective in conveying his feelings. Support your decision with examples from the text.

Q.2. Sometimes a poet says a lot by saying very little. Imagine yourself being the person in this poem, sitting on a long bench. Think about the city. How would you describe it?

Maurice Kenny

GOING HOME

Maurice Kenny is a distinguished poet of Mohawk ancestry. He was born in 1929 and reared near the St. Lawrence River in northern

New York State. He has written numerous collections of poetry and is the recipient of the 1985 American Book Award.

Poem, 1/2 page   p.40

This poem works well in conjunction with Luis Cabalquinto's "Hometown." Like "Hometown," Kenny's "Going Home" depends on imagery to convey strong sentiments about a place. Both poets feel a duality between urban and rural life; however, Kenny includes explicit details about the city that are more revealing about his feelings.

Even though both poems share a nostalgia about home, Kenny's poem reveals fear. Fear of having to open a door his father has shut and fear of being treated as a stranger in what he perceives as home. Finally, he fears alienation from what he seeks. You may want to discuss examples that illustrate his anxiety about going home.

Students may get a lot from a discussion that places this poem within an historical context that clarifies the poet's situation. Discuss the slow annihilation of Native-American culture by European colonizers throughout the Americas and the appearance of reservations.

Note the shift in tense from the beginning of the poem in the present to the end of the poem. Try asking the students if this shift to the past tense indicates that the concerns about going home no longer exist?

Suggested Assignments

Q.1. Poems and photographs are similar; each captures a world in a condensed image. The astute thinker analyzes the poem/picture for messages of a greater purpose. Think of the phrase in the poem "the Greyhound followed the plow" as a photograph. Think about this image. Is it just a funny picture? Or is there something more profound in it?

Q.2. The title "Going Home" suggests that the poet decided to open the door his father shut. Did he open it? If so, was he accepted or rejected? Provide explicit examples from the text to support your decision.

Student Encounter Activity

Choose a Native-American group near your area. Find out about this group's encounter with foreigners and describe it. How does the weight of this encounter affect a Native American's reality today?

Lorna Dee Cervantes

FREEWAY 280

Lorna Dee Cervantes was born in San Francisco in 1954, of Mexican descent. She is a poet and currently teaches creative writing at the University of Colorado at Boulder.

Poem, 1/2 page   p. 42

This poem's imagery and language point to two worlds, both experienced by the poet. One is where Spanish is spoken and old ladies use paper bags to pick greens. The other is the world of English, freeways, and neatly mowed lawns. You may want to open the discussion by noting the shift in the poet's attitude towards these two worlds. Where once she longed for the freeway and the rigid lanes, she now scrambles back over the wire fence. Discuss the significance of a wire fence to an illegal immigrant. Do the students see the poet's shift in attitude? Try exploring the shift by discussing what could have caused it; also ask the students if they relate to this shift yet. Or are they too longing for the freeway?

The Mexican-American experience provides a broader context for the poem. Situate the poem within this experience—for example, the migration patterns and the lure of the factory work away from the rural existence. The final image in the poem works well to explore how the poet feels about the future of her people and her identity. Explore any other images that point to the future.

A discussion of the details that depict the world she left behind and is now returning to and the use of Spanish is another way to approach the poem. Hispanic-American writers will often use Spanish in the text to depict the duality of their existence. Explore how it is used in this poem. Ask the students how they feel about the use of the language.

Suggested Assignments

Q.1. The word "Freeway" in the title of the poem is short and utilitarian. It is a name for a type of road. But the two words that compose it, free and way, are wrought with meaning. Based on your reading of the poem, what are the possible reasons for the poet choosing this title?

Q.2. Writing is a form of communication, but only if the other person can read. (Or so it seems.) The same can be said about language. Yet this poet uses Spanish words and phrases. Has she assumed that all readers understand Spanish? Why do you think the poet uses Spanish in the poem?

Student Encounter Activity

Take a drive on the nearest freeway for an hour and return on a small country road. Reflect upon the differences you sense driving on a freeway versus a small country road. How is home different for people living along each of these? Use details from each environment to support your observations.

Carter Revard

DRIVING IN OKLAHOMA

Carter Revard, part Osage, grew up on the Osage Reservation in Oklahoma and attended Buck Creek rural school. Eventually, he went to Oxford University as a Rhodes Scholar and later earned a Ph.D. from Yale in Middle English literature. He has published several collections of poetry.

Poem, 1/2 page   p. 44

Try opening the discussion of this poem in the context of the personal spiritual sense of home it evokes. The poem is about a chance encounter that creates an awareness of home in the poet. The poem is divided into two parts, visually marked by the verse "—a meadowlark." In the first part of the poem, we meet the poet content with his world of cement and machinery, a world that is fast, loud, and exhilarating. Ask the students to note the details that support this. The language of this part of the poem, full of density and metaphors, supports the overwhelming presence of the environment.

In the second part, after the encounter with the meadowlark, the language is simpler and full of clarity. The driver realizes that the weightlessness and simplicity of the bird and his song shape country and soul. The bird defines the earth and reflects the poet's soul. In this realization, the poet has found a new sense of spiritual home.

We've had success asking the students to contrast other elements of urban life with nature that can convey similar attitudes—for example, the clutter of a speed boat to the elegance of a dolphin at sea.

Suggested Assignments

Q.1. The "trappings of home" can reflect a person's way of life. They can also reveal a person's state of mind. Reread the first half of the poem. Identify and list the person's trappings of home. What do these say about this person's way of life and state of mind?

Q.2. Compare the power of the car to the power of the meadowlark. To this person, which is the stronger? Which is the stronger to you? Explain your choice.

Student Encounter Activity

Describe the trappings of a place you call home. Exchange this paper with another student. Infer, from the description provided, the person's way of life and state of mind. Share your findings with each other and analyze the power of description.

Edward Hirsch

IN A POLISH HOME FOR THE AGED (CHICAGO, 1983)

Edward Hirsch is of Eastern European descent. His poems have appeared in many journals and magazines. He has held various fellowships and won a number of prestigious awards for his poetry. He was born in Chicago in 1950.

Poem, 1 1/2 pages   p. 45

Students familiar with traditional poetry will likely feel comfortable with this poem. You may want to compare it to Richard Wilbur's "Love Calls Us to the Things of This World" or John Donne's "The Rising Sun," but here the waking is to memories of long ago and far away, to life tenaciously held onto instead of to a lover or an intense youthful moment. This is also a good selection for beginning to confront the issues associated with cultural loyalties and the conflicts among values in different traditions.

You may want to start by exploring the language. The second word of the poem, "sweet," an odd word to use in the late twentieth century, recalls the standard sensory word used by Shakespeare and his contemporaries to collate all kinds of pleasant sights, sensations, and feelings. Here the memories that add up to sweetness are diverse. Ask the students to identify and discuss them. At first glance, the contrast between the "sweetness" of the memories and the starkness of the "home" points to a nostalgic sentiment by a lonely aged person. However, it is important to note that the present is absent of bitterness. There is an acceptance that is reiterated in the concluding stanza.

Take time to explore the last stanza. What is this light that will be heavy yet nourishing as a pail of fresh milk? Ask the students to find clues that the past was not completely idealized, such as, "grand-mother's odd claim . . . brother was a mule," "cousin . . . was a poorly-planted tree," "dark caresses," and "the war." Discuss with the students what is meant by drinking the day slowly. Explore if the speaker of the poem has learned to drink the day slowly and if the old advice relates to the speaker's attitudes now towards savoring old moments and get-ting pleasure out of an acceptance of both past and present.

Suggested Assignments

Q.1. Memories of home are often fond ones. Yet reality can intrude and affect these, either by suffocating them or by idealizing them. Think of where the speaker lives and note the date and the city in the title. Are his memories/dreams influenced by his reality? Justify your answer.

Q.2. Reread the ninth line of the poem. Why would the speaker describe his grandmother's claim as odd?

Agha Shahid Ali

POSTCARD FROM KASHMIR

Agha Shahid Ali is a scholar and a poet born in Kashmir (now divided between India and Pakistan). He studied at the University of New Delhi and the University of Arizona. In 1984, he received a Ph.D. from Penn State. He now teaches at the University of Massa-chusetts, Amherst. He has written poetry in English since he was ten and has published several collections.

Poem, 1/2 page   p. 47

The image of the photograph, in this case the postcard, is central to this poem. The postcard evokes memories that connect the speaker to home. We find it helpful to discuss the use of the photograph in the literature of exile/migration, for it often works as a symbol of lost memories. Try using this poem to discuss memories of the students' or the poet's childhood home. Explore why photographs are so important, especially to one in exile. The speaker says the postcard is the closest he'll feel to home. Discuss why he says this. You can also ask the students to explore how memories can sometimes be more vivid than the reality of the place.

Note the contrast between the miniature size of the postcard that depicts homeland and the enormous Himalayas with the size of the memory depicted as a giant negative. As home is reduced and compartmentalized, memory expands to such a point that the two cannot be reconciled. The speaker is aware he is losing intimacy with the "real" home.

Suggested Assignments

Q.1. What makes a place home can be one's closeness, familiarity, and intimacy with it. In this poem, there is a reconciliation issue related to that closeness. The play with size has a lot to do with it. How does the speaker use size to expose his dilemma?

Q.2. In order to cope with conflicting emotional issues, the human mind often compartmentalizes the feelings associated with those issues. Keeping this in mind, decide what emotional issues the speaker is trying to cope with. Then describe the ways in which he has compartmentalized them. Decide if he is coping or avoiding dealing with his feelings.

Student Encounter Activity

Look at old photographs of your childhood. Contrast the sharp images of the pictures to your feelings about your past. How are they compatible? In what ways are they not? What has caused a change, if any?

Audre Lorde

HOME

Audre Lorde was born in New York, in 1934, to West Indian parents. She is the author of nine books, mostly of poetry, and a fictionalized memoir. She died in November 1992.

Poem, 1/2 page   p. 49

This poem can challenge your students' ability to analyze. The meanings are not obvious but can be inferred with attention to detail. There is a speaker and her companion returning to the parents' home after the death of a relative. Like most of the poems in this section, the main theme revolves around acceptance and reconciliation with one's roots.

The use of the past tense and the final line indicate that even though the speaker was at some point in conflict with her roots, her genealogy, it no longer matters. You may want to discuss if this has been resolved.

Suggested Assignments

Q.1. Accepting our past/roots/home can be a difficult process. Where one finds herself in this process can determine the reaction to a simple phrase. Given this, look at the phrase "you look *too* familiar." What sentiment does this comment evoke in the speaker? At one time, could she have reacted differently to this statement? If so, why the change in her reaction?

Q.2. Wars are fought for many reasons. There are many things lost and a few gained. Look at the last two lines of the first stanza. What reasons do you suppose there are for these childhood wars? What things have been lost and gained? Apply this to your own experiences in growing up. Discuss any similarities and differences.

Elías Miguel Muñoz
RETURNING

Elías Miguel Muñoz was born in Cuba in 1954 and was raised in California. He received his Ph.D. from the University of California at Irvine. He is a poet and a novelist.

Poem, 1 page   p. 50

This is an excellent poem to discuss the longing to leave home that one experiences especially at a young age and the consequences it may bring.

At the literal level, where you may want to begin, the poem deals with a Cuban boy in his homeland who dreams of the United States with its apples and chewing gum. In the United States, away from the tropical sun, his skin will be lighter and he will suffer no rationing lines. At the end of the second stanza, the poem begins to reveal how in abandoning his homeland he may lose things he cherishes, like a favorite game, *quimbumbia,* or *yuca.*, a Cuban staple.

At a deeper level, this poem deals with the human tendency to reject the present to dream about the future, a future that no longer satisfies us once we get it. The first half of the poem deals with longing for another place. The second half deals with longing for the past once we are in the new place. This part is filled with irony that culminates with the last four lines.

The last stanza, written in the conditional tense, serves to emphasize the possibility of regret in the decision to leave home. For once the speaker lands on North American soil, he begins to dream about returning.

Note the use of colloquial details to reveal the setting. We know the speaker is referring to the United States by the use of apples and chewing gum. His occasional use of Spanish also serves to reinforce intimacy with the land of his birth, in this case Cuba.

Suggested Assignments

Q.1. Imagine yourself as a person on the brink of leaving your homeland for the United States. Just as you are making your decision, a close friend already there mails you this poem. What do you suppose she is trying to tell you? Use excerpts from the text to explain your inferences.

Q.2. There are two cultures described here. Identify them by listing the attributes given for each one. Based on this list, are these descriptions positive or negative ones? Are they in opposition in the speaker's mind? Can the speaker reconcile both cultures?

Lucille Clifton

IN THE INNER CITY

Lucille Clifton was born in New York in 1936. She attended Howard University. She has written numerous children's books, a memoir, and poetry.

Poem, 1/2 page   p. 51

Explore with the students how this is a poem about reaffirmation. It is written from a position of power from a place that seems to be powerless. The power comes from its own reaffirmation, from its refusal to accept the view of the outsider. The poem redefines the inner city, reaffirming its life and vitality and rejecting the dominant terms.

After discussing the images used to describe "uptown" with its silent nights, dead houses, and pale colors, ask the students to discuss what these images imply about the inner city.

You may also want to discuss how such a simple poem can reveal much about the struggle between classes and races, a struggle that claims victory in the power of living as opposed to just existing.

Suggested Assignments

Q.1. The use of repetition in this poem reaffirms the position of its writer. Notice the words "we," "inner city," and "home." How many times are they repeated? Based on this repetition, what attitudes do you believe the speaker holds towards home?

Q.2. Discuss how this poem reveals the struggle between the insider trying to maintain the integrity of home and the pressure of the outsider questioning that integrity.

Wakako Yamauchi

AND THE SOUL SHALL DANCE

Wakako Yamauchi was born in California in 1924. She is best known for her short stories.

Play, 39 pages   p. 52

Yamauchi's play deals with two Japanese families trying to make a living as farmers in California in the 1930s. It deals with cultural and generational conflicts as well.

Setting is essential to the staging of this play and is a good point to begin the discussion of it. Discuss with students the physical appearance of the two houses around which the play revolves. Explore why the houses and the desert landscape are so important to the understanding of the existence of these Japanese families in California. Point out the name of the valley, Imperial Valley, and the name of prewar Japan, Imperial Japan. In what ways can this be significant?

The historical setting is also important. Note the details that reveal the treatment of the Japanese in California in the 1930s—for example, the fact that the Japanese could not own land, as well as the attitude of the waitress at the restaurant. Also discuss how this treatment worsened after the attack on Pearl Harbor when Japanese internment camps were created.

You can also use this play to explore the different attitudes adopted by immigrants towards their native land. Emiko represents the individual who lives in the past to such a point that she is annihilated by it. Kiyoko assumes Western ways soon after her arrival, perming her hair and wearing western clothes at the expense of Emiko. Though Oka supports Kiyoko's western ways, he does not transcend his own past. He still lives the humiliation of Emiko's family and the loss of his first wife which fills him with anger and resentment for her.

On the other hand, the Murata family appears to "bend" better like the bamboo. Though the parents miss Japan and plan on returning, like many immigrants, this wish does not embitter them. They lead a difficult life but one filled with hope and affection for each other. The daughter, Masako, is the observer who seems to adapt well to both cultural realities. Discuss with the students what home means to the characters. Is it different for each one? Can they have two "homes"?

Students may find it interesting to discuss the role of the wife in traditional Japanese culture: the expectations and the way marriages are arranged. Try asking questions such as these. Why is Emiko sent off to marry Oka though she is the beautiful one? Why does Oka send for Kiyoko only when she is 15 and able to cook and do other chores? How does Masako see her role as a female?

Note how this is a modern play that does not follow the classical dramatic structure and its rigid rules for staging, scenes, time sequence, plot development, and characterization. This play shares much with realist plays of the end of the nineteenth century and early twentieth century, with its slice of life and symbolic characteristics. It also shares with Asian theater its use of music, dance, and poetry to advance the movement of the play.

Suggested Assignments

Q.1. The play illustrates the tensions inherent in dealing with the two homes. These tensions are influenced by factors such as age, culture, experience, will, and desire. How these tensions are relieved depends on the ability to reconcile oneself with the two homes. Think of each character as being between two homes. Describe the tensions felt by each one. Use examples from the text to illustrate your descriptions. Rank the characters on a scale from most successful to least successful at reconciliation. Justify your ranking by using the text.

Q.2. Sometimes characters in a play, when taken as a whole, can represent a single being. Seeing a play this way can provide a greater understanding of each character and ourselves. In groups of three or four, discuss this idea and decide which facet of this "person" each character represents. For example, who is the soul of the play?

Student Encounter Activity

Based on your reading, draw the setting with the details provided in the stage directions. Exchange your drawing with a classmate. Discuss the differences and similarities in what each of you chose to emphasize. How important is the setting to this play?

Elise Sprunt Sheffield

THE "GENTLE WHOLENESS" OF HOME

Elise Sprunt Sheffield was born and raised in rural Virginia. She studied at Mt. Holyoke College and Brown University, served two years in the Peace Corps in Africa, and later earned a master's degree in Harvard Divinity School.

Essay, 2 pages   p. 93

Sheffield's essay works well to start a discussion about how often, in youth, we show disdain towards home. Yet later, after time away, we learn to appreciate what we left behind. Discuss how Sheffield feels about her home before and after her visit to Africa. Her life in Africa in a small mountain goat village, full of daily ordinary routines, made her aware of something within herself. She was able to look back at similar small-town behaviors at home, without the negative emotional attachments she previously held.

Note, however, how Sheffield reveals contradictory messages in the essay. Do students seem convinced that she really sees Virginia as her home, or is her return merely another experiment? Note that she says "so far, it works" as if the experience is a test. Also note how in the end Africa is still fuller, more whole, more fulfilling for her than Virginia where she "tries" to be happy. Point out the irony in these and other statements she makes, such as "deep in Africa." Why not "deep" in Virginia? Is her attitude of seeing what is foreign and exotic as more fulfilling typical of North Americans?

Another fruitful topic to explore with your students is her university experience which she blames for making her restless and unappreciative of home. Has she supported this claim sufficiently? Discuss the students' reactions to her view.

Finally, you may want to use this essay to discuss the use of narration as a primary technique in essay writing. The author uses personal anecdotes from her own life to present a discussion of home. Analyze the examples and descriptions given, in addition to the tone.

Suggested Assignments

Q.1. Often, two people can be telling us the same thing, yet we only hear the words from one. Keeping this in mind, read the last line of paragraph 6 and answer these questions: What makes the call different? What kind of call could she have had before? What was the call saying? Who was doing the calling?

Q.2. Many times in life, we make a choice and take the responsibility for it. In the essay, the person has made two choices concerning home. Identify the two choices and decide whether she has taken responsibility for each of them. Use the text to explain how she has done so. What does this say to you about the speaker?

Student Encounter Activity

Make a list of the features you like about your home community and another list of the features you dislike. What values about home do you hold as revealed by your lists?

Elena Padilla

MIGRANTS: TRANSIENTS OR SETTLERS?

Elena Padilla is professor of public administration at New York University. She studied at the Universities of Puerto Rico and Chicago and at Columbia University. This selection is taken from the final chapter of her 1958 book *Up from Puerto Rico*.

Essay excerpt, 5 pages   p. 95

Padilla's essay can work as an interesting portrayal of attitudes towards Hispanic migration in the 1950s. Furthermore, it serves as an example of the difficulty in trying to classify humans in their search for home. The terms used by Padilla easily date the text. Hispanics today use the term Latino rather than Hispanic and do not categorize Puerto Rican immigrants into such categories as settlers and transients. Today, the quest by Latinos is how to adapt to the new home without losing the cultural ties to the island.

You may want to point out how the researcher uses interviews to support her findings and how sociologists and anthropologists frequently use this type of evidence to formulate their conclusions. Also point out the rhetorical signals used to introduce the comments, such as "another informant," "for example," "on the other hand," and how this type of testimonial evidence can be helpful in an argumentative essay.

This essay provides plenty of material of a discussion of gender roles. The comments by the migrants reveal the attitudes of the 1950s towards gender roles. Explore the traditional values expressed. Do your students think Puerto Ricans in New York today would speak of men and women in the same way?

Suggested Assignments

Q.1. The process of selecting and settling a home is a profound one. It is wrought with major changes in many aspects of one's life. This essay deals with people in different stages of this process. Scan the text for the role emotions play in the process. What is going on emotionally with these people?

Q.2. Read the last line of the essay. Compare it to all the other quotes. Do they express similar sentiments? How so? In light of your conclusion, is the quote true for migrants today? Is it true for yourself?

Student Encounter Activity

Interview a second-generation immigrant and a recent immigrant. Ask them questions similar to the ones used by Padilla in her research. Discuss the differences and similarities in the answers given by each of the participants.

Edward Said

REFLECTIONS ON EXILE

Edward Said, a Palestinian, was born in Jerusalem in 1935. He attended Princeton and Harvard Universities and now teaches at Columbia University. He is the author of several books of literary criticism as well as books and essays on foreign relations.

Essay, 5 pages   p. 101

We find that this can be a good piece for a general discussion on the condition of exile. This essay by Said demands rigorous analytical skills from the student. There is much to question here. You may want to begin by discussing how Said distinguishes between exiles, expatriates, refugees, and émigrés. Explore with students if such clear-cut distinctions are effective, especially for the late twentieth century? We find that Said himself strays from these distinctions—for example, citing James Joyce as an example of an exile when Joyce *chose* to leave his homeland.

Discuss the importance of example in an argumentative essay. Does Said give enough examples to support his definitions and claims? For instance, ask the students to note the list of professions preferred by exiles, such as novelists, chess players, political activists, and intellectuals; then ask them to decide if Said provides examples to support this assertion. Do your students agree with his conclusion?

Ask the students to scan the text and list the characteristics he attributes to the exile. Explore with them if they find these to be realistic or romanticized. One example you may want to cite: "[Exile life] is nomadic, decentred, contrapuntal." Said sees advantages to seeing the entire world as a foreign land. Explore this point of view as expressed by Said and as perceived by the students. Is he validating the condition of being between homes, as opposed to being of one or the other? How does his view about home differ from the others expressed in this chapter?

Suggested Assignments

Q.1. List all the positive and negative attributes of being an exile according to Said. Based on this list, where would you say Said stands on exile? From where does he view the exile condition, from the level of a tower or from the level of the street?

Q.2. Imagine that this essay is a recipe for life. Would you follow its directions? Justify your conclusions with examples from the text.

Student Encounter Activity

Study an exile group, such as the Cubans or the Vietnamese, to discern whether their experiences in the United States reaffirm or contradict the views expressed by Said in the first two paragraphs of the essay.

The Craft of Writing:
SETTING

p. 107

Effective description of the setting is essential in establishing theme, mood, perspective, and even characterization. The stories, poems, and essays in chapter 1 illustrate this well for the students. We found it helpful to have the students read the Afterword section in the anthology because it reinforces the impact of setting. By writing their own descriptions of setting, students internalize the importance and the difficulty in accomplishing the task successfully.

The assignments in Writing about the Reading ask the students to describe a setting they are familiar with. This may seem an easy task at first, but we have found that in reality it can be troublesome for students. They often think that a random list of general details is sufficient. They need help in realizing first that the details must be specific and concrete and second that the details must be chosen to reveal a focused attitude about this place. We have found the following suggested activities helpful for the students. You may want to try them in your classroom.

To help with the details, have the students brainstorm a list that includes all the senses: sight, sound, feel, smell, even taste if applicable.

Have them reduce these details to their most specific level. For example, if they list a "large two-story house," ask them to add specific dimensions, color, materials used, etc. Find examples of specific and concrete details from the texts they have read in chapter 1: for instance, "wood-roasted river crab," from Luis Cabalquinto's "Hometown"; "We watched the cyp, too, profuse among the laden mango trees, and the redness of their rain-picked flowers was the redness of blood," from Michael Anthony's "Sandra Street." (Point out the metaphor in the last example as well.)

Ask them also to determine the viewpoint or attitude they want to reveal about this place. You can refer to the student poem at the end of the chapter to discuss whether the student was effective in focusing his or her viewpoint.

Once the viewpoint has been determined, ask the students to choose only those details that support such an attitude. Some details may need to be discarded.

Finally, ask students to add subjective details that emphasize their point of view; these may include metaphors and comparisons. You may want to spend some time pointing out subjective details and metaphors used throughout chapter 1. Some examples would include "On humming rubber along this white concrete," and "the windroar like a flash / of nectar on mind," from Carter Revard's "Driving in Oklahoma" or "The freeway conceals it / all beneath a raised scar," from Lorna Dee Cervantes's "Freeway 280."

Your main concern should be to make it clear to the students that the objective and subjective details should reveal the viewpoint and not be statements of opinion, such as "I liked the house very much." Remind them the essay is about "it" and not about themselves. Emphasize the old saying: "Show me, don't tell me."

Comments on Student Writing

p. 112

This student poem by Bao Gia Tran can be very helpful in discussing both the theme of home and the craft of writing. Explore with students the concept of home as revealed by Tran. To do this, highlight the examples the poet chooses to emphasize about the past. Why talk about first grade, mother's whipping, the river bank, friends, the war? The last stanza also reveals a lot about the poet's view of home as nurturing and comforting. Ask the students to explain how we know this.

In addition to the theme of home, discuss the techniques used by the writer. Note how the poem is divided into three sections. In the first, the writer introduces what home is not. Defining something by what it is not can be helpful. Is it effective here? In the second section, the poet lists examples and anecdotes about home. The last section summarizes the poet's definition of home. Note how the poet uses concrete and specific examples that allow the reader to see, hear, touch, and smell home. The poet also uses metaphors to convey his own values about home.

Note, however, how the poem might demonstrate a student tendency to say too much and thus create conflicting images for the reader. Ask the students to find opposing emotions or perspectives. For example, in the last stanza, if home "is in me," why does the poet wish to "return home"? This poem can be used to demonstrate the importance of editing. Contrast the student poem to others you have read in chapter 1, such as Luis Cabalquinto's "Hometown." Point out how "Hometown" is focused and concise, yet more effective in conveying a similar perspective.

2

FAMILY

About the Theme "Family"

A sense of family, whether an accepting or a rejecting one, is part of the equation that helps define an individual. We deal with the issue of family from birth to death. We spend our lives coming to terms with how our family impacts us. It is a process of communication that takes place mainly through our emotions—emotions, which in the family setting, are paramount.

Given the societal changes occurring in the late twentieth century in America, the relationships between families are often strained. The mobility of our society, the ever-present generation gap, the expanding suburban centers, the media culture, the influx of immigrants, and the clash of traditional versus modern values encumber familial relationships and the emotions associated with them.

Literature often explores the issues associated with family. The selections in this chapter deal with different facets of family through its members and the manifestations of feelings they generate. The works explore "the search to accommodate the self, the family, and the larger society."

Because the selections were chosen to emphasize familial relationships, characterization is central to the texts and is addressed in the Afterword. As the students read, ask them to look at the development of the characters. They should use dialogue, actions, and commentaries by other characters or the narrator to determine the traits of the major characters. After discussing the themes of the works, review the techniques used by the writer to achieve dynamic characterization.

Pre-Reading Activity

Before having the students read the chapter, explore with them their concept of family and their own personal relationships. Following is a suggested activity:

- Write the word "Family" on the board.
- After placing the students in small groups, have each of the students take five to ten minutes to write whatever comes to mind in relation to the word "family." Ask them to continue writing until you say stop.
- When the time is up, ask them to share their ideas with their classmates in the group. Ask them to form a group consensus of what a family is.
- Write each group's consensus on the board. Discuss the similarities and differences, as well as the difficulties inherent in the process of defining family.
- Based on the findings, explore the emotions revealed by the list. Ask what issues must be dealt with in discussing the concept of family.

Tony Ardizzone

MY MOTHER'S STORIES

Tony Ardizzone lives in Chicago; he is from Liechtensteiner and is of Italian-American descent. He has published two novels and two collections of short stories and he is the recipient of numerous literary awards.

Short story, 9 pages   p. 117

This story works as a prose elegy for a mother who is dying. The narrator describes the mother's life to us through a series of stories told to him by his mother. The story begins with her birth, a foreshadowing of the death at the end. We continue to hear about her childhood, her adolescence in Chicago, her "mixed" marriage to the father, her rearing of children, and her many years of illness.

The story deals with death and its effects on the family. You may wish to explore how the narrator uses the mother's storytelling techniques to face his own encounter with death. Look at the end of the story and how much is left unsaid by the narrator about the death of his mother. Students who have lost a mother or father may be particularly touched by the story, but all will probably relate to the possibility of loss at some moment. Explore their emotions and reactions to such a possibility. Can they empathize with the narrator?

You can also discuss how this story deals with communication, or the lack of it. Little is told to us that does not come in the form of a story from the mother; the father and the son (the narrator) are only witnesses, while she communicates only in stories. She is described as a natural at storytelling, with the ability to engender any expression to mask her face. These stories, we are told, are filled with unanswered questions. Though the narrator tells us that the details are important, many details that perhaps would allow for a greater intimacy are left out.

The following questions can be helpful to deal with issues of characterization. Ask the students how the narrator describes his mother. Does he go beyond a description of scenes and anecdotes? Does he show empathy for her? Has he allowed the reader to feel empathy for her and for himself? Ask the students if, after reading this story, they feel close to any of these characters?

You may want to spend some time reviewing the formal techniques of the story. For example, point out how the narrator switches time frames and alternates between the stories in the past and the present. Moreover, note how the author frequently begins paragraphs with short, direct sentences that clue the reader in on important points. For instance: "I stand here, remembering"; "She never tells the rest of the details"; "There were problems"; "Picture her, then"; "Details are significant"; "Forgive the generalities."

Discuss characterization in general and probe the students to see how effective it is. If details are important, what details are we given or not given to help the reader imagine the characters more or less vividly?

Finally, you may want to deal with the issue of "mixed marriages" as expressed by the narrator. Discuss what is meant by this and ask the students to cite examples that show the effects of the condition on the relationship. Point out how the Sicilian family felt about the mother, the absence of the "Ave Maria" at the wedding (as if the pianist refused to validate the marriage), and the use of German words in the text.

Suggested Assignments

Q.1. Death in the family is a difficult experience. Memories are triggered that reveal the type of relationship one had with the deceased. Reflect on what the writer remembers about his mother. Characterize their relationship in terms of emotions, intimacy, sincerity, and trust. Cite examples from the text to support your characterization.

Q.2. Communication among family members in the story takes place mainly through storytelling. Indeed, the author even communicates with the reader through storytelling. What are the advantages and limitations of communicating in this way?

Student Encounter Activity

Think of a deceased family member or one close to you still living. Reminisce about all the stories you have heard from/about this person. Choose three to five stories that would reveal the main traits you wish to communicate about this person. Retell these stories in writing.

Cynthia Kadohata

CHARLIE-O

Cynthia Kadohata is a Japanese-American novelist. She has published two novels and received a Whiting Writers' Award. She currently resides in Los Angeles. "Charlie-O" is an excerpt from her first novel, *The Floating World*.

Novel excerpt, 8 pages   p. 127

This is an initiation story which we find works well in studying characterization. The narrator draws a picture of her parents that allows us to share in her own discovery of the truth about them. In particular, the narrator shares her coming to terms with Charlie-O.

The narrator describes him in rather pathetic terms, perhaps picking up on how her mother sees him. He is short, loud, undignified, and boyish; he is also a bad painter and is easily disoriented. Furthermore, we are told he marries a woman he knows is already pregnant by someone else, raises and loves her daughter, and eventually forgives his wife's infidelity.

A good way for students to begin studying this work is to have them discuss the details provided about Charlie-O. We find this leads to a good debate as to what kind of a person is created. Ask the students if they empathize with the character at all? Does the narrator? If so, explore with the students what allows this attitude. We have found it useful to point out the comments and events that make us feel sorry for Charlie-O. For instance, "Yet I knew that sometimes my mother felt lonely and my father felt alone." Ask them to explore this sentence. An interesting topic to examine is the parents' relationship. We feel this is a relevant issue for many of our students today.

In this case, it can be important to analyze whether Charlie-O bears responsibility for the difficulties in the marriage. You may want to ask them the following questions. Did he not accept marrying the mother in spite of the lovelessness? Did he expect something in return? Was the mother able to give it to him?

The picture of the mother is not as sharply defined but we do have enough details to get a sense of her. Ask the students to describe her. How does the narrator feel about the mother?

Use the last sentence, "Promise me you'll never break anyone's heart," to discuss how the narrator gains a new understanding of the relationship between her parents. This new awareness helps her to realize the importance of compassion and truth in a relationship. Students will probably find it easy to talk about the narrator herself. Ask the students to describe how they see her. Ask them why the move to Arkansas is significant in this story. We have found it useful to contrast this story to the ones in chapter 1 where the actual move away from home, rather than the characters, was central to the story.

Finally, you will want to spend time pointing out the techniques used by the writer to develop the characterization, such as dialogues, scenes, and commentaries. How do we know that the characters and not the landscape are the primary element in this story?

Suggested Assignments

Q.1. How we begin, as children, to have a greater understanding of the world around us is called maturity. Our point of view begins to change. Select passages from the story that suggest a "typical" teenager is speaking. What feelings do these passages reveal about her world? How does she mature?

Q.2. Pretend that you are Charlie-O visiting your adult daughter. Imagine that she has left the house and that you accidentally find her journal with this story in it. You read it. Assuming this to be true, how would you react to the story? How do you think she sees you? How do you see her now?

Student Encounter Activity

Think back on an event in your life that hinted at a broader sense of the world than you had had before. Describe the event and explore how it marked a change in your awareness of things or people around you. Be sure to include the feelings the event evoked in you.

John Edgar Wideman

LITTLE BROTHER

John Edgar Wideman, an African-American novelist, was born in 1941 in Washington, D.C., and grew up in Pittsburgh. He is a Rhodes scholar, college basketball star, and author of many books including *Fever*, from which this story is taken.

Short story, 7 pages   p. 136

In this story, John Edgar Wideman characterizes an urban African-American family. He does so with no external narrative point of view, but rather through the dialogue of two sisters, Penny and Geraldine. This dramatic technique evokes the oral tradition, strong in African-American culture and literature. Oral communication is important: stories and dialogues that trace the lives of individuals. The author uses a colloquial dialogue to enhance the realism of the story. Discuss with the students their reaction to the language. Do they have trouble understanding it? Or do they find it comfortable?

We find it worthwhile to clarify the familial relationships between the characters mentioned before discussing the characters themselves. We learn the most about Geraldine. She appears to be a center for the family, and even the neighborhood, giving out candy and taking in stray Marky and the pups. Nevertheless, the story is truly a characterization of an entire family, anchored by Geraldine.

Through the comments and the anecdotes, we get to know the family. We see a strong matriarchal family, where the mother, and then one of the daughters, maintains the family unit. You may want to discuss the concept of a matriarchal and a patriarchal family and explore other matriarchal cultures. You may want to ask the students to discuss which is more prevalent in African-American families.

In light of the previous discussion, you may find it helpful to explore the role of the males in the family unit in the story. They seem marginal, almost on the periphery of all activities and decision making. Ask students what role does Marky play? Can he be compared to Little Brother, always staying outside? Explore the symbolism of the title and its relevance to the characterization of the males.

Finally, you can use this story to begin a discussion of race relations that can be ongoing throughout the term of the course. Ask students to react to the scene at Dr. Franklin's office. We have found that students enjoy role playing scenes such as this one. Ask them how would they have felt? Would they have reacted like the character in the story? Also ask them to explain why the white neighbor Vicky would not speak to Geraldine at Sears. Ask them how they would have felt in this situation as well.

Suggested Assignments

Q.1. Compare the female presence in the story to the male presence. What does this comparison show about the family? Justify your answer.

Q.2. Explore the role of loyalty as a value in this family unit. Give examples of loyalty and decide whether this is a positive or a negative trait in this family. Support your conclusion.

Student Encounter Activity

Would you classify your family as matriarchal or patriarchal? List specific attributes that would illustrate your classification. Are you satisfied with this arrangement? Discuss your feelings.

Simon J. Ortiz

MY FATHER'S SONG

Simon Ortiz, of Navajo descent, is of the Acoma Pueblo in New Mexico. He has taught at several universities and is an editor. He has published several books, including a volume of poetry and prose. He was the recipient of a humanitarian award for literary achievement in 1989.

Poem, 1 page   p. 143

This poem depicts a father-son relationship.

The structure of the poem is critical to its understanding. Begin by asking students to analyze who the speaker is in the first stanza and who the speaker is in the song. If the last four stanzas are "the father's song," then we are to understand that the speaker is the father referring to his own father. Yet the last stanza seems purposely to create ambiguity. It could be spoken by both the son and the father. Thus the father and the son fuse and become one. That is the heart of the poem.

Ask the students to look at the first line, "Wanting to say things," and the last line, "and my father saying things." The memory of the

father and his song brings peace and a sense of wholeness and rootedness to the son. Point out how the first stanza evokes a cradling feeling,
as if the father's song were a lullaby. You may want to discuss with the
students if they think this is an unusual association between a father
and a son.

To turn the discussion towards characterization, ask the students to
characterize the image of the father presented to us. Note terms such
as "gently," "tremble of emotion," "softness." Point out how the sand
is mentioned in all four stanzas of the song. The sand is home to both
corn and mice. It is the earth that nurtures and gives life, perhaps like
the father.

Use the description of the father's behavior toward the unearthed
mice to explore the attitude revealed towards the land and its creatures. From here, you may want to begin or continue a discussion of
Native-American culture, including its respect for the land and its oral
tradition.

Suggested Assignments

Q.1. A family can serve as a place of refuge when needed. When
the family is gone, its memory can offer comfort in difficult moments.
With this in mind, compare the first stanza to the last one. Describe
the speaker's state of mind in each one. What, if anything, has
occurred to the speaker throughout the course of the poem?

Q.2. In Native-American culture, the oral tradition is very central
to familial life. Important lessons are taught through stories and songs.
Read the song in the poem and describe what the father is teaching the
son. What details in the song support your inferences?

Student Encounter Activity

Choose a Native-American group. Research its oral tradition,
looking for one specific example of a lesson being transmitted. Contrast how this lesson is transmitted to how modern America transmits
its lessons to the younger generations. Decide which is the most effective.

Rhoda Schwartz

OLD PHOTOGRAPHS

Rhoda Schwartz has been co-editor of *The American Poetry Review*. She was born in Atlantic City and grew up in Elmira, New York. She is of Russian-Jewish and Midwestern descent.

Poem, 2 pages   p. 145

Schwartz's piece is rich in characterization. The image of the daring, devilish, vital, idealistic, and sensual Russian youth whom the speaker knew as her father, a salesman in America of imported goods, comes across graphically—almost photographically. Study how the poet achieves the effect through the details, anecdotes, and metaphors chosen.

In spite of the vivid characterization, however, the relationship to the father lacks intimacy; it feels remote. The use of old photographs creates this detachment for it limits the description to actions, behaviors, and scenes, all frozen in time. The treatment of events in Russia as being far away in space and time adds to the remoteness of the descriptions. Ask students to discuss if the father does not seem more like an historical figure than a father.

This poem also seems to have the kaleidoscope or montage effect of history. Ask the students to question this view with examples of "scenes."

Discuss with students the writing of history as a selective process. By choosing these particular photographs, what is the author trying to communicate?

Suggested Assignments

Q.1. How would you characterize the relationship between daughter and father in this poem? What images in the photographs support your characterization?

Q.2. Based on her selection of photographs, infer how the daughter feels about her roots.

Student Encounter Activity

Choose a member of your family. Select several photographs that illustrate your feelings about this person. Make a collage out of them and have other students give their views of this person. Do their views coincide with yours? Were you effective in the selection of photographs?

Eric Chock

CHINESE FIREWORKS BANNED IN HAWAII

Eric Chock, a poet, works in the Poets-in-the-Schools Program in Hawaii. His poetry has been published widely in many magazines.

Poem, 1 page   p. 147

Although this poem centers around a family gathering, it is really about the loss of tradition. The poem recreates a scene where family members unite to celebrate the last Chinese Fireworks to be held in Hawaii. Ask the students to describe the details provided: the aunts washing dishes, the uncles playing mah jong and drinking, the children playing. As the descriptions unravel, the speaker hints at the pain accompanied with the loss of traditions, here represented by the fireworks. Note the phrases: "jam the pole / into the bottom of your guts"; "into a silence that echoes"; "This is going to be history." How do these lines and the poem as a whole express the speaker's feelings about the loss of his traditions, his culture?

By the end of the poem, we realize this will be the last such gathering. You may want to point out the subtle mention of the styrofoam cup and ask the students to explore its symbolism. Have them compare the last scene to the rich tapestry of images that precede it. You may also want to discuss the meaning of the line "This is the family picture / that never gets taken." Does the speaker mean a literal picture of the family members and the actions? Or does he mean that no photograph can capture the sense of family unity, the emotions, the magic of such a night?

You may want to discuss the history of the Chinese presence in Hawaii, as well as the significance of the Chinese Fireworks to the culture. Knowledge of pyrotechnic mixtures existed in China for centuries before it spread to Europe. Fireworks played an important part in civil life in many celebrations and the Chinese devised elaborate and unique displays.

Suggested Assignments

Q.1. There are two pictures taken in this poem. One is rich in subjects and details. The other is stark with a single subject. Identify both images and compare the significance of their compositions to how the speaker feels about his place within the family.

Q.2. Which family picture is never taken? Why do you think it can never be taken? Why is this nonpicture mentioned? In what ways can a picture be "taken" without a camera?

Student Encounter Activity

Research the history of the Chinese Fireworks. Why is this tradition so important? Then choose a tradition that has been lost in your culture. Find out its history and its significance to your culture. Why has this significance changed?

Li-Young Lee
THE GIFT

Li-Young Lee was born in 1957 in Indonesia to Chinese parents. His family was forced to escape for political reasons and eventually settled in Pennsylvania, where his father became a Presbyterian minister. Lee has published two volumes of poetry, *Rose* (1986) and *The City in Which I Love You* (1990).

Poem, 1 page   p. 149

This is a moving poem about a son's gratitude toward his father. Its simplicity and lack of ego evoke the best of the Chinese poetic tradition.

Much is said through two images, one of the past and another of the present. Begin a discussion by asking students to describe the two scenes and what they have in common.

You may also want to explore with the class the characterization of the father, which in many ways resembles that of the father in Ortiz's "My Father's Song." Point out the details: "a low voice"; "lovely face"; "his voice still, a well"; "a prayer"; "tenderness." One way to characterize the father is to list the traits that the son hopes to emulate with his wife. Has the son succeeded? We have found it useful to determine this through the analysis of the second scene with the students. You may want to pose the following questions to your students.

Is the father the only person we get to know? What can the students tell about the son? What is he like? How does he feel about the father? About his wife? Is the love shared by both and the sense of peace and comfort provided by the father the gift?

You may want to explore the attitude toward religion in this poem. Knowing the poet's father is a minister and that the poet is an admirer of the Bible, can the students find any symbolism in the metal splinter in the palm, in the first line, and the words not yelled out by the speaker, in the fourth stanza? Could there be a religious implication intended? Is this poem only about relationships, or could it also be about faith and the strength it provides to transcend the adversities of life?

Suggested Assignments

Q.1. Read the last quote in the author's biographical sketch. Is this relevant information to the reader? Having read one of Lee's poems, decide if he has been effective in fulfilling his hope.

Q.2. In modern family life, much attention is given to the generation gap. Miscommunication is one of its major traits. In this poem, there are two gaps: one from life to death and one from child to adult. Yet given these gaps, much meaningful communication is taking place. What factors make this communication possible? Use evidence from the poem to support your answer.

Jimmy Santiago Baca

ANCESTOR

Jimmy Santiago Baca was born in 1952 in New Mexico. He has written several collections of poetry and won the 1987 Before Columbus Foundation American Book Award.

Poem, 2 pages   p. 150

"Ancestor" characterizes a father who is full of ambiguities. You may want to start a discussion by clarifying these ambiguities. One way we have done this in class is by asking students to list the father's negative and positive traits. Students may see him as an absent father and a gypsy on the negative side, and as one who owned true freedom and filled the house with love and safety, even if for a moment, on the positive side. Spend time discussing the father's lifestyle and traits. Ask the students to explore their feelings about the father. Then try and unravel the son's feelings toward the father.

You might ask students to determine if this is a poem about acceptance, forgiveness, and love, in spite of the failings of the other? Ask students to characterize the voice in the poem. You may want to guide the discussion by asking the following questions. Is this the voice of an adult speaker or a child still in need of love and acceptance from an absent father? Why does the speaker say "that made us grow up quick and romantic"? Is this a romanticized view of the father? Ask students to find examples from the poem to support their answers to these questions.

Explore the roles of the women by what we know of them. Ask the students why we are told about the grandmother and her role in the family. Have students contrast the women and the men in the poem. Ask them to explain the difference in the activities between the sister "working the cotton fields" and the brothers "running like deer." Would the sister and grandmother feel the same about the father as the son does?

Finally, emphasize the use of detail and especially metaphors to create a vivid and dynamic characterization. Note the metaphors, for instance, in the first few lines of the poem and elsewhere.

Suggested Assignments

Q.1. If the love this father offers is as a gypsy's "for a moment," then why is the voice in this poem not harsher? What sentiments toward the father is the speaker displaying?

Q.2. Coming to terms with the past is an important part of one's development. This dynamic within a family is a powerful one for an individual searching for meaning in life. Decide if the speaker is on a search. If so, what is he searching for? What has he found? Has a resolution of some sort occurred for the speaker? If so, how satisfying was it for him? Use examples from the text to support your views.

Elías Miguel Muñoz

LITTLE SISTER BORN IN THIS LAND

Elías Miguel Muñoz was born in Cuba in 1954. He was raised in California and attended the University of California at Irvine, where he received his Ph.D. in 1984. He has published various works on literary scholarship, three novels, a play, and a collection of poems.

Poem, 2 pages   p. 152

Muñoz's poem is about the loss of one's culture, expressed through the relationship between a brother and a sister. Ask students to list those elements associated with the speaker's childhood (hens nesting, excursions on foot, ravines, sweet potato pudding) and those of the sister's (space flights, expensive toys, foreign riddles). Does the speaker simply list the differences or does he pass judgment? Point out the negative connotations associated with the sister's world. For instance, "makes of you / of every child / a little clown / plastic and ridiculous."

Explore with students what the speaker reveals about himself in describing the sister's world. Ask them to describe his childhood. Have students compare and contrast the two worlds. You may also want to analyze the title of the poem. Is the title sincere or ironic? To determine this, it may help students if you ask them the following question. If the speaker is not reproaching the sister, who is he reproaching?

We have used this poem to discuss repetition as a poetic device. Repeating the same phrase or structure, as the poet does here, sharpens the focus of the poem and adds impact and musicality.

Explore the tone of the poem. Is the speaker angry at the sister, at the situation of having to leave his home, or at American urban culture? What does he mean when he says "your words / that will always be foreign / to our experience"? Is this reflecting a permanent inability for intimacy between the siblings because of the differences in upbringing? At this point, we have found it works well to open up the discussion to how cultural differences between family members can create conflict in familial relationships. In this case, it occurs between siblings, but more often, it occurs between generations.

Suggested Activities

Q.1. Change within a family can occur at different levels simultaneously. Our reactions to those changes define our attitudes concerning them. Change is occurring in this poem and the speaker is reacting to it. What are the changes? How does the speaker react to them? Based on this information, what are the attitudes of the speaker concerning these changes?

Q.2. Repetition is a poetic device used for impact and effect. Read the poem searching for the use of repetition. What impact does it have on you? What is its effect? Does the use of repetition in this poem add to or detract from your understanding of the poem? How so?

Sherley Williams

SAY HELLO TO JOHN

Sherley Williams is an African-American poet and novelist, born in 1944 in California. She is currently professor of literature at the University of California, San Diego.

Poem, 1 page   p. 155

You may want to use this poem to explore the role of humor in literature and particularly poetry, a genre less prone to humor, especially in the twentieth century. Analyze how the humor is achieved through the language, the situation, and the xaxa rhyme. Note how the poem is tightly controlled in its structure, with the rhyme already mentioned, and its seven 4-line stanzas. In humor, timing is critical. But you may want to begin by asking the students if they found the poem to be humorous.

As with John Edgar Wideman's story "Little Brother," the writer uses colloquial dialogue, again situating the work within an African-American oral tradition. If you did not discuss language with "Little Brother," you may want to do so now. Ask students if they feel the language is problematic or effective for the poem. Note how, when read aloud, the rhythm of the poem speeds up.

Finally, address the specific topic of the poem, the birth of a son. Discuss what the poem reveals about the family structure here and the relationships. Why do we need to know about Richard and what he tells the speaker? Why is the presence of males so weak here? How does the speaker feel about this son? Ask the students to show how they know what she is feeling.

Suggested Activities

Q.1. This poem makes one smile, if not laugh. But beware, for humor brings out the best and worst in us. What do you find funny in this poem? Why is it funny to you? Are you laughing with or at the people in the poem? What does this say about you?

Q.2. Is this poem confrontational in any way?

Student Encounter Activity

Imagine this poem was written by an Anglo-American. Would your interpretation of the poem change? What role would humor play then? How would you characterize the speaker?

Naomi Long Madgett

OFFSPRING

Naomi Long Madgett is an African-American poet who has published consistently since 1941. She is professor emeritus of English at Eastern Michigan University.

Poem, 1/2 page   p. 156

This poem can be used to explore the relationship between a mother and a daughter who is growing up. You will want discuss each stanza separately. In the first stanza, analyze the mother's intentions and her emotions as she sees her daughter grow. Can the students empathize with a parent's wanting a child to mature and improve on the original, without discarding it? The mother wants her daughter to blossom and fly higher than herself but without leaving her behind.

In the second stanza, explore the central image of the twig breaking. How is the grown daughter characterized in this stanza? How do these traits reveal the mother's attitude towards her daughter? How do we know she has accepted the maturity of the daughter?

Note how the two-stanza structure of the poem reinforces the shift from mother to daughter. In the first stanza, the mother is central; in the second, the daughter monopolizes the descriptions. The unmetered, unrhymed form here is worth addressing as well. Note how the placing of words such as "self" and "unfamiliar" allow for them to apply to both daughter and mother. Finally, examine the words of the last four lines and especially the final two one-word lines. How do they define the mother's vision of her daughter?

Suggested Assignments

Q.1. In familial relationships, often times things are not what they appear to be. Analyze the poem focusing on the characterizations of the mother and the daughter. What would you say makes them different? What makes them similar? Which is the most prevalent?

Q.2. The speaker wants quite a lot from her daughter. List what she desires. Then decide if she has gotten what she wanted.

Student Encounter Activity

Interview your parents. Ask them what they wish for you as you become more independent. Make a list. Do they reveal a strong presence in *their* plans for *your* independence? How do you feel about their desires?

Simon J. Ortiz

SPEAKING

Simon Ortiz, of Navajo descent, is of the Acoma Pueblo in New Mexico. He has taught at several universities and is an editor. He has published several books including a volume of poetry and prose. He was the recipient of a humanitarian award for literary achievement in 1989.

Poem, 1/2 page   p. 158

You may find it useful to teach this poem in conjunction with the earlier one by Ortiz. Both reveal a tender and gentle father-and-son relationship, as well as a respect for the strength and nurturing effects of nature. Explore these points in both poems. Ask the students how the simple scene between father and son in "Speaking" show much about the father. Analyze the repetition of the word "speaking." Might this reveal a father's hope of everlasting communication and understanding with his son? You may want to explore how both of Ortiz's poems depict the deep spirituality of Native-American culture.

After discussing the similarities between the two poems, ask the students to determine the differences. In "My Father's Song," the speaker looks back at his forefathers; in "Speaking," the speaker looks to the future with his own son. What role does nature play in this relationship? Note how this poem develops in two stanzas, similar to Madgett's "Offspring." As in her poem, the first stanza centers around the parent and the second around the child. You may find it helpful to ask students to explore why the speaker repeats the presence of the cicadas and the ants for millions of years in each stanza. Perhaps it's because nature gives permanence and continuity to their relationship.

Suggested Assignments

Q.1. If you were the nature presence in this poem, what would you say the father is telling you? What is the baby telling you? Why are they speaking to you about each other?

Q.2. This father is introducing his son to the world. As a father, what is his hope?

Student Encounter Activity

Find a way to spend an afternoon in the woods, far from urban life. Just sit still and listen to the sounds of nature. What do you hear outside and inside yourself?

Merle Woo

LETTER TO MA

Merle Woo is Chinese and Korean-American. She writes both fiction and drama and has lectured on Asian-American studies at the University of California, Berkeley.

Essay, 7 pages   p. 159

This essay, in the form of a letter, can provide the class with a number of discussion topics: the parent-child relationship, the Americanization of second-generation immigrants and the conflicts it creates, the politics of racism and sexism, addiction within the family network, and even tone in argumentation. It might help students if you begin by listing the main subjects addressed in the letter.

To discuss the parent-child relationship, ask the students to first explore characterization. What facts do we know about the mother? What facts do we know about the father? What do we know about the daughter's perception of both parents? What do we know about her? Ask the students to describe the author. We learn much about her through her attitudes about her parents. Ask the students if the daughter reflects a mature attitude or whether she is still looking for approval. Does she seem self-absorbed? Ask them to count how many times she uses "I" in the first two pages. Is this indeed a "Letter to Ma?"

The author appears to blame the parents for her alcoholism. Ask the students if they see this and, if so, to point out an example. Do the students feel she is being fair to her parents? In addition to all that her parents have suffered, doesn't the author add to their plight by condemning them for her upbringing? Or is it that the parents have never recognized her suffering?

You might also use the letter to discuss generational conflicts, in a family where the second generation is becoming Americanized. Ask the students to identify the indications of Americanization in the daughter and grandchildren. This can lead to a discussion of differences between cultures and the way they perceive gender roles. Explore the question of why Asian-American men accuse Asian-American women of denying their roots when they become feminists. Also note the differences in attitudes toward life and its adversities between parents and daughter.

Finally, it is important to discuss the tone of the letter. The author uses an angry, condescending tone towards the mother. Even though she talks about love and compassion at the very end of the letter, these sentiments are not expressed throughout the letter. When the author discusses politics, she also uses a very emotional tone that undermines the importance of her facts. This letter can serve to point out to the students the importance of tone, especially in a persuasive essay such as this one. Ask them if the tone of this letter does not work against the effectiveness of the ideas. Can there be a problem with lack of focus in the letter as well? If so, what does it say about the author?

It may be fruitful to your students in understanding this work to discuss the history of the Chinese presence in San Francisco in the latter part of the nineteenth century, particularly the importation of Chinese workers for the railroad, mines, and unskilled labor.

Suggested Assignments

Q.1. Striking a balance between saying too little or too much is central to constructive communication. This balance can lead to understanding and empathy. Decide whether Merle Woo has reached such a balance in her letter to her mother. How successful was she in terms of empathy and understanding? Give examples from the letter to support your observations.

Q.2. Based on Merle Woo's characterization of her mother, describe the kind of person "Ma" is. List her characteristics. Keeping these in mind, pretend you are "Ma" sitting at the little round white table, about to drink your tea. Furthermore, imagine you have just read the letter and are now going to answer it. Given that you are "Ma," how would you answer your daughter's letter?

Student Encounter Activity

Compare Asian-American prejudice as seen in this story to incidents of African-American racism you are familiar with. Describe the stereotyped image of each group. Given the hostile conditions many minorities have found themselves in, how do individuals in these groups survive behind the disguises of these stereotypes?

Marie G. Lee

MY TWO DADS

Marie G. Lee is a second-generation Korean American, born and raised in Minnesota. She is the author of essays and several novels, including *Finding My Voice*, which won the 1993 Friends of American Writers Award.

Essay, 3 pages   p. 167

Lee's essay can be taught in combination with Merle Woo's "Letter to Ma." It is the reflections of a Korean-American daughter coming to terms with her Korean parents, especially her father. The title "My Two Dads" refers to the same father who acts completely American in the United States, yet completely Korean while visiting his homeland. This is the most challenging part of the essay, trying to understand with the students why the father lives such a splintered life. Explore with the students why the father seems unable to synthesize his two cultures.

The daughter is surprised by this discovery in her first trip to Korea as an adult. She is different from him in that she is trying to be Korean, while he easily switches on and off his Korean-ness like a faucet. We are not told why he cannot belong to both cultures simultaneously. You may want to touch on the fact that he is a doctor and economically successful. Is being Americanized the price he paid for his status? Is being Korean degrading in the United States and thus motivation enough to avoid its traits? Discuss how economic status plays a role in adaptation. It would be interesting to compare this dad to the dad in Merle Woo's essay. You may recall how ashamed Merle Woo feels about him. Does Marie G. Lee feel the same way?

Explore the tone. Ask the students to determine whether the daughter shows compassion and understanding towards the parents. Analyze the statement: "Attempting to learn the Korean language, *hangukmal*, a few years ago was a first step in atoning for my past indifference." The daughter seems to be assuming responsibility for her cultural indifference, even though she is aware the parents never promoted the culture. How is this attitude different from Merle Woo's? Note other revealing passages, such as paragraph 14, where the daughter displays a new understanding for Korean culture.

You may want to ask the students to delineate what traits characterize Korean culture in the United States. Also, it would be helpful to talk about U.S. involvement in the Korean War in the 1950s and continued U.S. presence there.

Suggested Assignments

Q.1. In the essay, there are "three" family members, each with a different sense of home. Identify the members and describe each one's sense of home. Do they just visit each other's homes on vacation? Can these "three" people live together in one home? Support your answer with excerpts from the text.

Q.2. In some immigrant families, it is common for first-generation members (parents) to keep second-generation members (offsprings) from being "native." To this end, they embrace the host culture completely. Find examples of this dynamic in the essay. Develop a hypothesis as to why this occurs. Decide whether it is a benevolent or a detrimental act for the second-generation members.

Student Encounter Activity

Language and culture are closely interrelated. Re-read paragraph 5 in the essay. Note how she characterizes the Korean language. Analyze a second language or your own for indications of cultural traits. Then discuss how knowing this role of language can help you to better understand your own culture or that of others.

Fenton Johnson

THE LIMITLESS HEART

Fenton Johnson writes and teaches at San Francisco State University. He was born and reared in Kentucky. He has published a novel and numerous essays in national magazines.

Essay, 2 pages   p. 170

This is a moving essay about the power of love in the face of adversity. It is a good example of how when there is so much to say, it can be more effective to provide images rather than explanations. The essay could easily be taught alongside Li-Young Lee's poem "The Gift," in the spirituality of the message, as well as in the imagistic technique used.

The author goes through a learning process and through it is "transfigured." To guide students to this understanding, explore the first paragraph where he talks about his family and states, "There are limits to how much love one can give." What happens to him and causes him to end the essay with the statement that also becomes the title: "the limitless heart"? To analyze this, ask students to outline the various anecdotes provided: the death of his companion from AIDS, the Holocaust experience of his companion's parents, the fishing scene, the *abuelita's* acceptance of the grandson. Ask the students to determine what the similarities are in these experiences and what the author learns from these events. He feels lucky because of what he has been allowed to learn. Explore how this discovery feel similar to "the gift" Li-Young Lee refers to.

Note not only how these events demonstrate the strength of love, but that they do so in the face of serious difficulties; in addition, notice the parallels between the three groups included: gays, Jews, and Latinos. Explore how these three groups share a sense of alienation and persecution. Note the statement: "I need the company of men like myself—survivors, for the moment anyway, albeit of a different struggle." Ask students to analyze what the author means by terms such as "survivors" and "struggle."

Finally, point out how the power of this essay lies in the effectiveness of the anecdotes chosen and the clarity and precision of the images. Even with these glimpses, we sense an entire world. Also note how even the description of the landscape can be used to capture the mood of the character and enhance its depiction. For this, point to the second paragraph with its description of the trees.

Suggested Assignments

Q.1. Physical descriptions can be used to characterize the mood of the subject, in this case the narrator. Scan the essay for physical descriptions. Based on these, trace his mood throughout the essay. How effective was his use of physical description in conveying mood? Decide whether his mood has changed? Provide examples from the text to support your observations.

Q.2. The narrator says: "I am so lucky" to his dying companion. This statement seems contradictory. In what ways is he unlucky? Given these, how do you reconcile his statement to his companion?

Student Encounter Activity

Write your feeling about a group different from yourself with which you are not familiar. Visit a place usually frequented by that group of individuals, such as a Jewish temple, a Christian church, a gay establishment, a women's club, a Latino neighborhood, etc. Spend some time there. Back at home, write about how you feel after the visit. Have changes occurred in you before and after writing?

The Craft of Writing:
CHARACTERIZATION

p. 174

We have found it a meaningful exercise for the students to characterize literature as a process of communication with the hope of leading to an understanding between the writer and the reader. It will help them to realize that the more one provides in the communication process, the writing itself, the greater the chances of achieving understanding. In this context, characterization is of enormous importance. It is critical for students to understand how a writer develops the characteristics that define these individuals. In fiction, we call this technique *characterization*; nonfiction essay writing, what most of your students will be writing, also depends on the same techniques to describe the persons discussed.

By now, your students have had many examples of characters in the first two chapters. We have found the second chapter on family particularly helpful in illustrating effective characterization. We suggest that you refer to examples from the text as you discuss the techniques for characterization and to the Afterword section in the anthology. This strategy we find helpful to the students.

We often begin by pointing out to the students the main ways writers provide information about a character. Dialogue is probably the most revealing—though, since people themselves are often in denial or deceptive, as a reader the student must be cautioned to "read between the lines." The actions of the character can illustrate true motivation and even contradictions with the words said. You may want to show them how other characters can also provide facts and perceptions; the narrator can be a further source of information. Finally, the descriptions of landscape/environment can serve to depict the mood of the characters. Note Fenton Johnson's essay, as well as the short story by Richard Dokey.

In writing personal essays, such as the ones assigned in the Writing about the Reading section at the end of chapter 2, we have found that anecdotes can be most useful. In this section, students are asked to find stories and anecdotes that depict a parent or relative. We have had success asking students to practice brainstorming first. You can ask them to come up with numerous anecdotes, and then select the ones that best depict the attitude or traits they wish to portray. Determining viewpoint can be a difficult part of the process for students. Remind them how an author must always make choices and that these choices are central to good writing. In order for students to make these choices, they must first decide which traits they wish to highlight. Once they have focused on and selected the stories they wish to use, make sure they work on using enough specific and concrete details to create the images.

Students can also practice using dialogue within a narration. Often they assume that dialogue is appropriate only for fiction. Point out how the nonfiction essays in this chapter use dialogue, as well as anecdotes, to enhance characterizations.

Comments on Student Writing

p. 179

In order for the students to benefit from this sample student writing, they must first have read Merle Woo's "Letter to Ma." After reading the student essay, discuss with them the strengths and weaknesses of the piece. For example, the student is successful in creating parallels between Woo's experiences and her own. She effectively describes her own mother's plight as a servant in Colombia. The writing provides a good use of supportive evidence. The voice of the speaker also comes through clearly.

The essay demonstrates potential; however, there are areas that can be used to highlight weaknesses in student writing. One of the problems most common in student writing is maintaining a thematic focus. Such is the case with this sample. The writer brings up two or three different arguments, shifts back and forth, and does not establish a clear thread throughout the essay. The characterization of the author's mother could also be strengthened.

The power of literature to stimulate and comfort people and to allow them to open up to their own plight—in this case, a student—is clearly evidenced by this piece. In this sense, the sample can be useful as a model for your students to emulate.

⌐ 3 ⌐

HERITAGE

Many of us think of America as a mosaic, made up of individuals from many different backgrounds. The sum of the personal and cultural histories and traits that are part of an individual and a people is their heritage. Thus, to fully comprehend America's heritage, we need to become more aware of the growing voices of all of its members. The selections in this anthology will help students to become familiar with the variety of personal and cultural histories and traits that make up America. They will also help students to become more aware of their own heritage.

The editors in the introduction point out that our personal heritage can include many things inherited from our parents as well as from our ancestors, such as traits, mannerisms, attitudes, tastes, and customs. When we refer to cultural heritage, we include everything from the recent and remote past that affects our present lives. Our cultural heritage comes to us through stories, myths, art, religious beliefs, music, even food. Consciously or unconsciously, heritage defines who we are as individuals and as a people.

The selections in this chapter will illustrate how in modern American society, identifying heritage can be a challenging task. Old definitions and concepts no longer apply. Modern America has expanded its borders encompassing all and any groups. New immigrants arrive daily. These groups reinforce the new concept of heritage in America. We are a country made up of different backgrounds sharing the experience of arriving and having arrived. We live side by side: Hindus, Haitians, Cubans, English, Italians, Jews, Iranians, Mexicans, African Americans, Native Americans, and Western European Americans, to list a few. Understanding each other and our experiences, recognizing the different routes and the parallel ones, can be gratifying and fulfilling as well as frustrating and painful. The works in this chapter will attest to both.

Pre-Reading Activity

Before assigning readings from this chapter, we usually begin by asking students to take fifteen minutes to draw their family tree and include each country of origin by the name of the relative. You might be surprised how many of them cannot go back further than their grandparents, if that far. After the initial attempt, we ask them to research and draw a more comprehensive family ethnic genealogical chart. You can suggest that they have consultations with great- grand-parents, other older relatives, family Bibles, old photo albums, etc. Usually students get very excited as their knowledge expands.

William Saroyan

NAJARI LEVON'S OLD COUNTRY ADVICE TO THE YOUNG AMERICANS ON HOW TO LIVE WITH A SNAKE

William Saroyan, novelist, playwright, and short story writer, was born in 1908 in Fresno, California, and died in 1981. His play *The Time of Your Life* won the Pulitzer Prize in 1939. His first collection of stories, *The Daring Young Man on the Flying Trapeze*, was published in 1934. Several of his works have been published posthumously. There are recent signs of a revival of interest in Saroyan's works.

Short story, 4 pages   p. 185

This story often works well to begin the chapter discussion on the importance of heritage and the passing on of myths and tales that define a people. The story is about an the older man, Levon, who, when distracted by Aram's four children playing a board game on the linoleum floor, decides to tell them the story of the snake. Note how the firstborn son, who is the scorekeeper, is highlighted, as if it was his responsibility more than the others to carry on.

You may want to initiate the discussion by pointing out to your students that the symbol of the snake is first presented in a negative way on the children's board game. The wise snake in Levon's story, however, is a symbol of good luck. Ask the students to contrast the different ways snakes are viewed in each country. You may also ask them to brainstorm other items that may be viewed differently from culture to culture. Think, for example, of the sacred cows of India. These explorations can lead to a fascinating discussion of cultural diversity, understanding, and tolerance.

In spite of the differences, however, the story presents two parallel worlds that share "artifacts" such as snakes, the name Sevavor, two boys, two houses, and two families. Explore with students the significance of these parallel worlds and how the snake represents cultural heritage.

Another important issue you can discuss is the importance of storytelling as a vehicle to pass on cultural values and beliefs. The children in Saroyan's story are enthralled by Levon's tale, so much so that they stop arguing and abandon their game. This may be a good place to talk about the origins of storytelling from as early as *Gilgamesh*, the first recorded epic, told by the Sumarians and written down by the Babylonians.

Suggested Assignments

Q.1. Contrasting physical settings is a technique used by writers to get a point across. Often, by presenting opposing images, the readers get a clearer picture of what is being communicated. With this in mind, compare the setting of the boy, the firstborn, to Levon's house in his story. How are they different? What do these descriptions of place suggest? What might these images say about the boy's and Levon's heritages?

Q.2. What is in a name? The snake and Aram's family share the same name. Do they share anything else? Why does Levon give the snake Aram's family name? How do you think the boy takes this "coincidence"?

Student Encounter Activity

Make a list of five items such as animals, food, or musical instruments that have a different significance for different cultures that you know. Compare and contrast the significance and deduce why they may be different. Why is it important to know this?

Maxine Hong Kingston

NO NAME WOMAN

Maxine Hong Kingston was born in California in 1940. Her first book, *The Woman Warrior*, from which this story is taken, was published in 1976 and won the National Book Critics Circle Award. Since then, she has published *China Men* and *Tripmaster Monkey: His Fake Book*. She currently lives in Oakland, California.

Short story, 9 pages   p. 190

One of the aims of this anthology is to offer pieces seldom if ever anthologized; even if the authors of the pieces have been "canonized," the actual pieces chosen have not. Kingston is perhaps the only Asian American in the canon, and this is undoubtedly her most anthologized piece. It is included nevertheless because it represents so graphically the issues and origins of the noncanonical American literature that, by its significance and power, is forcing its way into the canon.

You may want to begin the discussion of this story by asking the students to describe the structure of "No Name Woman," revealing that it is a story within a story. Ask them to identify characters, setting, and time frame in each story. We find it a successful strategy to begin with the inside story first and then work our way out.

Try asking the students to narrate the details of the aunt's story. Help them to clarify certain issues. For example, they usually cannot understand the severity of the punishment against the crime committed by the aunt. We have found students to be very righteous and critical of the Chinese villagers. You can explain how adultery threatened the social stability of the entire village since the men needed to work away from home. Even though the author does not condone the actions of the villagers, she tries to situate them within a sociohistorical context.

You can also help students to understand by asking them to relate to a familiar contemporary situation—for example, teenage pregnancy, homosexuality, AIDS, alcoholism, or drug addiction. In their own lives, they may have witnessed or been party to the rejection of a family member suffering from one of these conditions. Ask them to discuss how in our own culture we may alienate or reject members of the community we find undesirable or threatening. This topic can lead to powerful and elucidating discussions in the class about our own contemporary society and its frailties.

You may also want to discuss how the women are portrayed in their expected roles as well as with their expected vanities. Finally, you may wish to discuss the way the aunt dies by jumping into the well. For the Chinese, this was one of the worst ways of dying and a curse to the entire village, especially since she polluted their drinking water.

After a thorough discussion of the inner story, we turn to the outer story. We ask the students to explain why we are even told the story of the aunt. Many students may not realize the narrator is told this story on reaching puberty. Ask the students why the mother chooses to tell the daughter about her aunt that day. At this point, you can discuss the role of storytelling as a powerful device to convey values and beliefs. You may also want to ask students which of them grew up surrounded by stories—that is, which of them were told stories that conveyed lessons on a regular basis. Students often share some fascinating stories themselves.

Finally, you can explore the title and the thrust behind this entire piece. Ask students to explore why the narrator is telling us this story about her aunt. Is it simply to reveal historical information on Chinese culture? Or perhaps to redeem the life and heritage of the aunt, the "No Name Woman?"

Suggested Assignments

Q.1. Different cultures often use stories to convey the beliefs and attitudes of the group. In this piece, the mother often tells the narrator stories. Why does she choose to tell her daughter the story of the "No Name Woman" at this particular time? What values is she hoping to instill in her daughter through the story? Do you think the daughter assimilated the values the mother intended? Why or why not? Support your answer with the text.

Q.2. This story is included in the chapter on heritage. How is this a story about heritage?

Student Encounter Activity

Think about a relative or friend who may be suffering as a result of an "unacceptable" reality in contemporary society (alcoholism, homosexuality, AIDS, drug addiction, teenage pregnancy, attempted suicide). Describe their situation. How are they being rejected or accepted by other relatives or friends? Explore your feelings toward them.

Leslie Marmon Silko

PRIVATE PROPERTY

Leslie Marmon Silko was born in 1948 in Albuquerque, New Mexico, and grew up on the Laguna Pueblo reservation. Her heritage is mixed—part Laguna, part Mexican, part white. She is a graduate of the University of New Mexico and now teaches at the University of Arizona. She is a poet and short story writer.

Short story, 7 pages   p. 200

Silko's story is full of themes and perspectives that can lead to stimulating discussions and even arguments. Nevertheless, we have found that the point of view can be confusing, so it may be helpful to distinguish for students the differences between the narrator's point of view and the point of view of the characters. Note the second paragraph as an example: The narrator tries to maintain a detached objective distance; however, we see a bias toward Etta.

You may want to begin by having the students list details of Etta's personal story, such as the fact that she is an orphan and that she prefers flowers and fences. Ask students to indicate ways we know the clan disapproves of these traits, and how the narrator judges the same traits and evaluates the rumors about her. After describing Etta and the community's reaction to her, ask students to explore if Etta has indeed changed to "white ways." You may want to note, if no student does, how the land was initially divided by the mother-in-law and not by Etta herself. At this point, it can help to bring in the introductory paragraph that speaks of the story of the orphan, like Etta. Ask students to find parallels between the initial story and Etta's life.

From a discussion of Etta, we have found it easy to jump into a discussion of "traditional ways" versus "modern ways." Ask the students to cite examples of conflicts that would illustrate the tension. The hardest part of this story is exploring the narrator's point of view toward Etta and what her desires represent. Does she represent the interest of the individual and her privacy, over the collective interest of the group? Or is she reaffirming the collective?

You may also want to explore the significance of the wild horses and their parallelism with Etta, as well as the infidelity of the husband. Why are we given this scene? Ask students to reflect on the women's attitude towards the man and his behavior. A discussion of this topic can serve to contrast the role of women and men in the community. You may need to call to their attention the fact that it's the women who pass down the house and property.

Finally, you may want to bring the entire discussion back to the chapter's theme, heritage, and explore what seems to be a conflict of heritages between Etta and the rest of the clan. Note, if no one does, how perhaps Etta's intrusion as an outsider may function as a vehicle for the others to reaffirm their own beliefs.

Suggested Assignments

Q.1. In families as well as in clans, boundaries between the members are flexible, yet maintained. However, the boundary between the group and the outside are inviolate. This is one aspect of Native-American heritage. With this in mind, review the story and note all the episodes of bickering, arguing, and stretching boundaries that take place. What do you think these, in the aggregate, represent? How does Etta fit into your observation?

Q.2. Look at the title of the story. Imagine it being a sign posted along a track of land. What normally follows these words on such signs? Now assume that the title alludes to heritage. Given this, and from a reader's perspective, whose heritage is posted Private Property?

Student Encounter Activity

Explore the idea of food as ritual. Research three different cultures in the United States where foods may have special functions as part of their heritage—for example, the gravediggers' meal in this story. Explain the role food plays in heritage and bring the class a sample from your own or your family's experience.

Lorna Dee Cervantes

HERITAGE

Lorna Dee Cervantes was born in San Francisco in 1954; she is of Mexican descent. She has published two books of poems and currently teaches creative writing at the University of Colorado at Boulder.

Poem, 1/2 page   p. 208

The question of heritage lies at the heart of this poem. The poet goes to the land of her ancestors, Mexico, but feels rejected there. Even though her body, her blood, is Mexican, her thoughts are American. This point is illustrated in the last two lines of the first stanza.

You may wish to begin the discussion by asking students to determine the tone of the poem. Ask them to explore how the poet feels about herself and her identity. Is she satisfied with her double identity or has she internalized the rejection? Ask students to give examples to support their answers.

To fully understand this poem, ask students to analyze what the poet means in several places such as "Blame it on the old ones" or "I didn't ask to be brought up tonta!" Ask them to explore whether the poet is placing blame for her condition and, if so, on whom. You may also want to ask them how the use of Spanish enhances the cultural tensions within the poet. You can also explore how the last line of the poem deals with the poet's conflict.

If your class includes students with mixed heritages—as most of our classes do; in fact, most of our students have mixed heritages—you may want to ask these students to share how they feel about being of two cultures. Ask if any of them has returned to the home of their ancestors and, if so, to share how it made them feel. You may use this to open up, now with a more personal engagement, the whole issue of heritage and its importance, or lack of importance, to them.

Suggested Assignments

Q.1. "Heritage, Heritage! Where art thou, oh Heritage?" is an apt paraphrase of a famous query. For second-generation cultural groups, a search for heritage can be elusive, painful, or seemingly irrelevant. Scan the poem looking for evidence of emotional pain associated with the speaker's search for heritage. Make a list of the words or phrases that indicate her pain.

Q.2. Let's say you are a good friend of this person. Based on your analysis of the poem, suggest ways to make her come to terms with her cultural reality. Write your suggestions in the form of a letter.

Linda Hogan

HERITAGE

Linda Hogan, a Chickasaw, was born in Denver in 1947. She has published several books of poems as well as a novel. She currently teaches creative writing at the University of Colorado.

Poem, 1 page   p. 209

This poem by Linda Hogan works well immediately following Lorna Dee Cervante's "Heritage," and has worked well for us in class.

As a transition, we begin by focusing on the contrast of color that plays in both poems. Dee Cervantes mentions "the dye that will color my thoughts"; Hogan contrasts the "white" of her mother to the "brown" of her father and his side of the family.

You can start by asking students to list the lines where either color is mentioned. Ask them to discuss the qualities attributed to each. You may want to point out how often in literature (and in language in general) white is associated with positive attributes, such as sunlight, and brown or black with negatives things, such as evil and the unknown. In this poem, however, the reverse occurs. White is associated with a "weighing down" and with shame, while the black of the saliva is nurturing. Ask students to explain why this may be so.

A discussion of color can lead into a discussion of the grandmother and her role in the speaker's life. The image of the grandmother's coffee can full of black saliva spilling on the white shirt of the young speaker dominates most of the poem. What does this image tell your students about heritage and the role of the grandmother in passing on the heritage? It is almost as if the spilling of the saliva were an induction ritual that allowed the speaker to feel a part of her people.

You may also wish to spend some time analyzing the last two lines of the poem. To help the students understand them better, you can first talk about Native-American hunting tribes and their nomadic way of life. For such a tribe, home was heritage, not a physical location. If so, ask the students what secrets the grandmother could have shared with the poet to help her come to terms with not having a home. Finally, you may want to ask them if home in the last line means just a physical place or is she expanding it to mean a cultural home as well.

Suggested Assignments

Q.1. What effect would line 16, "my father was told not to remember," have on a person searching for heritage?

Q.2. Read lines 45–46. Search the poem looking for literal evidence of "never having a home." Then search the poem for intuitive evidence. Based on your observations, decide where the speaker's home lies. Defend your conclusion with inferences from the poem.

Student Encounter Activity

Native Americans have a history of dispersion. Research an event like the Cherokee Trail of Tears tragedy. Having lost their homeland, how would you say Native Americans maintain their heritage today? Do they? Explain your answer.

Pat Mora

BORDERS

Pat Mora was born in El Paso, Texas. Her Chicana heritage and Southwestern background are central to her poems. She has published three books of poems and currently lives in Cincinnati, Ohio.

Poem, 1 page   p. 211

This poem deals with the obstacles to true communication, the danger of assuming we understand each other because we speak the "same language."

The epigraph is a good place to begin a discussion of the poem. Ask students what clues we are given here to begin to understand the poem. The poem, we sense, deals with gender and culture and the obstacles both present to people trying to understand each other.

To support the discussion, you may ask the students to take each stanza separately; however, this poem works almost like a puzzle, thus the picture is not clear until we see the whole. For example, ask students who the "we" is in the first stanza. Is it the "us" in the last stanza? If so, ask them what didn't the "we" notice. Did they not understand each other even though they had assumed it? You may need to spend time on the third stanza. Ask the students for clues that would explain why the "us" cannot communicate. Is it because of gender, as the epitaph may hint? Or is it because of culture, as the first stanza seems to focus on? Is it both? These questions can lead the class to an active discussion, even a heated argument.

Suggested Assignments

Q.1. Besides the differences in meanings of language, what other clashes do you think are occurring in the poem? In emotional terms, how would you characterize these clashes?

Q.2. After you have finished reading the poem, reread the first two lines. What is your answer to the question posed? What do you think is the speaker's answer?

Student Encounter Activity

Change the title of the poem from "Borders" to "America." Assume that the "we" and "us" in the poem refer to North America and South America. In groups of three, provide past and current information that would highlight the concept, as posed by the poet, of miscommunication between these two regions. Share your findings with the class.

David Mura

LISTENING

David Mura is a third-generation Japanese American. His book, *Turning Japanese: Memoirs of a Sansei*, won the 1991 Josephine Miles Oakland PEN book award. He is a poet, and his collection *After We Lost Our Way* won the 1989 National Poetry Series Contest. He is also a performance artist, playwright, and professor.

Poem, 1 page   p. 213

Mura's poem introduces the chapter's topic of heritage in a unique way, through the expected birth of a child. We do not see the central image until the end of the poem when we are told about a woman's belly and an imperceptible bump. You may want to begin the discussion by asking students to explain what is meant by these last lines. Once they comprehend the central image, understanding the rest of the poem should not be difficult.

You may want to explore with students the recurring images of water, such as rain, bay, sea, waterfall, stream, swell, and riverbed. After they have listed the images, ask them to explain what they represent. They may link the water images to the liquid in the womb, which is the central image. If so, ask them how memories of one's heritage are like the liquid in the womb.

An interesting activity you can try is asking the students to choose several of the images introduced in the first five stanzas and ask them to draw a scene. This helps them to visualize the places the speaker recalls in the poem.

Suggested Assignments

Q.1. A birth or a baby and a death or an elder are important markers of one's heritage. These events evoke reflection, a time for acquiring perspective. Based on this thought, what is the baby "saying" to the speaker?

Q.2. In the biographical sketch, we are informed that the poet is a *sansei*. Estimate how many years have passed between the "native" ancestor and the Americanized poet. With this in mind, reread the poem's last line. Would you agree that the past is romanticized by the speaker? What does this romanticized version reflect about the speaker's feelings toward his heritage? Be prepared to defend your decisions.

Student Encounter Activity

Interview your mother and your father separately. Ask each to reflect on how they felt about your eminent birth and what it meant in its relation to his/her individual heritage. Write down your findings. Are there any surprises? Compare the results with classmates looking for consensus and differences, and the factors which may influence these.

Muriel Rukeyser

TO BE A JEW IN THE TWENTIETH CENTURY (FROM LETTER TO THE FRONT)

Muriel Rukeyser was born in New York City in 1913; she died in 1980. She was a trained aviator, a journalist, and a poet. Rukeyser's poems often reflect her Jewish heritage and her powerful concerns for human rights.

Poem, 1/2 page   p. 214

"To Be a Jew" was written during World War II and is included in the Reform Jewish prayer book. It can be seen as a call to the spirit to accept the gift of suffering for the cause of human freedom. Both the historical and religious context of this poem will help students understand the power of the poem. You may want to use the line "the gift is torment" to explore the suffering of the Jews as a chosen people and the Holocaust.

The poem itself is a sonnet. Looking at this structure may help students understand the poem better. To comprehend its compacted verses, point out how the first eight lines depict the dilemma. The following three augment it, and the last three offer a resolution.

Also, you may want to take individual lines, such as "Wishing to be invisible, you choose / death of the spirit," or "Daring to live for the impossible," and use them as a springboard for philosophical discussions on the meaning of the sentences and their relationship to Jewish heritage.

Suggested Assignments

Q.1. There is a dual presence in the poem: the world of the spirit and the world of the flesh. List the characteristics of each. Decide which world the letter is beckoning the reader to choose. Justify your answers with textual references.

Q.2. This poem was written during World War II, a torturous time for Jews around the world. Given that many years have passed, would you consider this "letter" an artifact or a living document still applicable? On what grounds do you base your decision?

Student Encounter Activity

Imagine the following scenario. It is the late twentieth century. Somewhere in the Middle Eastern Holy Lands two soldiers, a Palestinian and a Jew, are facing each other with rifles drawn. The Jewish soldier hands this old poem to the Palestinian, who reads it. One of them says, "We are brothers." Who would say these words?

Maya Angelou

AFRICA

Maya Angelou is an African-American poet. She has an ongoing autobiography, has published numerous volumes of poetry, and has written a musical, a documentary, and a television series. She is active in national and international affairs in a wide range of subjects as well as being the official poet at the inauguration of President Clinton in January 1993.

Poem, 1 page   p. 216

The title of this poem, "Africa," lets students know from the beginning what this poem is about. You may want to start the discussion by analyzing each of the stanzas. Ask students to explore the metaphors in each. They should be able to discern the historical flow of the poem.

The second stanza can be fertile ground for a historical discussion on the slave trade. Some of your students may be more familiar with the facts than others.

You may want to explore with them the tone of the poem, especially as depicted in the last stanza. Ask students what the speaker means by "now she is striding." Is the voice optimistic about the future of Africa? If so, how can they tell and in what way?

Finally, you can ask the students if this poem is only about the continent of Africa or if it can also be about African heritage. Given this possibility, what can the poem be saying about the importance of history and remembering?

Suggested Assignments

Q.1. Finish the following analogy: Maya Angelou is to Robert Frost what "Africa" is to "_____"? Explain your response.

Q.2. One's heritage can be another's future. Given this, reread the last stanza of the poem. Discern who is being asked to remember and why they are being asked.

Ray A. Young Bear

IN THE FIRST PLACE OF MY LIFE

Ray A. Young Bear was born in Tama, Iowa, in 1950. He is from the Sauk and Fox tribe of Iowa, better known as the Mesquakies. He is the author of several collections of poems, a novel, and a collection of biographical narratives about Midwestern Native American culture.

Poem, 2 pages   p. 217

This poem, like others in the chapter, uses recollections of ancestors as the vehicle for exploring heritage. You may want to begin by discussing the images in the poem. Ask the students to describe the speaker's memories of the grandfather. You can point out how his strongest images are tied to birth and death, perhaps the reason why the poem has a dreamlike tone to it. For example, "i floated over the floor towards him" in the third stanza.

After discussing the grandfather, turn to the "bald-headed man" and ask students to identify him and his role in the family and the poem. This analysis should lead students to the last lines which hold the key to the poem. Ask them to pay special attention to the last line, "unlike ours." What is the speaker revealing about himself in this line?

Suggested Assignments

Q.1. As adults, we sometimes hold vague memories from our early childhood. These images may have special significance to our adult life. Looking back at the first remembrance in the poem, describe what special significance it holds for the adult speaker.

Q.2. Reread the last two lines of the poem. Keeping the tone of the poem in mind, how would you characterize the speaker's feelings about his heritage?

Student Encounter Activity

Think of an older relative in your extended family who left a distinct impression on you. Write a poem describing several vivid scenes you recall about this person.

Agha Shahid Ali

SNOWMEN

Agha Shahid Ali was born in Kashmir, lived in New Delhi, and now resides in Amherst, Massachusetts. He is the author of scholarly work, as well as being a published poet. He writes exclusively in English.

Poem, 1 page   p. 220

Like "Postcard from Kashmir" by the same poet, "Snowmen" is a concise yet powerful poem grounded on the central image of the snowman. Students will probably find the poem strangely moving, like the mysterious ancestor from Samarkand.

Some students may question the reference to the women as freezing under the snowman's embrace and then thawing. You may want to point out that in the world of the snowmen in the Himalayas, freezing is the natural order of things and that thawing (perhaps surviving, flourishing to old age) and "clear evaporation" can be seen as positive images, contrasted to the "melting" in the last line of the poem.

We find it useful to explore with care the last line, "on their melting shoulders." The first two stanzas emphasize clear images of strength and permanence, such as "skeleton," "passed / from son to grandson," "every year."

Yet the last stanza offers a stark contrast with the speaker seeing himself as being the "last snowman" on "melting shoulders." Ask students what this contrast could mean. Is the speaker suggesting that he will carry his ancestry with pride, even if he is the last to do so, until it disappears?

Throughout the discussion, you may want to ask students to clarify the metaphors used, such as "his skeleton under my skin," or "their voices hushed to ice."

Suggested Assignments

Q.1. Unless it is cold year-round, snowmen melt. Scan the first two stanzas looking for words which evoke a solid snowman. Then read the last lines. What do you think is happening to the speaker's heritage?

Q.2. Compare line 17 to lines 23 and 24. What accounts for the switch in the carriers? What can this reveal about one's heritage?

Virginia Cerenio

[WE WHO CARRY THE ENDLESS SEASONS]

Virginia Cerenio is a second-generation Filipino-American who grew up in San Francisco. She has published both poetry and fiction.

Poem, 1 page   p. 221

In Cerenio's poem, the emphasis on how blood, obligation, and custom inevitably affect character, even across oceans, is illustrated by the insistent Filipino phrases as well as the "natural" ties of childbirth. Get your students to discuss how the sense of inevitability is communicated, how customs are made to seem to grow out of biological and linguistic processes.

One way to discuss the issues of this poem, and perhaps return to the issues of parenthood and family ties you may have talked about in earlier selections, is to isolate the key words of the poem, pitting events of a single instant (heartbeats, breathing) against a sense of process, unvarying repetition, and permanence (seasons, shadows, desires, dreams). Note how much of the poem depends on the single word "carry" in line 1, how crucial women are biologically and emotionally to the process of passing on customs and values.

You may also want to explore the role of the individual. Ask students how much room the poem leaves for individual choice. Compare and contrast the sense of tribal control with that in other selections (for example, Woo's "Letter to Ma" or Silko's "Private Property") in which the need to express individual differences from family and tribe is asserted.

Suggested Assignments

Q.1. Draw a diagonal line from the first word "we" to the word "in" in the last line of the poem. Imagine the line as a fence between neighbors. Identify the neighbors on both sides of it and, in terms of neighborliness, describe their relations.

Q.2. Does the physical image of the poem reinforce the speaker's conclusion or contradict it? (Squint your eyes while looking at the poem.)

Yvonne Sapia

GRANDMOTHER, A CARIBBEAN INDIAN,
DESCRIBED BY MY FATHER

Yvonne Sapia was born in New York City in 1946. Her family comes from Puerto Rico. She has lived in Florida since 1956 and teaches at Lake City Community College. Her poetry has won various literary prizes.

Poem, 1 1/2 pages   p. 223

You may want to use this poem to explore point of view. Emphasize to the students how they must be careful not to assume that the speaker's voice is always the poet's. In this case, the title should give students a clue that the speaker is the father. Explore his voice. If this is a story of a father to his daughter, perhaps he is answering her questions. If so, ask students what those questions might be. What is the tone of his voice? The last stanza may help students to answer this. Also refer to line 4 in the first stanza. Why did the father have "no map" and how does he feel about that?

The grandmother is obviously important to the story. Ask students to describe her life and the events that shaped her attitudes. You may want to use the following questions to stimulate the discussion. Why was the grandmother "given the island / but no wings?" Why does she not come to the pier to say goodbye to her son? You may want to note that even though we learn more about the grandmother than anyone else, the poem is truly about the father and his decision to leave the island. What does the poem also say to us about the listener?

Get the students to discuss the conflict experienced by the speaker. He needs "to take care / not to exhume / from the mound of memory"; he loses his place in the "thatched house," yet is he satisfied with his decision to leave the island? The sentiments in this poem recall those of Elías Miguel Muñoz's "Little Sister Born in This Land." You may want the students to compare the two. Note how both poets come from Caribbean islands with strong traditional ties to the United States.

If you have not done so yet, you may want to give students background about the relationship between Puerto Rico and the United States. Students may not be familiar with the Commonwealth status of the island nor with the historical circular migration between the island and New York.

Suggested Assignments

Q.1. In understanding your individual heritage, you have to deal with your ancestors' individual heritages as well. Each ancestor has affected your own to varying degrees. Can this idea be applied to the grandmother, the father, and the listener in the poem? If so, pinpoint the specific phrases that illustrate transgenerational influences in each.

Q.2. To a Caribbean immigrant, "banana boat" is a derogatory term. Why is this so? Yet in line 42, the father uses the term. How would you explain this anomaly?

Student Encounter Activity

Make a list of derogatory terms used to describe the passage of an immigrant, such as "banana boat." Research the origins of these terms and explain how they have come to be negative terms.

Alberto Alvaro Ríos

MI ABUELO

Alberto Alvaro Ríos was born in Nogales, Arizona, in 1952. He is the author of short stories, poems, and a novel. He teaches at Arizona State University. His father was from southern Mexico and his mother from England.

Poem, 1 page   p. 224

"Mi Abuelo" is different from other poems in the chapter in its use of fantastical, and even humorous, images. However, it shares the view of elders as sources of heritage, with a mystical quality, almost like the one in "in the first place of my life."

Begin by asking students to describe the central image of the grandfather under the ground listening and talking through the pipe. In spite of the comical qualities of the image, what does it say about the grandfather's role in the family? Also ask students to point out the lines that describe the speaker's feelings about the grandfather, such as "mi abuelo is a liar." These lines reflect a skepticism toward the grandfather. Ask students why the speaker may feel this way about him.

Also try to get your students to evaluate the first and last images of the grandfather. Do they support or contradict the images in the body of the poem? Ask them how they feel about the grandfather in the poem.

Suggested Assignments

Q.1. If this poem reflects an argument between a skeptical spectator and a magician, then who would you say won the argument? Support your conclusion with specific passages from the poem.

Q.2. In what ways is the pipe like a feeding tube? Who is being nourished by it?

Dennis Scott

GRAMPA

Dennis Scott is from Jamaica. He is known as a playwright, a play director, and a skilled poet. He has published works of poetry and won numerous awards.

Poem, 1 page   p. 226

This is a sweet poem depicting the passage of an ancestor and the hope of the remaining one to meet again on a distant Shore.

You may want to start by asking students to divide the poem into two parts: the past with the recollections of the grandfather and the present at the death of the same grandfather. You may also want to spend some time discussing the use of colloquial language, to find out if it poses any difficulties for students.

Finally, ask the students to describe the grandfather and the sentiments the speaker bears towards him.

Suggested Assignments

Q.1. If birth and death are markers of one's heritage, and one is to take something of significance from these events, what then has the speaker carried away from this death?

Q.2. The poem depicts the death of an elder. How would you characterize the speaker's feelings toward this death?

Student Encounter Activity

Recall the death of a significant member of your family. What "gifts" did this individual leave you with for the rest of your life? Share these with your classmates.

Max Apple

TROTSKY'S BAR MITZVAH

Max Apple grew up in a kosher Jewish household in Grand Rapids, Michigan. He is regarded as an affectionate critic of American life and often writes about conflicts between different groups in American society. He is best known as a short story writer, but has also written plays and a novel.

Play, 6 pages   p. 227

The relationship of a grandson to his grandfather should be a familiar topic to your students by now. Many of the poems in this chapter deal with a grandparent as a source of heritage, wisdom, and at times irritation. This play by Max Apple picks up on many of the themes you may have discussed already. Nevertheless, it introduces a new dimension in a humorous way.

In some ways, the conflict is reversed since the child's father represents the traditional Jewish beliefs, while the grandfather is influenced by his Communist ideology. You may want to review some of the principles of the Communist ideology mentioned by the grandfather and who Trotsky and Stalin were. Note how Larry mentions the infamous deeds of Stalin, while the grandfather calls him a little Trotsky, separating himself from Stalin.

Students may also need help understanding what the grandfather means by saying he could have sent the boy to Cuba. Although today even liberal intellectuals have distanced themselves from Castro's revolution, and see him as another dictator who used a popular ideology to his advantage, in the early decades of the revolution some placed high hopes on Castro. They hoped he would carry out sincere changes to improve the fate of the Cuban people.

While discussing these issues, you may also want to probe students to find out if they are familiar with the Jewish custom of a Bar Mitzvah. Understanding the importance of this coming-of-age ritual for the boy is necessary to fully appreciate the play. The boy's desire for the grandfather to attend the event emphasizes the intimacy between the grandfather and the boy. Explore with students the relationship between the two. The following questions can be helpful. Why is the grandfather so stubborn? Why does he give in at last? Does it have to do with the boy's willingness to give up the party?

You may also want to discuss the tone of the play. How does the playwright achieve humor? Why does the playwright choose to use humor? How does the humor help the flow of the play? In discussing humor, you may also wish to discuss the role of the black assistant baker. He seems to fulfill the traditional "comedic relief" of the play. How so? and why? Is his role only for comedic effect?

Even though the boy's father and mother are only indirectly mentioned, we have found it worthwhile to discuss the tensions between them and the grandfather. Ask students what we know about this relationship and why the boy sees a side of the grandfather that nobody else sees.

Finally, you can ask the students to decide what they would have done if they were the grandfather. Perhaps the play makes it too easy to agree with the grandfather's decision. You can ask them to think of a situation in their life when they had to choose between a personal relationship and their beliefs. This may help them to understand the dilemma better.

Suggested Assignments

Q.1. Elders play an important role in our heritage. How is grandpa important to the boy in this drama? Provide examples from the play.

Q.2. Finish the following script:

Larry: You came to my grammar-school graduation.
Grandpa: Because education is a weapon.
Larry: You always come to my Little League games.
Grandpa: Because the revolution needs strong bodies.
Larry: You came to my Bar Mitzvah.
Grandpa: Because _____ .

Explain why you chose the words you did.

Student Encounter Activity

Given what you know about the histories and the relationships of these people from the play, as a group, continue the drama as it would evolve in the Bar Mitzvah. Try the round robin approach.

Margarita M. Engle

DIGGING FOR ROOTS

Margarita Engle is the daughter of a Cuban mother and an American father. She was born and raised in California. She has published an opinion column for the Hispanic Link News Service since 1983, and her haikus have been included in many anthologies in the United States and Japan.

Essay, 4 pages   p. 234

This can be considered a practical abstract for how to go about finding one's lineage. The essay is lucid and self-explanatory. You may want to assign it before asking students to draw their own family tree.

You may also want to explore what the author means when she says that "family history is much more than a series of names and dates." She says they are a window of understanding. Ask students what these windows open up to.

Finally, if you have not done so before, you may want to explain why the author is not able to return to Cuba. Some of your students may not be aware of travel restrictions to the island, especially for those of Cuban descent. Explore how this situation may explain a Cuban American's search for heritage.

Suggested Assignments

Q.1. Read the last line of paragraph 2. Take it as a nail in a coffin for heritage. How would the disappearance of heritage affect people?

Q.2. Read paragraph 14 again. Why is it important to this author to build a window for her descendants? Do you have such a window? In what way is the window important to you?

Student Encounter Activity

Interview an elder member of your family. Ask them to relate the connections between a branch of your family. Based on this interview, draw a window and in it list images that illustrate discoveries about your ancestry that came as a result of the interview. (You may also want to draw or cut out pictures to make a collage that evokes your sentiments.)

Judith Ortiz Cofer

MORE ROOM

Judith Ortiz Cofer was born in Puerto Rico in 1952 but grew up both on the island and in the United States. She has published poetry, a novel, and several collections of essays, including *Silent Dancing: A Partial Remembrance of a Puerto Rican Childhood,* from which this selection is taken.

Essay, 3 pages   p. 238

The interpretation of this essay pivots on the grandmother's act of getting more room. You may want to begin by asking students to summarize the story of the grandmother provided in the first half of the essay. Ask them to give details that depict the customs and attitudes of the family. How is this grandmother with her almost mystical herbal powers and her rosary and crucifixes similar to other grandparents seen before in the chapter?

In the second part of the essay, we discover how the grandmother tricks the husband into getting her own room. Ask students to describe the husband. Why is he referred to as a "benevolent dictator?" You may want to explore with students if he fits the stereotype of a Hispanic male. In what way does he or does he not?

From the discussion of the husband, you can analyze the roles of each gender. Paragraph 9 is a good place to start. Ask students to describe the behavior of each gender in this scene and how each feels about the other. Specifically, how does the grandmother feel about the husband? At this point, you may want to ask them why they think the grandmother wanted her own room.

Get students to read over the last paragraph carefully. You can use the following questions to help them. Are the views expressed here the point of view of the grandmother or the granddaughter? Would the grandmother describe her actions in the way the author describes them? If not, are we finding out more about the author and her attitudes toward gender roles than we imagine at first glance? Is the action by the grandmother of getting more room the heritage she leaves her granddaughter?

Suggested Assignments

Q.1. Understanding a momentous action taken by an ancestor can help us to clarify our own motivations. In the essay, Mamá kicks Papá out of the bedroom. How does the speaker interpret this action by the grandmother? What can this interpretation tell us about the speaker?

Q.2. In extended families, to criticize is often taboo. Everyone acknowledges the assigned roles given to each family member. To an astute outside observer, behavior becomes paramount in discerning truth. Identify the statements made about the persons in the story. Note the actions taken by all of the people. Do the statements and the actions mirror each other or are they paradoxical? Explain your observations.

Student Encounter Activity

Take a mental tour of your grandparents' home. Describe the objects that you vividly recall from this tour. What could these artifacts be saying to you about your heritage?

Gail Y. Miyasaki
OBACHAN

Gail Miyasaki is a third-generation Japanese American born in Hawaii. She has taught ethnic studies, and has worked as a journalist and editor for Hawaii Public Television. She has written several books of Asian ethnic studies.

Essay, 2 pages   p. 242

This narrative in many ways lies at the heart of the major issue in this chapter: the personal ties between family members separated by generations and cultures but tied together by deep love. The narrator's love for the grandmother is presented tenderly and indirectly but deeply and movingly. You may want to explore this tone with the class, and ask them to point out how the narrator subtly reveals her love to the reader, as in paragraph 5.

The cultural gulf between the narrator and the grandmother first surfaces with the kimono but appears most clearly in the story of the narrator's Aunt Mary. Here again there is indirection: the narrator never openly states her feelings about Mary's marrying a Caucasian sailor, but we can understand, it seems to us, her responses through her mother's. You may want to discuss other pieces in the chapter that introduce individuals separating from the clan, such as the father in Sapia's poem "Grandmother" and the sister in Silko's "Private Property." Ask the students to compare and contrast the attitudes of the individuals and the clan's response to them.

The combination of love and cultural difference is encapsulated in the title, the Japanese word for "grandmother," both loving and, for English-speaking Americans like the narrator, "foreign." You may want to point out that it is common for second- and third-generation Americans to use the language of "home" to evoke strong familial connections. This is particularly true for the names of close relatives such as parents and grandparents.

Suggested Activities

Q.1. Journeys away from our heritage can distance us from it. They can also bring us closer to it. With this in mind, compare the grandmother's journey to a new land with that of Mary's. How are they similar? How are they different? Given this, was Mary acting within her family tradition? Why is the grandmother opposed to Mary's journey? How is the journey viewed by the other family members?

Q.2. Imagine you are Mary and that your daughter reads this story to you from her copy of this anthology. Being Mary, how would you react to it? In light of this information, what would you say to your daughter about her heritage?

Student Encounter Activity

The Japanese presence in Hawaii has a long history. Research the factors that would explain this presence up to the present day. How are these factors similar to those of other immigrant groups elsewhere?

The Craft of Writing:

POINT OF VIEW

p. 246

The Afterword in chapter 3 presents an interesting and informative discussion of point of view that can be helpful to students. We would recommend having students read it before assigning the selections in the chapter. That way, you can ask questions about point of view as you read the pieces.

Most of the Writing about the Reading assignments ask students to describe a relative, their family, or their ethnic group. If you are following the order of the chapters in the anthology, you will probably have already discussed the importance of setting and detail in creating an effective description. (If not, you may want to read the Craft of Writing sections for chapters 1 and 2 in this guide and review the suggestions discussed with your students.)

With this chapter, you can emphasize the importance of point of view. We work extensively with students helping them to realize that selecting a focus for their description is not sufficient; they must also select a point of view. You may wish to spend some time distinguishing between fact, opinion, and point of view. Point of view is the position from which the details are perceived and related to the reader. It is the filter that controls how the reader perceives the details. Facts and opinions do not generate interesting perspectives in writings. Points of view do.

To clarify the issue of point of view for students, we have found it helpful to compare the writer to a painter. We discuss how an artist must choose not only the subject—the focus—of his painting, but also the perspective—the point of view—he wishes to convey. For example, if an artist wants to paint a seacoast, he must determine the mood and attitude he wishes to evoke with the painting. This will determine his choice of colors, textures, sizes, and even shadows. Likewise, a writer must have a point of view toward the object she is describing. This point of view will determine her choice of details, the physical position from which the speaker sees the object or action, the descriptions, and even the comparisons.

Finally, we spend some time discussing consistency in point of view. Some of our students have trouble maintaining the point of view. The trouble may include something as simple to fix as person and number or as subtle as attitude.

Comments on Student Writing

p. 251

This essay by Lisbeth Sivertsen is a good example for students to illustrate how they can use literature as a springboard to a personal discussion on attitudes and values. In this case, the student has used Maxine Hong Kingston's "No Name Woman" to discuss the issue of cultural heritage and the responsibility of an immigrant to maintain or discard this heritage.

At first glance, your students may find the essay challenging, even difficult to follow. You can help them by discussing the basic structure of the essay. In the first paragraph, the author introduces the arguments. Ask your students to point out the questions to be resolved. The second paragraph introduces the issues as presented in the short story. Again, you may want to ask students to enumerate the main points discussed in this paragraph, especially since it is long. It may be helpful to spend some time analyzing the author's discussion of "roundness" since it is central to her attitude about conformity. The third paragraph brings in American values in order to contrast them to those of the short story; the conclusion discusses the author's personal reflections in an attempt to answer the questions presented in the introduction.

After reviewing the organization of the essay, and clarifying issues for the students, you may want to ask the students how they feel about the style of the essay. If they find it difficult to follow, ask them what suggestions for changes they have. They may suggest that the writer should use shorter paragraphs with more directed topic sentences and clearer transitions. Even though this could be true, you may want to discuss personal style and the way the author builds a case to offer an explanation in the end. Though not as easy to follow, it is a valid and popular technique for developing a complex issue such as the one here.

If you have not done so in your earlier discussions, you may also want to have the students express their opinions about the author's conclusions. Do your students agree with her observations about China, about the United States? Do they agree with her views of immigrants? How do they feel about the rejection of one's cultural heritage?

4

LANGUAGE

Language is the most intimate form of communication with ourselves and with others. How we think as individuals tells each of us how we are as individuals. We cannot think without language. As the editors point out in the introduction, language shapes who we are and how we perceive others. As such, language is intricately tied to our culture. So, in a sense, language is part of our being as well as part of our culture.

Without language we cannot fully communicate; as the selections in this chapter illustrate, it is a necessary vehicle for all facets of our lives. Whether we want to fit into a profession or a social sphere, language plays a pivotal role. It is a conveyor not only of words but also of values, attitudes, beliefs, and desires. Our desires for professional acceptance or social mobility may ask us to make adjustments, even choices about the language we speak. If a person belongs to two cultures, a common situation in the United States today, these choices can be difficult.

For the writers in this chapter, making a choice is critical since language is the instrument of their art. In choosing a language, they often face personal, cultural, and professional dilemmas, which frequently become the subject of their work. This chapter presents several examples of this situation.

Apart from the personal dilemma that an individual, whether a writer or not, may experience, language can be a barrier at a cultural level. It can be the source of misunderstanding and conflict, as well as the scapegoat for prejudices and other abuses. People will use differences in language to justify deeper fears and resentments. The selections that follow explore the power of language in these various aspects. In the end, though, they attest to language as our most important communicator.

Pre-Reading Activity

Before assigning the selections in this chapter, you may want to have the students explore the concept of language and how it can encompass different realms. In addition to its traditional concept, language also refers to the "language" of a profession, a trade, a science, or a geographical region with its unique accents and expressions.

Try dividing the class into groups and assign a different realm to each group. Have each group discuss the advantages and limitations of language in each realm. For example, how does the "language" of medicine help medical professionals to communicate more quickly among themselves, yet at the same time become an obstacle to the patient?

Hugo Martinez-Serros

"LEARN! LEARN!"

Hugo Martinez-Serros teaches Spanish at Lawrence University and has published a collection of short fiction.

Short story, 9 pages   p. 260

Language as a weapon is at the heart of this story by Hugo Martinez-Serros. Both of the main characters use language as a way to manipulate others and empower themselves.

In order to understand the use and abuse of language in this piece, you may want the students to characterize each of the main characters. Students will probably point out how different these two individuals are physically and culturally. Yet, you may help them see that the characters share some traits as well. Even though from different countries, they both speak Spanish and use it to their advantage. Father Tortas uses it to seduce his parishioners in his bulletin and at church. José María uses it to show his superior linguistic standing in relation to others.

Both characters also share professional frustration and disappointment in their daily condition. Ask students to explain this point. If this is true, ask them how both employ language to release the tension and insecurity of their lives. Could this explain the passion they both attach to their "linguistic" attacks and their constant use of foul language, surprising for men of such linguistic purity?

You may also want to discuss expectations and stereotypes and how they control people's reactions to others. The priest has decided what José María is like without having met him and, likewise, José María never gives the priest a chance. They respect each other's linguistic abilities and share the same obsession with the purity of language, yet they cannot transcend the limits of their own expectations about the other. Ironically, though they speak the same language, they cannot understand each other. They use language against each other, rather than to communicate. To clarify this point, you may want to ask students to come up with examples of situations where people "throw" words at each other.

Suggested Assignments

Q.1. If José María dominates the use of language so well, why does he write the letters anonymously? Why does Father Tortas not pursue the identity of his co-writer to its logical conclusion? What role do you think anonymity plays in the story?

Q.2. Language and how we use it can reflect our inner feelings about our place in the world. Based on this idea, decide what is wrong with the relationship of the two men. How does each man feel about his place in the world? Given this, can you find anything right about their relationship?

Student Encounter Activity

In groups of three talk about language in your home. Talk about the role language played in your childhood, if any. As each of you speaks, have the other two note what differences exist in intonation or accent from one student to the next. Write down expressions or puns that may be unique. Did you find many similarities or differences? Discuss your findings with the class.

James Alan McPherson
I AM AN AMERICAN

James Alan McPherson was born in Savannah, Georgia, in 1943, of African-American descent. He graduated from the Harvard Law School in 1968 and received an M.F.A. degree from the University of Iowa's Writers Workshop where he now teaches. He won a Pulitzer Prize in 1977 for his collection of stories *Elbow Room*.

Short story, 12 pages   p. 270

We would recommend teaching this story as a vehicle for exploring stereotypes and how language plays a role in promoting these. You may want to begin by seeing the story as an unfolding mystery. Get students to detail how things are revealed or held back. Then move to the characters, and lead the discussion to considerations of how uses of language, especially by Leroy, lead to judgments. So many stereotypes appear here that they force themselves into the discussion. Try to get to the self-conscious qualities of Leroy, his self-deprecation, his sense of his own awkwardness and limitations of perceptions. The study guide questions should help guide students in these directions.

After you have discussed Leroy's qualities, try discussing the concept of the "Ugly American" tourist. Which characters could be described as such? Ask students to support their claim with examples. You can also explore the concept of provincialism, of seeing no place as better than our own. Again, get students to provide examples.

Finally, discuss language and the role it plays in the story as a communicator or a barrier to understanding.

Suggested Assignments

Q.1. The language of stereotype is very prevalent in our society. It is also a barrier for true understanding among peoples of different backgrounds. Explain how the story supports these two statements. Use examples from the text to support your conclusions.

Q.2. Given that stereotypical language is an obstacle to understanding, why do you think the characters in the story cling to it?

Student Encounter Activity

Pair off with the person in the class who appears to be the most different from you. Make a list of stereotypical statements that would characterize each of you. Afterwards, get into groups of five or more students and create a master list of stereotypes that would describe all the members of the group. Share your findings with the rest of the class.

Salli Benedict

TAHOTAHONTANEKENT-SERATKERONAKWENHAKIE

Salli Benedict is director of the Akwesasne Museum on the reserve of the Mohawk Nation in upstate New York.

Short story, 1 1/2 pages   p. 283

"There is great importance in a name," says the old man in this story. You may want to begin discussing the story by writing this line on the board and asking students if they agree or disagree with it. Get them to give reasons for their position. Then ask them to discuss what the characters in the story feel about names. Students may find the names in the story absurd, but point out the European tradition of using names that reflect a trade, such as Smith or Hospital. East Indians today officially have the name of their village as their last name.

From here, you can jump into a discussion of expectations and how language, specifically a name, creates expectations that can be to our advantage or to our detriment. How does the name work for and against the boy in the story? Can your students come up with examples of situations when their names worked for or against them?

You may also want to discuss the tone and style of the story. Ask students to compare the language in the story to other things they have read, such as parables or fairy tales. In the previous chapters, you have probably discussed the importance some cultures place on storytelling for passing on values and customs. If so, ask students to explore what values or attitudes are being conveyed through this story.

Finally, ask students to explain the use of humor at the end of the story. What is its function? Does it enhance or detract from the story?

Suggested Assignments

Q.1. What's in a name? A name can at once reflect history and project the future. In what ways does the boy's name accomplish both of these things?

Q.2. Naming an individual is a moment of significance. Think of when the boy was first named by his parents. Then think of his name after the old man's first visit. Keeping this in mind, what desires can you infer from the parents' choice for a name?

Student Encounter Activity

Find out the last names of both your maternal and paternal grand-parents. Do some research on the root and meaning of the last names. Prepare a presentation where you discuss the meaning, origin, and evolution of each name for the class.

G. S. Sharat Chandra

STILL KICKING IN AMERICA

G. S. Sharat Chandra was born in Mysore, India. He has been liv-ing in the United States since the 1960s and currently lives in Kansas. His books include *Heirloom*, *Immigrants of Loss*, and *Family of Mirrors*.

Poem, 1 page   p. 286

This is an interesting poem that may offer your students a chal-lenge. You may want to begin the discussion by asking students to find natural divisions in the poem.

First, the speaker talks about himself and how others would ques-tion him about his good English. Then the Polish wife is introduced. Understanding her function in the poem is essential. Ask students to explore what is meant by the long lines and the dictators, as well as the kicking. In the last stanza, the speaker focuses on himself again through the image of the "vegetarian calves."

You may want to direct the discussion of the last stanza by asking students questions such as what is the tone of the speaker? Why would Gandhi be ashamed? Is Gandhi the one ashamed or is the speaker? What would the speaker have to be ashamed of?

Finally, return to the title and explore its meaning. Ask students to decide who is kicking still: the Polish wife? the speaker? You may want to point out how in this poem, similarly to other poems in this section, the issue of language is very important. The speaker here seems to be self-conscious about his good English, as if somehow it was a reflection of an inability on his part to stand up and kick the powers that be. Was he perhaps too successful at assimilating? You can explore with your students what this poem may be saying about the limits of assimilation.

Suggested Assignments

Q.1. Reread the first two lines of the poem. Consider them as a statement of solidarity. In this light, how does the rest of the poem validate these opening lines?

Q.2. Imagine an Indian woman trying to make a life in the United States. She is watching a night show and a comedian is getting tremendous laughs mocking an Indian speaking English to a policeman. As the television laughs, she closes her eyes. Given this scene, infer the influence language may have on her "dreams or desperation."

Gustavo Perez-Firmat

LIMEN

Gustavo Perez-Firmat was born in Cuba in 1950 and grew up in Miami. He studied at Miami-Dade Community College, the University of Miami, and the University of Michigan where he earned his Ph.D. in 1979. He currently teaches at Duke University and writes works of literary criticism and poetry.

Poem, 1/2 page   p. 287

Try to start the discussion of this poem by exploring the use of the Spanish within the English text. Point out how the Spanish is reserved for the more familiar and familial elements: water, mother, cookies, warmth. This would seem logical if we see language as a symbol of those cultural and familial traits the speaker misses, now that he has moved away from where he grew up.

The speaker is moving his son north and inland to where "y'alls and drawls" are spoken, to North Carolina where he has lived and yet "never lived." Ask students what the speaker means by this. The speaker feels an angst "knotting his tongue" because his son will be raised away from his cultural roots. Does the son feel the same angst? or does it belong primarily to the father?

You can also explore what seem to be markers of cultural identity and rootedness in the poem. In addition to the actual language, the speaker mentions items from popular culture such as the Latin Pop singer Chirino, El Farito, a popular beach in Key Biscayne, before the hurricane, and Dadeland Mall. While considering these elements of popular culture, it may be interesting to point out to your students how the author, who is Cuban born, makes references to Miami, and not Cuba, as his roots. For many Cuban Americans, Miami has indeed become the symbol, if not the reality, of home away from home.

Suggested Assignments

Q.1. Language is sometimes treated as an heirloom to be inherited by the next generation and preserved intact. Would you agree or disagree with this statement? Use specific lines from the poem to support your contention.

Q.2. Make an argument to the speaker that moving David will "broaden" his tongue rather than "knotting" it. List four points that support your argument. List four counterpoints from the poem (stated or inferred). Who has the better argument?

Student Encounter Activity

Watch three days of television shows. Make a list of the different kinds of native English you hear. Look for differences in intonation, accents, colloquialisms, dialects, etc. Decide what these people are communicating about themselves depending on their use of English. What emotional reactions do these different ways of speaking English evoke in you? Now, listen to or imagine a recent immigrant speaking so-called "broken" English. Does your reaction change?

Lorna Dee Cervantes

REFUGEE SHIP

Lorna Dee Cervantes was born in San Francisco in 1954, and is of Mexican descent. She has published two books of poetry and currently teaches creative writing at the University of Colorado at Boulder.

Poem, 1/2 page   p. 288

This poem can be taught as a companion to Cervantes' earlier poem in chapter 3. In this poem, the speaker brings up once more the issue of her name, "I am an orphan to my spanish name." She focuses specifically on language, and how her inability to feel at home in Spanish makes her feel like an orphan. From this point, you can discuss the last stanza. Ask students to explore what the image of the refugee ship that will never dock refers to and what it has to do with language deprivation.

You can also use the poem to bring back some issues discussed in earlier chapters concerning ancestry. Ask students to contrast the first two stanzas. How does the speaker refer to each of the relatives? Is the tone the same for both? Try to get the students to talk about the parent's role or responsibility in maintaining language for the children. How does the speaker feel in this poem? How do your students feel? These questions can lead to a lively discussion since students usually have strong feelings about language retention and parental pressures.

Suggested Assignments

Q.1. How important is language to the speaker's sense of self? Where do the speaker's linguistic strengths lie? What does the language of the poem reveal to you?
Q.2. Why doesn't the speaker just get off the ship?

Rita Dove

PARSLEY

Rita Dove was born in 1952, in Akron, Ohio, and is from African-American and Chicano descent. She has been a Guggenheim Fellow and a Fellow of the National Endowment for the Arts. She now teaches at the University of Virginia. She has published fiction and poetry, including *Thomas and Beulah* (1986), for which she won the Pulitzer Prize.

Poem, 2 pages   p. 289

This is a powerful poem with strong political overtones. To help students fully understand it, have them analyze each section separately. Ask them who is the focus of each part. The visual images that establish the contrasts are also very important. You may find it helpful to get students to write a story based on the poem. Doing so can deepen their understanding and prepare them for exploring the more subtle issues.

The most obvious issue is that of political corruption and the excesses of power. Get the students to explore their feelings about the general. Why is his method of choosing a word such a powerful image? Furthermore, explore why the speaker emphasizes the blacks' inability to pronounce the r's and how this ties in to the general's choice of words. What might the poet be saying about racial issues?

If you are interested in the social and political dimension of the poem, you may want to discuss the historical background to it. General Trujillo was a dictator of the Dominican Republic from 1930 until his death in 1961; that is the reason he speaks Spanish. It may be interesting to suggest researching Trujillo's mixed racial makeup and its implications to the poem.

Further information can be helpful to better understand the context of the poem. The Haitians are often imported to cut sugarcane since the Dominicans do not want to cut the cane themselves. There are strong anti-Haitian sentiments in the country and the Haitian workers live in deplorable conditions. You can also point out how Jamaicans are recruited in Florida to cut sugarcane as well. It's very hard and dangerous work that many do not want to perform. Very recently, the number of Jamaicans coming to Florida has been reduced because of mechanization.

Suggested Assignments

Q.1. The general is full of rage. Characterize his rage according to your reading of the poem. With this in mind, what are his motives for killing the cane cutters?

Q.2. Are there any allusions in the poem to the general's mother being like the Haitians? If so, how would this knowledge affect your reading of this poem?

Student Encounter Activity

Research General Trujillo's ancestry. How do your findings give you a new understanding of the poem?

Louise Erdrich

JACKLIGHT

Louise Erdrich is of Chippewa and German-American descent. She grew up in North Dakota and now lives in New Hampshire. Her best-known novel, *Love Medicine*, won the National Book Critics Circle Award. She is also known for her poetry collections.

Poem, 1 page   p. 292

In this poem, a story is told purposely full of ambiguities. You may want to start by discussing how writers, especially poets, will use a story or an image that evokes or implies meaning but does not openly state it. The image or story works as an extended metaphor.

In this case, you can begin with the epigraph which should offer students a clue to the ambiguity. Ask them to discuss who "we" and "they" are literally; then ask them who they could be figuratively. To help the students, ask them to list words associated with each. Are there sufficient references to deduce that this is a poem about seduction? Is it about gender differences? Or is it about two cultures separated by the edge of the woods, by two distinct visions of life? Ask students to explore the different possible interpretations and how, depending on the meaning chosen, we can read the line "It is their turn now."

You may want to ask students to discuss the advantages or disadvantages of using a technique such as Erdrich's to explore a point.

Suggested Assignments

Q.1. Assume that the edge of the woods is a boundary line between two worlds. With this in mind, what values do you think are encompassed by each world? Use details from the text to support your answers.

Q. 2. In this story of encounters, who has had the advantage? Provide inferences from the poem to justify your choice.

Li-Young Lee

PERSIMMONS

Li-Young Lee was born in 1957 in Jakarta, Indonesia, to Chinese parents. He grew up in Pennsylvania where his father became a Presbyterian minister. Lee has published two volumes of poetry.

Poem, 2 pages   p. 294

This is a sensual poem that illustrates the power of the word and the image. One word or incident leads to another, thus demonstrating the power of association. You may want to point out to students the importance of the two words confused in the first stanza: *persimmon* and *precision*. Is this a coincidence? Besides sounding similar, what does *precision* have to do with *persimmon*? Ask students where else each word appears. Explore the function of these words in the poem.

The event in the class brings the speaker to his father. Ask students to explore how the father's words in the last stanza relate to the rest of the poem. In addition to exploring the sensuality and imagery of the poem, you can also explore the speaker's attitude toward the role of language.

The speaker talks about words getting him into trouble—trouble that seems to stem from others' perceptions or misperceptions. The speaker seems to be indicating how we often worry so much about the words that we forget the true purpose of language: to bring us closer to the sensuality and physical reality of the object or scene. What is important is the intimacy with the world and not the word.

Some of us forget that, as, for example, does Mrs. Walker. She obviously knows less about persimmons than the speaker, yet she is disturbed by his inability to use the "right word." She can't or refuses to move beyond his mistake. You may want to ask students if this incident could be viewed as culturally prejudicial.

A poem by Li-Young Lee appears in chapter 2. If you have already taught the poem, it may be worthwhile to return to it now to notice what distinctive uses of language your students find in poems by the same author. You may even ask them which poem they like best and why.

Suggested Assignments

Q.1. Consider this idea: To possess the word, or the language, is to retain power. With this in mind, in what ways does the poem illustrate a power struggle? How has each side manifested his or her reaction to the other's action? How can this poem be considered a microcosm for cultural assimilation in the United States?

Q.2. Critique the speaker in the poem as if he were a teacher. What techniques does he use? How effective are they? How would you describe his style of teaching? What lessons is he trying to convey? How successful was he as a teacher?

Student Encounter Activity

Gather newspaper clippings that report the 1980 Mariel boat lift from Cuba to Miami, Florida. Focus on those articles dealing with the tensions in that city due to the major influx of refugees. Also focus on articles reporting on the English Only movement in Miami that same year. Why do you think language was chosen as a battlefield?

Ricardo Pau-Llosa

FOREIGN LANGUAGE

Ricardo Pau-Llosa was born in Cuba in 1954 and came to the United States in 1960. He is an art historian, curator, and English professor at Miami-Dade Community College, as well as a poet. His first book of poems, *Sorting Metaphors*, won the national Anhinga Poetry Prize.

Poem, 1/2 page   p. 297

The title of the poem, "Foreign Language," reveals its focus. The rest of the poem is a series of metaphors that serve to capture the speaker's perception of a foreign language.

You may want to begin discussion by asking students to list each of the metaphors individually in order to decipher its meaning. Then ask them to look for verbs or adjectives that may share a common attitude. For example, "opens a crack," "barge through," "a kill," "opens," "rumble," "teeth tear," "plane crashing," and "hit you." In addition to suggesting violent behavior, these words share a sense of suddenness and intrusion. What might these terms reveal about the speaker's attitude toward a foreign language?

Amid these violent images, students may notice other images of seduction and sensuality such as "caresses" and the "wet white word." How do these images add to the complexity of the poet's view of a foreign language?

Finally, you may want to probe your students to see if they feel that this poem speaks only about language, or perhaps about a foreign culture as well.

Suggested Assignments

Q.1. Consider this analogy: foreign language is to the speaker what the apple was to Adam and Eve. Do you agree or disagree with it? Support your decision with references to the poem.

Q.2. Reread the poem looking for images that evoke the speaker's feeling about a foreign language. Based on these images, what do you conclude is his opinion about speaking a foreign language?

Nora Dauenhauer

TLINGIT CONCRETE POEM

Nora Dauenhauer is a native Alaskan. She comes from a family of noted carvers and beadwork artists. She is a linguist and an author of instructional materials in her own native language and has published a collection of her poems, *The Droning Shaman*.

Poem, 1 page   p. 299

Even though your students may enjoy this poem, it could be hard to get a discussion going. You may want to ask them to describe what they see and then probe them with questions such as why an apple? why a worm? What is the relationship between these two forces opposing each other? You may want to point out how the choice of apple may be an unusual choice for an Alaskan. What then could be its meaning in terms of the dominant American culture or its mythical, religious allusions?

Explore the issue of language and the fact that the poet uses her native tongue for the poem. Why? Ask the students how this poem is like, or unlike, other poems, and why. Let them wander into the visual arts and analyze their visual response to the poem.

Suggested Assignments

Q.1. Compare the power of the apple word to the power of the worm word. Which is the stronger word? Which is the weaker word? What could this power relation be saying about power and culture?

Q.2. Squint your eyes and look at the poem. Which part draws your attention most quickly? What does that part of the poem communicate to you?

Student Encounter Activity

Get in groups of three or four. Each group must bring one of the following items to class: a toaster, a shoe, a plate, a banana, and a bag of rice. Imagine that each item is a concrete poem. What does each item communicate to you? Share your findings with members of the other groups.

Linda Hogan

SONG FOR MY NAME

Linda Hogan, a Chickasaw, was born in Denver in 1947 and grew up in Oklahoma. She earned an M.A. in English and creative writing from the University of Colorado where she now teaches creative writing. She has published several books of poems and a novel.

Poem, 1 page   p. 300

This poem is similar to Pau-Llosa's "Foreign Language" in that it offers a series of images that evoke an object—in this case, a name. Ask students what characteristics the images in this poem share.

There are many references to color. Ask students to imagine this poem as a painting. In what shades would they paint it? What images would they include? What do these images say to them about the Native-American culture being depicted in the poem? How does the speaker feel about the relatives in the poem?

This poem can also launch, quite beyond an analysis of how the poem itself works, a discussion of how names operate in life and in literature. It can be useful to recall some of the fictional names provided by authors in poems, stories, and plays you've already read, and spend time on how the names worked to create particular kinds of expectations. Then move to "real" names or names that claim to be real in nonfictional works: what claims do these names make about their significance in some larger world? In what ways do "works of art" imitate beliefs about the significance of names in the real world?

Suggested Assignments

Q.1. Imagine you have figured out the speaker's secret name. Based on your reading of the poem, how would you describe her reaction to you once you know her name? Why would she react this way?

Q.2. What would a poem about the speaker's known name be like? What would it show about her? Why does the speaker need two names?

Student Encounter Activity

Think about "real" names that have caught your attention. What was implied by these names? Think about your own family names.

What do they reveal about you, your family, your culture, or your ancestry? Do you have or desire a secret name that no one will ever know?

Derek Walcott
A FAR CRY FROM AFRICA

Derek Walcott was born in San Lucia in 1930 and attended the University of the West Indies in Jamaica. He is a poet and playwright and has taught at numerous American universities including Columbia, Howard, Yale, Rutgers, and Boston University. He was awarded the Nobel Prize in Literature in 1992.

Poem, 1 page   p. 302

Derek Walcott's powerful poem will probably surprise students as well as challenge them. To understand the strength of its visions, students will need to comprehend the historical situation the poet is depicting. Ask students to read the footnotes and relate them to the incidents described in the poem. Ask students to explore what the speaker refers to in lines 7 and 8. You may want to stop here and probe your students to see what they know about European colonial policies in Africa. Then get students to explore why these policies are insignificant to the "white child hacked in bed."

After studying the first stanza, discuss the philosophical points introduced in the second stanza. You may want to begin by asking students to discuss the contrast presented between animals and humans. Also, ask them what role color plays.

The last stanza will probably be more accessible to your students. Here the speaker is more personal and reveals the conflict he encounters. Ask students to define the conflict by using specific references from the poem. This stanza can lead to a lively discussion of double identity and how to come to terms with them, especially if an individual belongs to two cultures that have been in conflict in the past.

Finally, you may want to point out the precision of Walcott's language and how he controls the tone and power of the poem with his direct choices of images, situations, metaphors, allusions, or reflections. This precision reflects his power over the English language—the language of the colonizers—which he uses to express profound sentiments that put him in conflict with this language.

Suggested Assignments

Q.1. Return to the last two lines of the poems. How do they encapsulate the speaker's theme? How do you think the speaker would answer these questions? How would you?

Q.2. Compare and contrast Walcott's view of language to Sharat Chandra's. How do they each feel about the "foreign language"?

Student Encounter Activity

Research the encounter between the United States and Somalia. Imagine the actions taken by both sides as if they were words being spoken. If this were so, what would each be saying to the other? How well would each understand the other?

Israel Horovitz

THE INDIAN WANTS THE BRONX

Israel Horovitz was born in Wakefield, Massachusetts, in 1939. He was educated at the Royal Academy of Dramatic Art in London, the New School for Social Research, and the City University of New York. He has won numerous awards for his plays including an Obie and a Grammy.

Play, 19 pages   p. 303

So many different languages come up here—and are staged quite theatrically—that this play can provide an easy summary of the issues of language illustrated throughout the chapter. You may want to focus, however, on a new type of language introduced here: the language of violence.

Your students may be familiar with the play *West Side Story*; if so, you can contrast how in that play the violence seldom becomes language, even though the violence is ritualistic. Here, however, all the rituals of violence express something quite specific. Spend time with students getting them to explore what is being expressed through the different acts of violence, from horseplay, to verbal abuse of Gupta and the women who do not appear on stage, to the physical abuse of Gupta, to the breaking of communication by cutting the phone line. Ask students how the physical actions reflect inner states.

Get them to discuss their feelings about Joey and Murph. What details can they provide about these characters? What details do they know about the other characters mentioned in the play?

Staging is important here. If you have had students do exercises earlier on how they would stage a particular scene or set of moments in another play, it is worth following up here by having them consider how they would create effects based on characters who are important but don't appear—for example, the two women and Gupta's son.

You may also want to discuss the power of intimidation and the vulnerability of Gupta. Ask them to explore how the boys intimidate Gupta; encourage them to include physical appearance and language in the discussion.

The study questions here will raise so many issues for class that you may need to assign them selectively depending on how much time you have to devote to the play and how you wish to focus the discussion.

Suggested Assignments

Q.1. From time to time, Joey refers to Murph as a Jap. What does he mean by it? How does this reference bear on the activities in the play?

Q.2. Sometimes language can serve as a barrier rather than as a facilitator of communication. How does the play illustrate this statement? Give specific examples to illustrate your answer.

Student Encounter Activity

Think back on a time in your life when you felt intimidated by someone. Explore the reasons the episode occurred and how you felt about it. Write a theatrical scene that reveals the details of the event. Make sure to convey your sentiments about the incident through the behavior and dialogue of the characters.

Richard Rodriguez

ARIA: A MEMOIR OF A BILINGUAL CHILDHOOD

Richard Rodriguez was born in San Francisco in 1944, and is of Mexican heritage. He received a B.A. from Stanford University and an M.A. from Columbia University. He is the author of two collections of essays, *Hunger of Memory: The Education of Richard Rodriguez* and *Days of Obligation: An Argument with My Mexican Father.*

Essay, 16 pages   p. 326

While this anthology has attempted to introduce new, nonmainstream voices, or less-known pieces by familiar voices, this essay by Rodriguez, frequently anthologized, has been included because it is recognized as one of the strongest proponents of assimilation and anti-bilingualism. Rodriguez's arguments have won him favor among many; nevertheless, his views are very controversial especially among Hispanic intellectuals and writers.

Before opening up the class to debate the issue of bilingualism in schools, you may want to explore various issues. The most important of these would be the contrast Rodriguez proposes between private and public worlds. Get the students to define the two realms and to isolate examples of elements that belong to each. Then ask them to explain what Rodriguez means by "intimates." Ask your students to decide if they agree with the author's position that the "intimates," not language, is what matters.

You may also want to clarify other terminology used in the essay, such as "assimilation" and "melting pot." In addition, you may want to explore why Rodriguez repeatedly distinguishes between middle class and lower class children. Ask students what class has to do with the point the author is trying to make. Would a middle-class Hispanic have a different position on this issue? Why?

Bilingualism is an emotional topic in our city; since both of us also grew up with this separation between our linguistic private and public worlds, we often offer anecdotes about our own experience. You may want to do the same, or ask students in the class to do so. We are sure they will offer poignant anecdotes. If you do get students with similar experiences, ask them how these have affected their views of bilingual education.

This essay lends itself to the discussion of many issues and can probably be extended to at least two class meetings. Other topics you may want to touch upon include self-esteem and how language affects it, the child's feelings towards parents who cannot speak the public language properly, and the possibility of maintaining strong public and private linguistic and emotional worlds simultaneously. For the latter you may want to explore the differences between cities and demography and how that can affect one's attitudes towards language retention and assimilation.

Suggested Assignments

Q.1. It is sometimes difficult for family members to accept a public language in a private realm. When this happens, they treat the perpetrators as if they were traitors to the family and the culture. In this essay, the relatives use the term *pocho* to refer to the author. What is the purpose of the nickname? How does the author feel about it?

Q.2. Even though the author is rejecting bilingualism in schools and promoting quick assimilation, he seems to recognize the price he had to pay to get it. What was that price? Would you agree it was a price worth paying?

Student Encounter Activity

Even though we may speak the same language in public as in the home, other elements may distinguish our home life from our public life. This may include religious values, eating habits, musical tastes, clothing, etc. Think about your "private world" and if it is different from your "public world." If so, discuss how, and what effects it has on your life on a daily basis.

Gloria Naylor

"MOMMY, WHAT DOES 'NIGGER' MEAN?"

Gloria Naylor is of African-American descent and is the author of four acclaimed novels, including *The Women of Brewster Place*, for which she won the American Book Award in 1982. She is a native of New York City, where she still lives and teaches.

Essay, 2 pages   p. 344

Naylor's essay can bring the class back to the issue of racial or ethnic slurs discussed earlier. It adds a new dimension to the discussion by suggesting that one way to neutralize a slur is to possess it, to confront it as a community and create a new context for it. In this case, the African Americans in the community she describes have empowered themselves by possessing the word "nigger."

Get students to discuss the difference between the way the word is referred to by the family and the way the small boy uses it to humiliate the child. How does the word change for the child? Students will probably want to contribute personal anecdotes to illustrate the same point.

These can lead to a volatile discussion; be aware that you will be treading in sensitive waters.

You may want to spend some time discussing the relationship between language and cultural attitudes and values. Students may not realize the power of language and how much it shapes and reveals the values and attitudes of a group. For example, the Eskimo have twelve words to refer to snow; obviously snow is a central part of their world and they must be able to distinguish it in its numerous forms.

Suggested Assignments

Q.1. If language indeed reveals cultural attitudes, what attitude is the child's classmate revealing with his use of the word "nigger"? Is race what is bothering the boy? Or could some other factor be bothering him more? If so, what does this say about using race as an excuse to reveal loss of power?

Q.2. If labels can influence identity, how could this child's discovery of a new meaning for "nigger" affect her self-identity? If you were her mother, what would you explain to this child about the slur?

Student Encounter Activity

Choose an ethnic or racial group and make a list of jokes or puns you have heard about this group. What similarities do these share? What attitudes do they reveal? Some people would say these are "just jokes." Would you agree? Explain your answer.

Rudolph Chelminski

NEXT TO BRZEZINSKI, CHELMINSKI'S A CINCH

Rudolph Chelminski was born in Connecticut in 1934. He graduated from Harvard University in 1956. He was a reporter for *Life* magazine for many years and now works as a freelance writer.

Essay, 2 pages   p. 347

This brief essay will be fun for your students. It will offer them a welcome change of pace from the previous two essays and introduce humor as an important technique in coping with the frustrations of daily life.

In addition to getting students to share their own anecdotes about their names, you may want to share your own. With names like Carolina Hospital and Carlos Medina, you can imagine that we have plenty of our own.

You may also want to discuss the more serious aspects of the essay which include cultural identity and self-esteem. Ask them why a name is so important. Why are some people willing to change their names while others are repulsed by the thought? Is this essay only about tolerance with names or about cultural tolerance and sensitivity as well?

Suggested Assignments

Q.1. When the author arrives in Warsaw, he discovers that he too had been mispronouncing his own name. How does he react to the discovery? Would you have reacted in the same way?

Q.2. Some people seem to be very attached to their names and even get defensive if you mispronounce them. Why do you think the name is so important to them? Do you attempt to pronounce a name as its owner prefers it? Or do you always use your own English version of it? Explain your motivations.

Student Encounter Activity

Family names can be very important to individuals. In many cases today, women have opted for maintaining their family names after marriage. Find a woman who has done so and interview her to discover her motivation. Then explore your reaction to her decision.

The Craft of Writing

WORDS

p. 350

The Afterword in this chapter gives a comprehensive and interesting overview of language, as both an oral and a written medium. You may want to assign the Afterword to your students before assigning the literary samples in the chapter. It will help students relate better to the pieces if they have an understanding of the importance and significance of language in all its variations.

You may also want to talk about the language of writing. We have found that students often rely on speech as their main vehicle of communication; consequently, they have trouble understanding why their writing skills leave much to be desired. They don't understand why writing demands skills different from those of speech.

In order to illustrate this point, we have found various activities helpful. For example, you may want to act out certain attitudes without speaking a word, such as frustration or anger. The students will immediately understand. They will be able to identify body language as one of the main advantages to communication that is inaccessible to the writer. Other advantages are tone, pitch, and intonation. All these provide information that the writer cannot. Consequently, the writer needs to find other tools to substitute.

Probe your students to see if they can come up with a list of techniques writers use to enhance their written language, such as sentence variety, unusual word order, variety in sentence length, etc.

In order to further emphasize the differences between oral and written language and the need for precision, you may try a few demonstrations. For example, you may want to call out a student's name and ask him or her to "bring the *thing* over there." The student will most likely look at you perplexed and do nothing. Repeat the command, but the second time point to an object in the classroom, such as a garbage can. Right away students understand the inaccuracy of oral speech and why in writing it is necessary to be specific and precise in language.

We also find it helpful to talk about the role of reading. Reading is the main medium for improving writing, for it immerses the reader in the language of writing. This concept of the language of writing can be very helpful in clarifying many issues for the students. For example, beginning writers may feel awkward trying out new techniques in their essays. The new language of writing may seem unnatural to them. Remind them that when we learn a new foreign language, we feel unnatural when we first hear ourselves; however, with time and practice, the new language becomes more and more natural. The same is true for writing.

Comments on Student Writing

p. 357

This student essay by Steven Krueger is powerful, succinct, coherent, and well-supported. We would recommend that you assign it after the students have finished reading the play. It will help them to understand better the issues of language revealed in the play.

You may also want to use the essay as an example of a tightly organized essay response to the reading. To best illustrate this, ask students
to write an outline to correspond to the essay. Ask them to include the
thesis statement, the three main points expressed in the topic sentences
and the supporting examples for each main point. They should not
have much trouble seeing the organization.

The conclusion introduces linguistic terminology not used in the
rest of the essay. After discussing the meaning of these terms, you may
want to ask students if these terms enhance or detract from the thesis
of the essay.

Finally, get students to note the strength of the final line. You can
use it to discuss the importance of an effective conclusion and some of
the common techniques authors use. You can also discuss the content
of the statement and whether the students agree with it or not. If so,
get them to discuss what repercussions this could have on a society and
the implications for linguistic assimilation.

┌ 5 ┐

ALIENS

Aliens is the term we use to refer to creatures from other planets; however, it is also the term we use in this country for people arriving from other lands. Foreign nationals are called aliens because they are socially and culturally different. As the editors point out in the introduction, encountering such a person is a common American experience. Encounters of the foreign kind have occurred from the time Native Americans first laid eyes on the Spanish explorers to South Floridians watching Haitians arrive on their shores.

As the selections in this chapter illustrate, encounters with the "Other" can be unsettling for better or for worse. They can lead to individual and societal growth through understanding; they can also lead to misunderstanding and intolerance. By reading these pieces, your students will see how the history of America is one of constant encounters between "aliens," as it is a favorite landing site for people from around the world. Consequently, America can be characterized as a land of commotion among different people.

Because America is a land of commotion, it is important to comprehend the impact of these constant encounters if we are to get along. The stories, poems, and nonfiction prose pieces in this chapter reflect and explore the plethora of issues concerning encounters between "aliens" at home and abroad.

Pre-Reading Activity

To prepare the class for this chapter on encounters between different people, and what these signify to an individual in society, we recommend trying the following field trip activity.

Ask students to leave the classroom and wander the campus for thirty minutes. They are to search for and take notes on "aliens" roaming the campus. "Alien" should be defined according to what each student perceives it to be.

Regroup in the classroom, and ask students to describe their "aliens." Make a list on the board and infer from the list what individuals in the class perceive an "alien" to be.

Margaret Atwood

THE MAN FROM MARS

Margaret Atwood was born in Ottawa in 1939. She has published six novels and more than a dozen books of poetry, short stories, nonfiction, and children's literature.

Short story, 15 pages   p. 364

This story is useful as a beginning to the chapter. It thrusts the students directly into the issue of explicit and implicit racism. As a result of a chance encounter, the main character is forced to deal with the "other."

You may want to begin with the mother's attitude and work your way to Christine's. The mother doesn't seem to mind the young man when she thinks he is French, but things change when she finds out he is of a different race. The mother's attitudes towards "others" are also illustrated in her comments about the maid. Ask students to explore attitudes toward house servants. If your students are from different cultures, they may provide a variety of attitudes and anecdotes to illustrate them.

Christine's attitudes are more subtle and complex. Explore her behavior with your students. Why does she give the student her name, agree to the tea, allow him to follow her for so long? In order to understand her better, get students to talk about Christine's physical appearance and the way her family and friends view her.

Get students to find parallels between Christine and the oriental student. Help them to see the irony in the similarities. Both Christine and the student are outcasts, yet Christine finds no camaraderie with him. She treats him as harshly as she is treated. Is it that she is blind to their similarities or is it that the similarities remind her of her own inadequacies? Get the students to explore these issues.

You may also want to discuss the abundance of racial stereotypes used in the story, so many that the Asian student never seems to transcend beyond a caricature. Do your students think the author does this to magnify the stereotypes or perpetuate them? The students may possess some of these stereotypes themselves. Probe them to find out if this is true, and if so where they acquired them. Most likely they will admit that they came from the media. You may want to mention the film *Sixteen Candles* where an oriental student is depicted in exactly the same way.

Finally, you can explore how many of these stereotypes against Asians emerged and were promoted during World War II and how these attitudes are present today.

Suggested Assignments

Q.1. Scan the story looking for explicit and implicit racial attitudes and beliefs held by all characters surrounding the oriental student. What picture is drawn of him? What purpose is served by the use of such an overwhelmingly racial stereotype?

Q.2. Compare Christine to the Asian student, noting all possible similarities. With this in mind, what would you say is ironic about these characters? How do you feel about this irony?

Student Encounter Activity

With your close friends, draw up a list of prejudicial remarks concerning race, gender, sexual orientation, and nationality that each of you use, whether in jest or not. Now think of classmates and other persons you are acquainted with who are representative of the people your list alludes to. When comparing the remarks to actual persons, consider this statement. "Prejudicial remarks deny an individual's humanity." How is this statement valid for both the listener and the speaker of the remarks?

Becky Birtha

JOHNNIERUTH

Becky Birtha is a poet and writer of fictional narratives. She has published two collections of stories and currently resides in Philadelphia.

Short story, 4 pages   p. 381

"Johnnieruth" is a coming-of-age story, a story of self-discovery. It is written in the colloquial voice and language of a fourteen-year-old girl who senses she is different but incapable of verbalizing this difference.

You may want to begin the discussion by asking students to characterize the girl. Ask them what details are provided to help us understand what she is like. Get them to talk about how she is different and when she first begins to realize that her old world is not all there is.

Explore the symbols used in the story such as the speed bike, the Plaza, and even the women in the park who tell her "Catch you later." How do these provide clues to the greater meaning of the story?

With this story, you will want to discuss the issue of homosexuality and how it often serves to separate people as much as race and culture do. This piece works well in dealing with this subject because it can disarm the reader's preconceptions, if any. Since this story is included in the chapter on aliens, you may want to ask students who the aliens are in the story. Does the girl feel alien? If so, in what way?

Suggested Assignments

Q.1. How would you describe Johnnieruth's self-esteem? Does she feel herself an alien? Could this be because she is fourteen years old and innocent or has she intuitively known something all along? Defend your conclusions with excerpts from the story.

Q.2. To what degree is this a happy or sad story? Why do you think so?

Student Encounter Activity

Think of when you were an early teen. What discovery about yourself did you make at the time? As an older individual, how has the discovery panned out?

Neil Bissoondath

THERE ARE A LOT OF WAYS TO DIE

Neil Bisoondath was born in Trinidad of East Indian descent. He is the nephew of two well known writers, V. S. and Shiva Naipaul. He has published three collections of short stories and currently lives in Toronto.

Short story, 12 pages   p. 387

If you have already covered the chapter on "Home," this piece should offer an interesting perspective to your students. The story focuses on the main character's disappointment at returning home. He is idealistic and nostalgic about the island; however, he soon discovers that his memories were not always true to reality. Usually we see a character longing for home. It is unusual to find a piece such as this that deals with the disillusionment of home.

You may want to center the discussion around the central image of the Pacheco house. Ask students why the author spends so much time describing this house and its history. What does it have to do with the central theme of the story?

You may also want to ask students to chart out the values and customs associated with each setting: Trinidad and Toronto. From the first paragraph, we get a clue of the wife's attitudes when she says, "That's all very well and good for Toronto, but you think people here care about that kind of thing?" Get students to explore the attitudes of the different characters, including the wife, the best friend, and the main character himself.

You may want to explore the title, as well as some of the symbolism in the different characters' names. Furthermore, you may consider the possibility of a strain of self-contempt in Joseph throughout the story. Consider the LeNoir memory and Joseph's view of the others on the island. Could Joseph be a man trapped between cultures, and if so, why? Are his perceptions of the island reliable?

Suggested Assignments

Q.1. If we listen just right, sometimes we can hear the words of an inanimate object. They tell us many things about ourselves. Think back on the LeNoir window. What was it saying to Joseph as a boy? What was it saying to him as a man? Did he ever listen to it? In your opinion was the window a friend or an enemy to Joseph? Why do you think so?

Q.2. "To be an alien to oneself is to hate oneself." Agree or disagree with this statement using Joseph's story to support your choice.

Student Encounter Activity

Think of an aspect of your culture that you cannot stand but that is still present in your daily life. What is it that you despise about it? Do you despise yourself for it? Share with your classmates how you can accept or reject this cultural aspect and achieve peace with it.

Diane Burns

SURE YOU CAN ASK ME A PERSONAL QUESTION

Diane Burns is a painter and illustrator, educated at the Institute of American Indian Art in Santa Fe, New Mexico, and at Barnard College. She lives in Wisconsin.

Poem, 1 page   p. 401

This is a clever poem that your students will probably enjoy. The clarity of the message allows for easy discussion of Native-American stereotypes, as well as an exploration of the deeper sentiments expressed. You may want to begin with the tone of the poem. Ask students to explore how the speaker feels about the subject of the poem. You can also ask students to express their own perceptions of the two individuals involved. Help them to determine if their own perceptions are based on stereotypes.

We find that taking a few of the lines individually and exploring their meaning in more depth is also very helpful to the overall discussion of the poem.

Suggested Assignments

Q.1. Describe in terms of empathy, understanding, and respect how each person will walk away from this conversation. What insights have you carried away from eavesdropping on this conversation?

Q.2. Where do you visualize this conversation taking place? Describe the setting. Now describe the two people talking. Compare your description with that of others in the classroom. Has anyone perpetuated a visual stereotype?

Perry Brass

I THINK THE NEW TEACHER'S A QUEER

Perry Brass was born in 1947. He has published several books including *Survival Kit: A Complete Guidance Manual for Gay Men* and *Mirage*.

Poem, 1 page   p. 402

With this poem you can reintroduce the topic of homosexuals as "aliens." You can also add to the discussion the issue of violence as a response to encounters, an issue you may have discussed already with the play "The Indian Wants the Bronx," in chapter 4.

You may want to begin by distinguishing the speakers in the poem. Ask students who is saying the first line and who is saying the rest. The students will probably want to focus on the teacher and his sentiments, understandably so. But you may also want to explore the speaker of the first line. Get the students to describe such a person. How do they feel about both?

Finally, this poem can be used to discuss how often the characteristics associated with the "alien," in this case the homosexual, can evoke such strong reactions in others that it hinders their ability to be objective. For example, traditionally teachers represent a place of respect and authority in the classroom. In this case, however, the teacher has been robbed of such a place because of his fears of being discovered and the consequences of such a discovery.

Suggested Assignments

Q.1. How would you characterize the student who says the first line of the poem? What do you think the student means by the word "queer"? Why does the student need to say this?

Q.2. How indicative is this poem of the concept of a person being treated as an "alien"?

Student Encounter Activity

Suppose you find out that a teacher/professor you admire is gay. What effect would this have on your learning, your admiration for the person, and your feelings about yourself as a person?

Mitsuye Yamada

LOOKING OUT

Mitsuye Yamada was born in Japan and raised in Seattle, Washington. She was interned with her family in a concentration camp in Idaho during World War II. She attended New York University and the University of Chicago. After 23 years of teaching, she is now retired but still teaches creative writing and Asian-American literature in southern California. She has published several collections of poetry.

Poem, 1/2 page   p. 404

This incisive, brief poem is also a profitable one to read aloud and around which to center a discussion of tone. But we also like to use it as a portable, succinct example of how literature often leads, urges, or forces us to leave our own selves, our own pair of eyes, and imagine ourselves "over there," looking out from other eyes toward ourselves. To us, this is the moral as well as aesthetic center of the literary experience.

If you have not done so in earlier discussions, you may want to bring up the historical context of the poem. We find it helpful to create contemporary examples as possible repetitions of the World War II event. For example, since many of our students are Cuban Americans, we set up a scenario where the United States goes to war with Castro on the island. How would Americans look at Cubans here? Would they find them a threat as they did the Japanese in World War II? We ask the Cuban-American students how they would feel if they were interned in concentration camps for the duration of the war. This scenario usually leads to passionate discussions in the class.

Suggested Assignments

Q.1. When you "look out" do you see others like yourself? Do you feel like a minority? Do others look at you as one?

Q.2. Does reading the biographical note about the poet that precedes the poem help you to understand the poem better? If so, how?

Marcela Christine Lucero-Trujillo

ROSEVILLE, MINN., U.S.A.

Marcela Christine Lucero-Trujillo, a poet of Mexican-American descent, was born in Colorado in 1931 and taught Chicano/Chicana studies at the University of Minnesota. She died in 1984.

Poem, 1 page   p. 404

This poem can work well as a companion piece to Diane Burns's poem. They both deal with stereotypes. With this one, you can also speak of the language of alienation. The juxtaposition of the abuela, suggestive of the Mexican heritage, and the "culmination / of her cultural perpetuation" measures semantically how far the speaker has come (for better or for worse). And there's the twist, of course, of the grandmother being unhappy with the granddaughter's behavior.

You can also explore the perception of the two worlds, one South-western Mexican, and the other "gringo," as being two separate realities. You may want to talk about the name of the town and the ironies that the name itself might hold.

Suggested Assignment

Q.1. The moniker "alien" serves a purpose to societies that horde a homogeneous power. The U.S. government calls its immigrants by the official name of "aliens." To those threatened, the word "alien" is a call to action. From the poem, list the many facets of the term "alien" that are stated and implied. To the "other" residents of Roseville, what does their use of alienation language reveal about "them"?

Q.2. Describe how a native resident of Roseville—say a member of the Rotary Club—would be proud of the town's name.

Sharon Olds

ON THE SUBWAY

Sharon Olds was born in San Francisco in 1942 and educated at Stanford and Columbia universities. She has published four volumes of poetry and is the recipient of numerous literary awards.

Poem, 1 page   p. 406

The voice of "On the Subway" can be read as one of white fear couched in an *apologia*. The speaker is talking to herself and feeding her fears with a long list of metaphors that are classic clichés about blacks. Ask students to dissect the poem and identify these stereotypes. What similarities do they share? What do they reveal about the speaker's perception of this black boy and black men in general?

Even though the speaker is describing the black boy, the poem is really about her and her attitudes. Ask students what her views reveal about her. Do we really know much about the black boy? If anything, what? Does his voice ever come through?

You can easily use this poem to explore expectations, the literary element discussed at the end of the chapter. To do so, we would suggest not assigning the poem as homework, but instead reading it in class. If so, stop periodically as you read the poem, for example after line 9, and probe the students' expectations about the rest of the poem. This exercise can lead to discussions of more general racial issues.

Suggested Assignments

Q.1. In what ways is this poem a classic example of the one-way apology characteristic from a member of a power elite? Does the apology succeed in terms of empathy and understanding?

Q.2. Does the speaker in the poem hold any prejudices against the boy? If so, what are they? How does the speaker attempt to overcome them?

Student Encounter Activity

Make this encounter a conversation between the two people, like the one in Diane Burns's poem "Sure You Can Ask Me a Personal Question." What would the boy say to this woman's thoughts?

Tato Laviera

TITO MADERA SMITH

Jesus Abraham Laviera, or "Tato," as he is normally called, was born in Puerto Rico in 1950. Ten years later he moved to New York. He is the author of five volumes of poetry, one of which won a Before Columbus Foundation American Book Award.

Poem, 2 pages   p. 408

Tito Madera Smith is a fictional character, half Puerto Rican, half African American, portrayed in the book *Enclave*. Laviera is a Nuyorican poet who belongs to a strong group of poets concerned with exploring political, social, and cultural features of Puerto Rican life on the island and particularly in New York. They are influenced strongly by Latin music, as well as the literary Afro-Caribbean tradition begun in the early twentieth century with writers such as the Puerto Rican Luis Pales Matos and the Cuban Nicolas Guillen. Interestingly, these contemporary poets write within an English tradition as well. For poets such as Laviera, the oral, colloquial sound is essential to the poem, and we encourage students to read the poem aloud.

We suggest you begin the discussion by asking students to list the cultural values and customs depicted in the poem. Do these belong to only one cultural heritage? Then ask students to describe Tito Madera Smith. How do they feel about him? What kind of a man do they think he is? What characteristics does the speaker seem to admire in him?

After discussing the character and his cultural traits, you can end by discussing the last lines which hold the key to the rest of the poem. Ultimately, this is a poem of affirmation. Tito Madera Smith's last lines reveal this. Ask the students to explore these last lines. You may also want to ask them if this is a poem about Tito Madera Smith only, or also about the cultures he represents.

Suggested Assignments

Q.1. From an "alien" point of view, how can this poem serve as a "call to arms"?

Q.2. How to adapt to a society that seeks to exclude is a harsh challenge for the one seeking inclusion. This dynamic is prevalent in many parts of the United States and the world, where various cultures seek to make room among themselves. The process of inclusion takes on many forms. Identify the technique Tito Madera Smith uses to demand inclusion. Decide to what degree it is effective. Justify your response using excerpts from the text.

Student Encounter Activity

Reflect on the times you have excluded someone from your group. What were your reasons for excluding the person? Were they justified? Now think of a time when you have been excluded. How did you feel? Share your responses with others in the class and decide what is the true purpose for exclusion.

Leslie Marmon Silko

[LONG TIME AGO]

Leslie Marmon Silko was born in 1948 in Albuquerque, New Mexico. She grew up on the Laguna Pueblo reservation. She is a poet, a writer of stories, and a storyteller. She recently published a novel, *Almanac of the Dead*.

Poem, 5 pages   p. 411

This poem has a peculiar physical shape. Could it be a totem pole? In a totem pole, the bottom figure is the most important. If so, ask students to explore how the last stanza is the most important in the poem. We find it interesting to work this poem backwards. After exploring the last stanza and how the story cannot be untold, explore with students how the curse could have been avoided so that the world could have stayed in its original state of paradise. Get the students to examine how evil begot evil. The witches were not satisfied with their animal skins and fell to temptation.

After studying the structure of the poem, you may want to discuss the way the "white people" are presented. Ask students how they feel about this depiction. You may want to remind them of other pieces by Native Americans where whites are depicted in similar ways. Ask them why this seems to be a common theme for Native-American literature.

Finally, you may want to highlight "the power of narrative" and the imagination. Talk about the power of storytelling and prophecy in this poem.

Suggested Assignments

Q.1. Given that the current population of Native Americans in the Americas is at pre-Columbian levels, approximately 50,000,000, would you say therefore that the witches' spell was broken? Or would you say that it makes no difference? Give reasons for your response.

Q.2. Why does the poem include "native" witches as part of the beginning of the end of their world? How does this relate to the actual history of the destruction of Native American cultures?

Student Encounter Activity

Compare the physical and cultural decimation of Native Americans to that of Jews in the Holocaust. Compare the perpetrators of each horrific event. What aspects of their reasoning in justifying so much death and destruction do they share? What can you say to refute any future protagonist of mass death and destruction?

Carter Revard

DISCOVERY OF THE NEW WORLD

Carter Revard, part Osage, grew up on the Osage Reservation in Oklahoma and attended Buck Creek rural school and the University of Tulsa. He is a Rhodes Scholar, has published three collections of poems and is a professor of English at Washington University, St. Louis.

Poem, 2 pages   p. 417

The strength of this poem lies in the analogy of a "space discovery" for a European discovery of America, the "New World." Some of the students will be clued in right away from the title; it may take longer for others. Their expectation of what's coming and what the poem is about will influence their perception of the poem.

Most students will probably empathize with the Native-American cause and the culpability of the explorers and settlers. The most interesting thing here is exploring how the author works this analogy to reveal the details and perceptions of the events. You may want to dissect parts of the poem and ask students to explain how the analogy works, how the description applies to the historical event. For example, note how the reference to heart attacks and cancer can be substituting for the diseases western civilization visited upon the natives, such as tuberculosis, pneumonia, and venereal disease. Ask them to find other parallels such as this.

Students may also find it fun to go back through the poem conjuring all the "space man" details.

Suggested Assignments

Q.1. Imagine the writer of this poem as he is writing his first draft. Think of the emotions he was feeling at the time. Write the poem as it may have looked before this final version. Why does the poet polish his words? What are his expectations?

Q.2. How can the mention of General Sherman be significant to a non–Native American reader of a poem?

Student Encounter Activity

In groups of three, imagine yourselves being space aliens desiring the Earth. Make a list of the aspects of the Earth your people covet.

Design a strategic plan detailing how you will go about acquiring what you desire. Your plan is limited to three venues: a psychological approach, a physical approach, and a spiritual approach.

Grace Nichols

WE NEW WORLD BLACKS

Grace Nichols was born in Guyana in 1950. She now lives in England and is a poet, anthologist, and author of children's books.

Poem, 1 page   p. 419

"We New World Blacks" is obviously referring to blacks if we are to go by the title. However, without the title, the poem could apply to any group that separates from its original group. This original group could be family, class, culture, or nation. The poem explores identity and how one feels in spite of change. It's about feeling pulled back by origin and roots, no matter how far one travels physically, culturally, economically, or psychologically.

Get the students to explore these issues, first concerning blacks and then generally. You may want to begin by asking students to refer specifically to the elements included in the poem, such as "timbre," "tongue," "echoes," "the river stone," etc. Ask them why the poet chooses these particular images and details. Also ask them to note loaded words such as "betray" and "decayed." What insights do they gain from these? What expectations are created with their use?

Suggested Assignments

Q.1. According to your reading of the poem, how would you characterize a "New World" black person? How would you characterize an "Old World" black person? What are the differences? Why are they significant to the speaker? How are they significant to you?

Q.2. Many emotions well up when immigrants cross the line to assimilation successfully. How would you describe the emotions of the speaker with regard to her assimilation? Use specific references to the poem in supporting your opinions.

Etheridge Knight

HARD ROCK RETURNS TO PRISON FROM THE HOSPITAL FOR THE CRIMINAL INSANE

Etheridge Knight was born in 1931 in Corinth, Mississippi. He became a poet while serving a sentence in the Indiana State Prison, prior to his death in 1991. He wrote numerous collections of poems and won many prestigious awards including Guggenheim and NEA fellowships.

Poem, 1 page   p. 421

You may want to begin by asking students to narrate the details of the poem in a story form. Ask them to describe Hard Rock before and after "the doctors had bored a hole in his head." Since the other prisoners looked up to him, spend some time discussing why. Then talk about the others. Why would they admire such a man? How do they feel about what happened to Hard Rock?

After discussing the specifics, you may want to talk more generally about prison practices, and about practices for the mentally insane in general. Probe the students to find out how much they know about the treatment of the mentally insane now and in earlier decades.

You may also want to spend some time looking at the metaphors in the poem and their power for creating visual images—for example, "His eyes empty like knot holes in a fence." We usually ask our students to choose other examples they find particularly powerful.

Suggested Assignments

Q.1. Assume that Hard Rock is an immigrant returning to the old country. If so, what is he doing to cause so much distress in his countrymen's hearts?

Q.2. Knowing the author to be an ex-prisoner, and Hard Rock to be a "hard-core" prisoner, are you influenced by these facts in your reading of the poem? If so, in what ways? What do these reveal about you?

Jack G. Shaheen

THE MEDIA'S IMAGE OF ARABS

Jack Shaheen was born in Pittsburgh in 1935. He teaches mass communications at Southern Illinois University and is the author of *The TV Arab* and *Nuclear War Films*.

Essay, 3 pages   p. 422

We recommend you ask the Study Questions before you assign this essay. Since it is short, we prefer reading it in class after we have probed students for their attitudes about Arabs. This essay is particularly important because unfortunately it presents a valid depiction of how Arabs are viewed in this country. Sometimes, students react at just hearing the author's last name in class. If this happens, we try to deal with it openly, for this chapter is about "aliens" and how we perceive those we categorize as such.

This essay can be very effective for exploring stereotypes in the media not only about Arabs but about a variety of groups. We use it to discuss the power of the media and its influence on culture. You may find that students disagree with the author when he says that the media presents more realistic depictions of Jews, Hispanics, and Italians. If so, explore media depictions of these groups as well. Ultimately, the strength of this essay lies in exploring how often our perceptions of a group are based exclusively on what we encounter in the media and not in our own lives.

You may also want to use the essay to illustrate effective essay technique. Pay special attention to the introductory techniques, the lucid thesis, and the effective use of examples and personal anecdotes throughout the essay to support the thesis.

Suggested Assignments

Q.1. If the media controls our perceptions of groups such as Arabs, what does this say about the power of the media? Furthermore, if the media has such power, does it also have a social responsibility? Be sure to explain your answer.

Q.2. The author states, "[These] images of the lazy black, the wealthy Jew, the greasy Hispanic and the corrupt Italian . . . are mercifully rare on today's screens." Do you agree or disagree with the author? Support your answer with examples from the media.

Student Encounter Activity

Choose an ethnic group you know little about. Write down your perceptions of this group. Then study the depiction of this group in the media for a week. Compare and contrast the views you have with those demonstrated in the media. How close are they?

James Fallows

THE JAPANESE ARE DIFFERENT
FROM YOU AND ME

James Fallows is Washington editor for *The Atlantic* and lived in Kuala Lumpur, Maylasia, where he wrote a series of articles for the magazine. He has also published two recent works on the differences between the United States and Japan.

Essay, 11 pages   p. 426

Since this is one of the longer expository essays in the anthology, you may want to spend some time analyzing the structure and techniques used. Similarly to the previous essay by Shaheen, Fallows begins with a provocative first sentence that grabs the reader's attention. We spend a lot of time in class emphasizing the importance of beginning with a strong technique that attracts the reader. We even spend time listing and illustrating popular techniques used by writers; so, whenever we can, we use the essays to highlight effective introductions.

You can discuss the anecdote about Mrs. Trollope and its function in the essay. Ask students how the story helps the author to set up his thesis. You may want to ask the class to outline the essay. This may help them see how the author first highlights the positive qualities of the Japanese and, in doing so, satisfies our expectations. However, he then surprises the reader by discussing two traits he finds offensive, the open use of pornography and the Japanese concept of racial purity.

Both of these topics demand scrutiny. In discussing the issue of pornography, you may want to explore if this knowledge in some way affects students' perception of the character in the story "The Man from Mars." You may also want to discuss the final sentence in paragraph 16 when the author sums up his concern for pornography as creating "an atmosphere that gives most Westerners the creeps." This

statement seems to trivialize the subject. Has the author explored sufficiently the effects that pornography can have on male attitudes
towards women? In fact, there is little discussion of female roles in the
home, in public or in sexual affairs in Japan. The author makes an
assertion about the absence of sex crimes in Japan. Could other factors
explain the absence of sex crimes? Furthermore, you can explore with
students if physical crimes are the only crimes that can be perpetrated
against a group.

In his second point, Fallows switches to an indictment of Japanese
society as being closed, insular, and parochial. He contrasts it to our
own open, though imperfect, society. This point can bring the discussion back to the issue of "aliens." In this case, we see how the Japanese
see others, such as the Koreans, as "aliens." It is interesting to contrast
how individual Japanese suffer as "aliens" outside their country (a topic
surely to have been discussed in earlier classes) and how they treat others as "aliens" at home.

In discussing this final topic, you may want to be careful that the
class does not end up feeling hostile toward the Japanese. You may
want to remind the class that the essay is about Japanese culture and
society, not a definition of what a Japanese man or woman is like or is
worth. In this regard, the title can be misleading and a little dangerous
in its ambiguity. Ironically, from the title and the criticism of Japanese
culture, the essay can be construed as racist, the last thing that Fallows
wants.

Suggested Assignments

Q.1. Reread the first two lines of paragraph 21. The author seems
to be implying that perception can be just as powerful and influential
as reality. Would you agree or disagree? Use this essay to support your
answer.

Q.2. Compare the way Japanese treat the Koreans in Japan to the
way Americans treat the Japanese in the United States. What do these
comparisons say about both cultures? Do you agree with the author
that Americans are more open than the Japanese? Support your answer
with examples.

Student Encounter Activity

Interview members of the community to find out their perceptions
of Japanese culture. What aspects of Japanese culture are they more
familiar with? Can you deduce why this is the case?

Mark Salzman

TEACHER WEI

Mark Salzman is a graduate from Yale University with a degree in Chinese language. He spent some time living, studying, and working in China. He has written two books, one of which was turned into a feature film. He lives in Los Angeles, California.

Essay, 8 pages   p. 438

Salzman's piece on Chinese culture is a good followup to Fallows's essay which emphasizes traits of Asian culture he finds distasteful. In this autobiographical essay, Salzman depicts certain Chinese traits prevalent in daily life. The young narrator adapts to these in an accepting and unquestioning manner. Perhaps because of his youth, we perceive a bit of brashness in him, especially in his lecture on *E.T.* You may want to spend some time asking students how they feel about the narrator, particularly if we see him as representative of American culture.

His impatience and extroverted manner contrasts with the subtlety and indirection, humanity, and warmth in relationships, an unselfishness that stands in contrast to our sex-and-success public life. This contrast surprises even Salzman, the student of things Chinese who by his academic and other choices has tried to realize different kinds of relationships.

This essay works well with Fallows, as well as with Shaheen, because the first sentence has the same eye-grabbing introductory technique of the other two essays. Yet the structure in this one reverses that of Fallows by beginning with a negative depiction of Chinese buses and ending with more positive observations. Even the initially negative scene of the bus dissolves when the man cheerfully pays half his fare.

After looking at the first two paragraphs, you can ask students to outline the essay and, in doing so, list all the unexpected or strange events described in the story, beginning with the man who cheerfully pays half his fare after having had the bus door slammed shut on him halfway in the vehicle. Then you can ask students to explain the rationale for each of the behaviors. This should lead to interesting discussions of Chinese customs and values.

Suggested Assignments

Q.1. Focus on paragraph 53. Think of one of your professors as "a teacher in the Chinese tradition." How would you react to the professor's concerns with your development as a person (as characterized in paragraph 53)? Should U.S. educators teach in the Chinese tradition? Why do you think yes or no?

Q.2. Deciding to accept a stranger into one's culture is a delicate and serious affair. Some cultures accomplish the task through ritualistic means. Others do so in more subtle ways. Some embrace a stranger very openly. Describe the ways in which Teacher Wei and Dr. Li accept Salzman into their culture. Focus on the details. What did their techniques have in common? Would you classify these as ritualistic, subtle, or open? Why do you think they utilize these ways? Are these ways agreeable with you?

Student Encounter Activity

Have you ever had a foreign professor or teacher who practiced unusual behaviors? Describe these. What could have been the teacher's motivations? How did you feel about his or her differences?

Maya Angelou

MY BROTHER BAILEY AND KAY FRANCIS

Maya Angelou is an African-American poet, actress, and dancer. "My Brother Bailey and Kay Francis" is from the first volume of her autobiography, *I Know Why the Caged Bird Sings*. Angelou read her poem "On the Pulse of Morning" at the inauguration of President Bill Clinton in 1993.

Memoir, 4 pages   p. 448

Students usually have little trouble taking off on a discussion of this piece. They may focus on racism in the South, depicted in the last scene at the movie house, or on the family relationships. Even though the piece is an autobiographical memoir, the excerpt reads like a short story with characters, plot, and suspense.

As such, the story revolves primarily around Bailey and his loss, as well as his coming of age. In discovering the sameness on the screen, Bailey actually realizes the differences. The first paragraph with its metaphors gives us a clue. He is caught between his desire to be a little boy in his mother's arms (the reason for his bedtime prayer) and his need to be a man, detached from the rest of the family and the future that awaits him. In this vein, you may want to ask your students to interpret the line, "Children's talent to endure stems from their ignorance of alternatives."

You can also explore other provocative lines such as "Southern Blacks until the present generation could be counted among America's arch conservatives," and "I laughed because, except that she was white, the big movie star looked just like my mother."

Suggested Assignments

Q.1. Describe life for Southern Blacks as depicted in the story. Why were Saturdays so special?

Q.2. In some ways, this story reveals a coming of age for Bailey. Find details in the story that would support this statement.

Student Encounter Activity

How much do you know about life in the South for Blacks in the early decades for the twentieth century, before the civil rights movement? Interview members of the community or do some research in the library to uncover details about daily life. Do these approximate the lifestyle depicted in Maya Angelou's story?

The Craft of Writing:

EXPECTATION

p. 454

The Afterword for this chapter examines how a large part of reading involves expectations on the part of the reader. The anticipations and expectations of the reader can enhance or detract from the reading experience, but they always affect it. For this reason, it is important that students realize the power a writer holds in controlling the expectations of the reader.

As students write their own papers, you may want to discuss the power of expectation by reviewing different elements of the essay that create expectations. For example, unless we insist, our students will often leave out a title. Nevertheless, titles are important in that they are the first source of anticipation; if not well chosen, they can also confuse the reader. Sometimes the ambiguity can be intentional to create surprise later in the essay. What we emphasize to students is that the writer must be in control. Ambiguity should not exist randomly; it should exist only if it serves a function.

We have students work hard on the introductions to their papers because we feel it is probably the most important section of the essay in creating expectations. The introduction not only introduces the focus of the essay but also establishes the tone, diction, and mood of the essay. If the rest of the essay does not satisfy the expectations of the introduction, the reader will be confused and disoriented and the writer's credibility will diminish.

Similarly, topic sentences will create certain expectations within individual paragraphs. Readers expect that all the examples, facts, and anecdotes included in a particular paragraph will be placed within the framework created in the topic sentence.

In order to help your students develop the essays assigned in the section "Writing about the Reading," you may also want to discuss the importance of strong examples in topics such as these. Most of the assignments ask students to explore ethnic groups other than their own. Get them to distinguish between perception and reality. Ask them to gather concrete data, statistics, etc. to counter the effects of media perceptions.

In your discussions of the pieces in this chapter, your students will hopefully have become more aware of their own stereotyping and biases against certain groups. Encourage them to write about the groups with which they have the most trouble. It may help them to distinguish expectations from reality. After all, what good is reality, if perceptions govern?

Comments on Student Writing

p. 460

Jennifer Johns's essay can be useful in three ways. First, you can assign it as a companion piece to Carter Revard's poem. It will provide students with the historical background to help them understand the parallels in the poem between the space creatures and the Native Americans. In order to do this, the student did some research and incorporated it into her essay, which she then documented. Using her paper as an example of research and documenting is also useful for students.

You can use this essay to emphasize to students the need for research. In writing about topics such as this one, where controversial or ignored issues are addressed, it is critical that students support their points with data and experts' testimonies. We find that we need to remind our students that when they write their own essays about stereotypes, they need to get concrete data to distinguish myth from reality.

Finally, in addition to pointing out the research orientation and organizational techniques of the essay, you may want to use this essay to illustrate expectations. For example, in the first line, Johns establishes the tone of the essay and lets us know the angle the essay will take. The quote by Francis Jennings in the second line establishes the introductory technique, and the thesis at the end of the paragraph reaffirms the expectations that will control the entire essay. In other words, it is easy to expect what is coming. I would point out to students, however, that being too blunt can also be a stylistic disadvantage for it can alienate readers who disagree with the thesis too soon.

⌐ 6 ⌐

FENCES

The editors have titled this chapter "Fences." In Western literature, fences have often represented the end of a lifestyle where openness and freedom predominated. This was particularly true in the nineteenth century, when the railroad brought with it development and fences. Today, fences have become a normal part of the urban and even rural landscape. They mark borders and intimidate people from crossing them. Obviously, they are not absolute barriers, but rather warnings that entrance is not acceptable.

As the editors indicate in the introduction to this chapter, fences also exist at a social level. We create them to keep others from coming in, while protecting and offering security to the members within. As such, they can have both a positive and a negative impact.

The editors go on to summarize the roles of types of fences. By establishing criteria and borders, symbolic or metaphoric fences can provide clarity, comfort, and support to a group's members. They can also serve to constrain and intimidate those who would want to be different and dare to cross the fences. Some of these individuals cross fences for courageous and noble reasons; others do so simply to rebel or to be adventurous.

This chapter presents the concept of fences in all its dimensions—sometimes to celebrate them, other times to denounce them. Mainly, they explore the motivations and consequences of these fences in society.

Fences can ultimately lead to conflict, and conflict appears more frequently and insistently in this chapter than in any other section of the book. The idea of constructing barriers between people, for whatever reason, leads repeatedly to confrontation. The Afterword in this chapter relates conflict to structure; you may want to read it before discussing the selections. We have found that using conflict as a basis for discussing the structure of the pieces is helpful for our students.

Pre-Reading Activity

Before assigning this chapter's selections, you may want to explore the concept of fences with your students. The following activity can be helpful.

Organize the class in groups of four or five. For the first ten minutes of class, ask students to free write an answer to the following question: What defines groups in our society as different?

After they have written individually, ask them to read their answers to each other in the group. Ask one of the members to serve as a secretary and generate a master list for the group. After this list has been discussed and created, ask another member of the group to read their list to the class.

After you have completed the presentations of each group, repeat the same exercise but with a new question: What methods do you and the members of your family use to distinguish yourselves from others outside the family?

Both these questions should generate interesting perspectives on fences.

Toni Morrison

"RECITATIF"

Toni Morrison was born in 1931, of African-American descent. She grew up in Lorrain, Ohio, and was educated at Howard and Cornell universities. She teaches at Princeton University. Her many novels include *Song of Solomon*, *Tar Baby*, *Beloved*, for which she was awarded the Pulitzer Prize in literature, and *Jazz*. She won the Nobel Prize for literature in 1993.

Short story, 15 pages   p. 467

The strength of this story lies in the direct way it addresses racial tension: not as an abstract issue, but as a condition that affects the lives of individuals. The story revolves around two women—one white, the other black—who meet as children at a shelter. Even though they have already been introduced to racism, they find support and friendship in each other. The first part of the story revolves around their similarities. Get students to find these and list them. For example, their reasons for being at the shelter, their instability, their unwillingness to find permanent beds, and their vulnerability in front of the big girls.

At the beginning, we are not told the race of each girl. The details given are not conclusive. You may find it interesting to discover how your students reacted. Did all the students assume Roberta was black at first? If so, why? Did the African-American students have the same expectations as the other students in the class?

The story is structured around four major encounters that shape the relationship between the two girls: encounters at the shelter, at the Howard Johnson's, at the school, and at the diner. Review each of these situations with the class and ask them what each reveals about the characters as well as about the society in which they live. These encounters are riddled with conflicts. Ask the students to identify these as well, and the participation of each character in each case.

The episode with Maggie at the shelter serves as a thread that runs throughout the story. Ask students to explore the function of the incident. Do we, as readers, have enough evidence to uncover the truth?

Suggested Assignments

Q.1. The narrator of this story is Twyla, yet the story revolves around two main characters. Do you think the author develops the two characters equally? Do you empathize with one character more than with the other? Do your feelings towards the characters change throughout the story? If so, explain your answer.

Q.2. Often a writer uses characters and specific incidents in their lives to introduce the reader to general, even universal, issues in a more personal way. If this is true in Morrison's story, what issues would you identify as important and universal? Support your answer with examples from the text.

Student Encounter Activity

You may be surprised to find how many individuals, especially of your parents' age, have similar stories to tell, stories where societal pressures and expectations made them question or even end a friendship. Interview several people, looking for examples of similar situations. Discuss with the class their examples and any you may have of your own.

David Leavitt

A PLACE I'VE NEVER BEEN

David Leavitt was born in Pittsburgh in 1961 and attended Yale University. He is the author of three novels and two collections of short fiction, and has been writer-in-residence at the Institute of Catalan Letters in Barcelona, Spain, for several years.

Short story, 11 pages   p. 483

One of the most challenging aspects of this story for your students will probably be figuring out the relationship between the two main characters, Celia and Nathan. Celia is the speaker of the story, but is she the main character? The following questions may help you probe students: Is this a story about Celia's feelings toward Nathan? Or is this a story about how Nathan copes with being gay in a world of AIDS? Who are we supposed to relate to? Who are we to sympathize with? Might reactions to the story change depending on the gender and sexual inclination of the reader?

You may also want to discuss the conflict in this story. Depending on who we choose as the main character, the conflict will be different. For Celia, the conflict lies in her love for Nathan but her inability to find fulfillment in their relationship. For Nathan, the conflict stems from his being gay and afraid of AIDS. Is either conflict resolved?

Finally, explore the chapter's concept of fences. What fences exist between Celia and Nathan? Between Nathan and the rest of the world? Between Celia and the rest of the world? Hasn't she let Nathan become a fence, too? Other minor characters in the story also suffer as a result of their differences. Ask students to identify them and their own reactions to them.

Suggested Assignments

Q.1. We don't often see depictions of homosexuals in literature and in the media unless it's to reinforce stereotypes about them. Does this story fit that category? Is Nathan stereotyped in any way? Support your answer with examples from the text.

Q.2. If we viewed the game Deprivation as a window into the life-styles and expectations of a generation of college students depicted in the story, what would it tell us about them? What were their expectations while in college? Have these changed? If so, how? Be specific with your answer. How do these compare with your expectations?

Student Encounter Activity

Brainstorm a list of expectations you had in high school. Categorize these into personal and public desires. Brainstorm a list of expectations you hold as a college student. How do these compare? What do the results say about you? Can you identify any "fences" along the way?

Wayne D. Johnson

WHAT HAPPENED TO RED DEER

Wayne Johnson grew up in Minnesota and lived for many years in the West. He has published a novel, *The Snake Game*.

Short story, 14 pages   p. 495

This story works well to look at the way people cope or fail to cope with ostracism and alienation. Red Deer is an interesting character because he feels isolated from both his Native American tribe and outsiders. Basically, he is on his own and temporarily finds refuge in his ability to play baseball.

Characterization is central to this story. Before opening up the class to a discussion of Red Deer, you may want to begin by discussing Litani, the stepfather, and Freddie. Each of these minor characters plays a role in rounding out Red Deer's personality. Ask your students to describe the function of each of these minor characters. Then get students to talk about Red Deer.

How much do your students sympathize with Red Deer? Enough to condone the final action? Get them to explore the conflicts and tensions that lead up to the end. Does the depiction of Red Deer in this story reinforce their expectations or stereotypes of a Native-American male? Try to probe them on this issue.

Another approach is to begin by asking students to outline the structure of the story. Explore with them how the technique of flashback is effective in creating tension in the story. Ask them if this technique helps or hinders us in determining which events are more or less significant in the life of the main character.

Suggested Assignments

Q.1. Red Deer's final action could be interpreted as the result of his inability to cope with external pressures. If so, can you think of alternatives or solutions to his dilemma?

Q.2. Even though Red Deer experiences pain as a result of taunting at the baseball games, why does he continue to play the game? Why doesn't he walk away from the pain? the anger?

Student Encounter Activity

Get into groups of four or five. For five or ten minutes write individually about those things that make you so angry. Share these with the group. After listening to all the members, determine if there are common elements to the things that make us the most angry. Are any of these things the same as those that made Red Deer so angry?

Pat Mora

SONRISAS

Pat Mora is of Chicana heritage and was born in El Paso, Texas. She is a poet with three published collections of poetry, and lives in Cincinnati.

Poem, 1/2 page   p. 510

This poem relies on crisp, concise, clear images as well as a binary quality to dramatize the speaker's plight. The poem works well for a formalist analysis. Your students will probably have no trouble seeing the structure or themes because the contrasts are so directly established.

Ask the students to describe the two worlds depicted and to note the shifts in clothes, colors, food, sounds, facial expressions, etc. You may want to point out how in the first stanza, the speaker uses the word "hear" and in the second stanza "peek." Ask them to analyze the contrast in the images and choices of words in order to interpret their greater meanings.

Suggested Assignments

Q.1. Living in the doorway allows the speaker to observe two worlds. Is the speaker more familiar with one than with the other? From the poem, can you deduce which she would most likely step into if she had to? Why do you think so?

Q.2. Compare the act of hearing to the act of peeking. In terms of impressions and communication, is one more powerful than the other? How does this affect your understanding of the poem?

Cathy Song

LOST SISTER

Cathy Song was born in Hawaii in 1955. She is a poet and anthologist. Her collection *Picture Bride* was the winner of the Yale Younger Poets Award in 1982.

Poem, 2 pages   p. 511

You may want to begin the discussion of this poem by describing its dual structure. The first part should elicit interesting reactions by your students concerning the treatment of Chinese women. You may need to clarify some of the references, especially those to the "shoes / the size of teacups" (the ancient Chinese tradition of binding women's feet). Get students to note the images chosen in the first part. Even though the women had difficult lives, the speaker uses terms such as "Jade," "stone," "moisten," "healing," "glistening," "grateful," "patience," and "surviving." Ask them what these terms have in common and what they reflect about the speaker's attitude towards women in China.

After analyzing the first part, move on to the second and ask students to do a similar exercise. They should be ready to note a severe contrast in images with such terms as "loneliness," "meager," "flimsy," "snake," "spewing black clouds," and "dough-faced." The contrast of these specific images should help them to understand the speaker's attitude in the last stanza.

Discuss the irony of the last stanza and how the speaker seems to imply that the loss of rootedness is the price to pay for the gain of freedom. Explore this point with your students. How do they feel about the ambiguity expressed?

Suggested Assignments

Q.1. The poem presents parallel themes of travel. Identify the lines that identify the idea of traveling. Compare the two and decide to what degree they are different.

Q.2. If in China the "shoes / the size of teacups" steal the ability to move freely, and if in America "the possibilities / the loneliness / can strangulate like jungle veins," then what recourse is left for the speaker?

Student Encounter Activity

Have you or do you know someone who has taken a journey in search of a freedom (to another land or even another city or home away from home)? Describe the journey with its trials and tribulations. What was gained and what was lost? Was it worth it?

nila northSun

UP & OUT

nila northSun was born in Schurz, Nevada, in 1951 of Shoshoni-Chippewa heritage. She is a poet and coauthor of two collections.

Poem, 1 page   p. 513

This poem makes an excellent followup to Cathy Song's "Lost Sister." Even though the cultures and settings are different, the speaker is reflecting similar attitudes. Explore these similarities with your students.

We find the best way to deal with the poem is to ask students to make a list of each of the items the speaker associates first with the reservation, and then with the city. Discuss the contrast and why the speaker has changed her mind. The Study Questions should help to set up the discussion. You may also want to discuss what values expressed here have been seen in earlier works by Native Americans.

Suggested Assignments

Q.1. In what ways does the poem attest to the old saying that "the grass is always greener on the other side of the hill"? How can this poem also reflect non–Native-American feelings towards city life?

Q.2. In your opinion, can the speaker return to the reservation after having lived in an urban culture?

Student Encounter Activity

How many times have you yearned to live in or visit another place? Once there, how did the place compare to your expectations? What made for the differences or similarities between the two? How were you affected by these?

Ricardo Pau-Llosa

SORTING METAPHORS

Ricardo Pau-Llosa was born in Cuba in 1954, and came to the United States in 1960. He resides in Miami where he is a professor of English at Miami-Dade Community College. He is also a poet, art historian, and curator. In addition to publishing extensively on art, he has published three collections of poetry, the most recent of which is *Cuba*.

Poem, 2 pages   p. 515

"Sorting Metaphors" can be a challenging poem for your students. We would suggest you begin by discussing the nature and function of a metaphor. Continue by asking students to mark the shifts between the metaphors in the poem. Ask them to decipher what each metaphor refers to; then ask them to find what the metaphors have in common. In other words, help them to systematically sort out the metaphors in the poem.

Ultimately, this is a poem about fragmentation. Both the epigraph and the abrupt shifting of metaphors reaffirm this perception. You may want to explore with your students the cause of the fragmentation (exile, displacement, etc.). The "two unyielding and unseen boundaries," plus the references to Havana, should give them some clues.

Suggested Assignments

Q.1. How does the speaker feel about life between unseen boundaries? List the emotions evoked. Which lines in the poem support your list?

Q.2. Compare this poem to Pat Mora's "Sonrisas." How are the poems similar? How are they different? In your opinion, which is the more effective poem in conveying ideas or sentiments? Why?

Rita Mae Brown

SAPPHO'S REPLY

Rita Mae Brown was born in Pennsylvania in 1944. She is a novelist, poet, and political activist. She has published many novels, three collections of poetry, and nonfiction on the craft of writing and on feminist/lesbian politics.

Poem, 1/2 page   p. 517

For students to understand this poem, they will need to know that Sappho was a Greek poet from the seventh and early sixth centuries B.C. who wrote amorous and passionate love poems. She was a noblewoman and ran a school for girls devoted to the study of music and poetry. Some consider her the first poet to express lesbian tendencies.

After knowing this, it should be evident to your students that Sappho's voice is being invoked as a source of strength throughout the ages. You may want to explore with your students the metaphors used by the poet to depict the situation of the "lovers" in the poem.

Suggested Assignments

Q.1. Who was Sappho? Apart from the obvious, why do you think the poet utilizes this person?

Q.2. In your estimation, who is Sappho answering? What is being asked? Is her reply effective in making her point?

Madeline Coopsammy

IN THE DUNGEON OF MY SKIN

Madeline Coopsammy was born in Trinidad and Tobago. She is a poet with two collections of poetry; she currently teaches English in Winnepeg.

Poem, 1 page   p. 518

This poem can work well to bring students back to the topic of fences. It seems everywhere she travels, the speaker encounters "fences" that prevent her from being accepted. Ask students to explore these and the solution the speaker seeks in the last stanza. Is she satisfied with her solution? Get students to decipher the metaphors in the last three lines. What do they reveal about the speaker's attitude? Pose to them the following question. Is she the victim of fences or has she, perhaps, created her own?

Suggested Assignments

Q.1. To liberate oneself from bonds and boundaries would seem to be a great accomplishment. One becomes universal, a whole, rather than a part. With this in mind, scan the poem. Has the speaker become universal? Is this possible to attain? Should it be a sought-after goal? Explain your reasoning.

Q.2. Who is the keeper of the dungeon?

Student Encounter Activity

Research the race classifications of the colonial governments of Spain or England. Why were they so detailed? How do they influence modern-day race relations in former colonial nations? Choose one nation as an example.

Dwight Okita

IN RESPONSE TO EXECUTIVE ORDER 9066: ALL AMERICANS OF JAPANESE DESCENT MUST REPORT TO RELOCATION CENTERS

Dwight Okita, a poet, was born in Chicago in 1958. He has also written music and written for the theater. He is active in the performance poetry community of Chicago and has published one book of poems. During World War II, both his parents were sent to relocation camps for Japanese Americans. The following poem is written in the mother's voice.

Poem, 1 page   p. 519

The speaker in this moving poem is "straddling the fence," a fence of two cultural worlds. Up to now, she has been allowed to do so, but with the coming of the war she is forced into a corner by those closest to her.

There is a subtlety to the poem worth exploring with students. For example, the tomato seeds act as a recurring image. Ask students to explain their function in the poem. You can help by reminding them that Janet calls them "love apples," yet the father says "where we're going / they won't grow." Ask them why not. The tomato seeds and the final gesture in the poem reinforce the tone of the poem, which stands in contrast to the anger visible in the best friend Denise. The tone of this poem is so deftly managed that its effects are powerful. It is a good idea to get the class to try to account for the poem's ability to do so much emotionally in so little space.

You may also wish to explore line 7, where the speaker says, "if it helps any." Ask students to determine why she says this. The speaker reveals a considerate attitude towards "the others," the Americans who sent the order.

If you have not discussed the historical context of the poem earlier in the course, you should probably do so before analyzing the text. It is important that students be aware of the incarceration of Japanese and Japanese Americans in concentration camps during World War II.

Suggested Assignments

Q.1. Compare the language of the title to the language of the response. How does each sound to you? What is intended with the juxtaposition of these different tones?

Q.2. Identify and describe all of the possible "fences" surrounding the people in the poem. Tell how each individual copes with the fences surrounding him or her. In your opinion does any particular individual cope better than the rest? Use examples from the text to support your answer.

Student Encounter Activity

Imagine yourself a student on the campus of Kent State University in 1970. The campus is alive with student demonstrations against the Vietnam War and for social justice. You have just read the executive order given by the governor allowing the National Guard to remove the demonstrators from the campus. Four of your fellow students are shot. Keeping the poem in mind, write your response to the executive order.

R. T. Smith

RED ANGER

R. T. Smith, Scotch-Irish and Tuscarora, was born in Washington, D.C., in 1947. He has published ten books of poetry and has won numerous prizes for his work.

Poem, 1 page   p. 521

This is a powerful poem that reveals the despair and, of course, anger of Native Americans towards their plight. The poet describes scenes from three different tribes to emphasize the common experience of all the Native American tribes in the United States. The power of the poem rests, however, not in a retelling of large historical events, but in the depiction of everyday elements.

Get students to make a list of all the words that can be associated with a negative experience. After they have isolated the words, ask them to read them aloud. This activity should reinforce, if that could be possible, the dark side of the Native-American experience.

Some students may offer suggestions to the dilemma of the speakers, assuming each speaker is different since they come from different tribes. In doing so, they may be avoiding dealing with the anger of the poem. Spend time exploring the line "I nurse my anger like a seed," since most non–Native Americans may have trouble with the concept of nurturing anger. We are taught to dissolve our anger, not to nurture it.

Finally, students may not be familiar with the trail of tears mentioned in the last line, yet they must understand the reference to understand ultimately the last line and the entire poem. We have found it helpful with our classes to review the historical background.

In the end of the nineteenth century, President Andrew Jackson gave an executive order to relocate Native-American tribes, such as the Cherokee of North Carolina and the Seminole of Florida, to Oklahoma. While some individuals resisted by hiding in the mountains or in the swamps in the South, the majority complied with the order but suffered many casualties on the way. For example, of the 16,000 Cherokees removed from North Carolina, one-fourth died on the way to Oklahoma, a journey they made on foot, refusing to ride the white man's wagons. This journey, the "Trail of Tears," is what the poem refers to.

Suggested Assignments

Q.1. Why does the poet sketch brief scenarios from the three tribes rather than describing one tribe or one event in more detail? Explain your answer.

Q.2. Before reading the poem, consider its short title. Close your eyes and visualize the images the title evokes in you. Write these down. How do they compare with the text of the poem?

Student Encounter Activity

Imagine a concerned individual giving the following suggestions to the poem's speakers.

> Write a letter of complaint about your school's
> poor conditions. Get a petition going! Save
> your money and send your mom to an eye spe-
> cialist. I'm sure you are eligible for some kind
> of government assistance. Declare your rights
> as a citizen! Your dad is an alcoholic . . . but he
> has a job! As for you, with your experience in
> fast foods, you should get into the management
> program at Big Burger Corp. With your
> minority status, you'll fly through it. Then you
> can get everybody the heck out of the reserva-
> tion, or even buy into it!

How would you characterize these suggestions? What do they reveal about the individual giving the suggestions? How would the speakers of the poem react to these suggestions?

August Wilson

FENCES

A major American playwright, August Wilson was born in 1945. He grew up in Pittsburgh and is a poet as well as a playwright. *Fences* won a Tony Award and a Pulitzer Prize.

Play, 51 pages   p. 523

We suggest three different approaches to this play: one emphasiz- ing the theme of this chapter, one involving characterization (the characters here are not only clearly and firmly drawn; the playwright takes bold chances with type characters that he goes on to individuate carefully), and one focusing on the play's staging and dramatic structure.

A discussion of theme can grow most naturally out of the fence on stage. In plain sight in its unfinished state throughout most of the play, the fence is a visual reminder of intentional barriers as well as of incompleteness and lack of control. The fence here, even in Troy's intentions, stands for something different from a lot of the fences in the selections earlier in the chapter. In defining exactly what it represents to Troy, to Rose, and to us as audience, you can run back over the possible symbolism suggested by what fences stand for—or stand between—in other pieces of writing. The Study Questions will set up this discussion quite well for the class. Indeed, you may have set up the discussion more fully than you expect if you have varied, in your teaching of other selections, your emphasis on the idea of how barriers work and how different kinds of people use barriers for their own psychological reasons. (You will no doubt wish to discuss in some detail the fences between generations, genders, and friends; in fact, a good strategy to begin the discussion is to get your students to list all the kinds of fences they can think of that appear literally or metaphorically in the play.)

Our favorite character to use to show how subtly the play develops its characterization is Gabriel. In a way, he is a pure stage "type"—the "crazy" who is not all there but is sweet and innocent. Gabriel performs the role admirably, his simplicity offering at several crucial places a relief from the human complexities that "regular" characters can't cope with. But let your students show each other how much more complex Gabriel turns out to be. Get them to point out where he becomes a complication, even a pain in the neck to the audience as well as to the Maxons. Several other characters also work off "type" models but are well individuated. If you have taught other plays earlier in the course, you might wish to use whatever character you choose to isolate here as a vehicle to note how, in different plays, different authors individualize figures who begin with some burden of type but become complicated by their function in the play.

The Afterword to this chapter will serve as a reminder to your students about the traditional terms used to describe dramatic structure; once you have the play's theme and ideas on the table, you may want to have the students point specifically to divisions in the play that correspond to classic structural divisions. One thing that may confuse them at first is that structure is put in terms of a five-act play, whereas Wilson has divided his play into only two acts, presented in the way most contemporary plays are with a single intermission. Get them to reconcile the two conventions; let them know that act division is only a convention while structural matters transcend such obvious formal markings. The point is to get them to see that the action does in fact rise, come to a crisis, then fall to a point where a resolution and closure can occur.

Some discussion of visualization seems necessary for this play; for us, the most convenient way of leading into this discussion is to return to the issue of the fence. A question you can pose to the students as profitably at the end as at the beginning is how to stage the fence, using it as a silent commentary on the action taking place all around it but without making explicit reference to it. If you begin with a thematic discussion of fences and end with dramatic structure, you can do a kind of afterpiece on staging that picks up those two threads.

Suggested Assignments

Q.1. Sometimes passing down behavior from generation to generation can have a positive and/or a negative influence on an individual. Given this, list the ways in which cross-generational fences are mended or torn down in the play. Support your answer with specific examples from the play.

Q.2. Does the play present any values that are in conflict with your own? List them, if any, and give one reason for each as to why they are in conflict. Do these conflicts affect your reading of the play in any way? How so?

Student Encounter Activity

What aspects of your past do you feel you need to free yourself from? In a brief essay, describe the specific aspect, your feelings toward it, and the steps you need to take to move on.

James Seilsopour

I FORGOT THE WORDS TO THE NATIONAL ANTHEM

James Seilsopour was born in California in 1962. He spent most of his early life in Iran but returned to the United States in 1979.

Essay, 2 pages   p. 576

We find that this unpretentious essay is strangely moving to students—even when feelings towards Iran were at their most feverish high. Maybe the fact that Seilsopour wrote this from the perspective of a high school student is responsible; more likely it has to do with the fact that almost all students have experienced (or feared) this kind of isolation, for whatever reason, from their peers that Seilsopour describes so vividly here.

Still, the emotional and political issues are so entangled here that your students may feel inhibited from public discussion. Students may brood about the piece later. A writing exercise, using this essay as a model, can be very helpful. You may ask them to share a personal experience or let them invent an incident that demonstrates a similar isolation.

You may want to relate this essay to the poem by Dwight Okita, earlier in the chapter, dealing with Japanese internment during World War II. Even though the historical context is different, the experiences are similar. Ask your students to discuss how this is so. By doing so, you may help them to detach a bit from their emotions towards the specifics in this essay.

Suggested Assignments

Q.1. Seilsopour says he is not bitter. Yet his subsequent actions seem to contradict his statement. In your opinion, is he bitter or not? If he is, does he have a right to be so? If he is not, how can he not be, given his experiences? Use specific examples from the text to support your observation.

Q.2. In moral and legal terms, what are the differences between how the U.S. government and a segment of its citizenry treated Seilsopour's family and the way they treated the Japanese-American population in World War II? In your opinion, to what degree are the differences significant?

Student Encounter Activity

Think back on your own high school days. Can you think of an incident when you felt ostracized by your peers? Describe the incident, your feelings, and your subsequent reactions to it. In the long view, what did you learn by it?

Laurence Thomas

NEXT LIFE, I'LL BE WHITE

Laurence Thomas teaches in the philosophy, political science, and Judaic studies departments at Syracuse University. He is the author of two books and numerous articles on moral theory and social philosophy. He has received numerous awards and fellowships.

Essay, 1 page   p. 578

This is a powerful and moving essay that may challenge some of your students' expectations and beliefs, as well as their prejudices. They will probably react emotionally to it; in some cases, we have found that their emotional reactions may interfere with their analysis of the issues presented.

Since the essay is short enough to read aloud in class, we would suggest the following approach. Without giving out any information on the essay or the author, begin by writing on the board several lines that may outline some of the arguments. For example, "white males have committed more evil cumulatively than any other class of people in the world"; "white males generally regard themselves as morally superior to all others"; "one of the benefits that come with living morally—namely, the public trust"; "the truly moral person is indifferent to the public trust"; "psychology is constantly telling us that being affirmed by others is indispensable to our flourishing"; and "the victims are made to feel inadequate for insisting upon what their oppressors enjoy and routinely take for granted."

Each of these phrases can lead to stimulating discussions without necessarily dealing with the issue of race head-on. After exploring the meaning and validity of each phrase, read Thomas's essay aloud. We have found that students are more open to his ideas after understanding his principles outside of the racial context.

In any case, after reading the essay, you can also discuss the examples the author provides to demonstrate the lack of public trust that exists for black men in general.

You can also use this essay to point out how Thomas's philosophical arguments are strengthened by the power of his examples. We find that student writing doesn't truly come alive unless they understand the power of effective examples, regardless of the topic or approach of the essay.

Suggested Assignments

Q.1. Is the title of the essay ironic or literal? What makes you think so? Use examples from the text to justify your position.

Q.2. Read the last sentence of the essay. Identify one group, other than African-American, that would serve as an example supporting the idea. Using your example, explain the motives of the oppressors for making the victims feel inadequate. In what ways can (and do) victims overcome their oppressors?

Student Encounter Activity (If the class makeup permits this.)

As an experiment, get into teams of two where one student is white and the other is nonwhite. Visit a local grocery store and take turns walking near patrons of the store while the other person observes the patron's behavior. After doing this several times, study your findings. Do you find a change in the patron's behavior toward each of the team members? What accounts for the change? Present your findings to the class.

Michelle Cliff

IF I COULD WRITE THIS IN FIRE
I WOULD WRITE THIS IN FIRE

Michelle Cliff was born in Kingston, Jamaica, and educated at Wagner College and the Warburg Institute in London. She is a novelist, poet, and essayist, as well as the recipient of numerous fellowships. She has also worked as a reporter, researcher, and editor. She lives in California and teaches in Connecticut.

Essay, 13 pages   p. 581

This essay usually generates a powerful reaction in the classroom. The students are interested in the points and see their relevance. The difficulty is in getting them to talk rationally and in terms of the sources of the essay's rhetorical effectiveness. The immediacy of emotion, freshness, and sincerity are easy to respond to, but students are apt to think that powerful effect comes from powerful feeling, period. Get them to compare other selections that are more restrained, in which anger seeps or bursts through, with the directness here.

Get them to see the calculations in this essay, how pieces of the long-ago past are interwoven with more recent events and bursts of emotion. You may want to ask students to outline the essay, pointing out the transitions and the places where transitions are notably, calculatedly omitted. Get them also to list the self-conscious gestures of spontaneity and immediacy, such as "an interesting face," "a true story," and "there is no ending to this piece of writing." Ask them to list all the themes and topics covered and explain how they are interrelated. The challenge is to get students to see what a complex, finished piece of writing it is when everything, from the title on, presents itself as if it were offhand, just an outburst of feeling. Starting with the title—a good idea with many selections—is particularly useful to suggest the rhetorical stance the author assumes from the start.

In analyzing the rhetorical techniques, you risk that students will move too far away from the emotional power in the essay. Get them to analyze the source of the anger, not just its rhetoric. Throughout the various topics and anecdotes presented, there seems to run a thread that culminates in the last line: "we/they/I connect and disconnect— change place." Ask students to explore the meaning of this line and how identity or the search for identity seems to be at the core of the essay. Besides the conflict with being light and dark, victim and oppressor, what other conflicts could the speaker be confronting or avoiding? Ask students what her lesbianism has to do with the rest of the issues in the essay.

Suggested Assignments

Q.1. In your own words and using specific details from the text, explain Cliff's problem. Compare and contrast your explanation with the others in the class. Is it possible to arrive at a class consensus?

Q.2. Given that most rates of exchange are 10-to-1 U.S. dollars or higher in Third World nations, what would you say to a family living in such a nation, earning U.S. dollars, and paying their domestic workers Third World wages?

Student Encounter Activity

If you have visited, or are from, or know about a Third World city, then you know that even the poorest shanty home has a TV with an antenna. Furthermore, the favorite programs are U.S. made. Among some intellectual circles, this phenomenon is considered high-tech colonialism. Among others, it is seen as visual cultural diffusion.

Attribute a positive or negative effect on the people of the city to each of the two points of view expressed above. Which do you defend? Justify your response.

The Craft of Writing
CONFLICT AND STRUCTURE

p. 595

The Afterword in this chapter provides an interesting overview of conflict as a constant condition in society and a requirement in literature, at least in narrative and dramatic literature. The editors discuss how conflict manifests itself in several of the pieces in the chapter, such as the play "Fences" and the short story "Recitatif." In addition, the editors review the role of structure in literature in general.

Form and structure remain pretty abstract terms to most students, and yet they are useful terms for understanding. As readers, students need to be sensitive to how writers manipulate the structure of a piece in order to achieve the effect they want. It is also important to help students see the differences between the outward appearance of a piece of writing and the internal structure that provides cohesion and strength. The essay "If I Could Write This in Fire I Would Write This in Fire" can be useful for illustrating this point.

As writers, students must realize that they too control the structure of their own writing. We have found that students shy away from this responsibility and prefer to develop their essays intuitively. Though this may work well enough for the stronger writers, especially those who are avid readers, most students will benefit from an understanding of the differences between free writing and a structured essay. The structure and shape given to the creative and intuitive ideas that originate in the initial free-writing exercises will make a better essay.

Because this chapter deals so much with conflict and motivation, most of the assignments at the end ask students to explore causes and/or effects of conflicts. We recommend you use this opportunity to review some of the guidelines for writing cause-and-effect essays. For example, students must first identify the condition, in this case the conflict. After identifying the conflict, students should explore the actual, probable, and possible causes and effects associated with the conflict. Make sure they understand the differences between these categories. Furthermore, they must be sure there are obvious links between the causes and the effects and not just coincidences.

Finally, we recommend you discuss the difference between distant and immediate causes, as well as immediate and long-term effects. We have found that students often underestimate the complexities and subtleties of such an analysis. The story "Red Deer" will be helpful to distinguish between the immediate and distant causes of the main character's anger.

Comments on Student Writing

p. 601

The strength of this student essay resides in the writer's intimacy with the text. Through her discussions and examples, she demonstrates that she has thoroughly familiarized herself with the poem and the ideas it expresses. You may want to use this essay to discuss the importance of reading a poem carefully. The economy that characterizes poetry means that each part of the poem carries significance and impact. For this reason, each aspect demands attention. Point out how the student writer observes carefully the different elements of the poem she is analyzing. The following questions can help your students to begin their task:

- What does the title tell about the poem?
- What do individual words in the poem mean, and what do they suggest?
- Who is speaking in the poem?
- What are the setting and the situation in the poem?
- What is the subject of the poem?
- What is the theme?

Point out to your students that these questions may be hard to answer at times; however, once they are answered, they will be on their way to a meaningful reading of the poem.

After reviewing these questions, go back to the student essay and discuss the various elements introduced by the author, such as language, imagery, wording, and implications. The student gives numerous examples directly from the text to support her observations.

In addition to showing an effective, careful reading of the poem, this student essay shows how students can use a poem as a springboard for an insightful and moving discussion of their own related issues.

⌐ 7 ⌐

CROSSING

About the Theme "Crossing"

In the introduction to this chapter, the editors elaborate on the theme of the chapter, "Crossing." The sense of togetherness, familiarity, and belonging is comforting for many people. Within our own particular group, we feel secure. It is a cultural comfort the group members depend on. The boundaries of these groups, whether they be a small family or a larger society, are flexible yet they are usually not crossed.

Tension arises when an outsider crosses the boundary or when an insider leaves the group. The editors offer several reasons why an individual might leave a group—such as the need to assert one's individuality, to seek greater opportunity, or simply to explore.

Two of the most common and intense crossings are courtship and marriage. These are also the most intimate and, because of this intimacy, the most threatening to a group. Many of the selections in this chapter, therefore, deal with sexual relationships. Other works present varying dimensions of the theme of crossing, such as the clash of values.

Pre-Reading Activity

It is important for students to explore their own ideas about the theme of crossing before reading the selections in this chapter. Through written assignments and oral discussions, you can probe their views about the theme.

Have the students read the editors' discussion on the theme of crossing.

At home or in class, ask students to free write for fifteen minutes their reaction to the introduction.

Write the word "crossing" on the board and ask students to describe the images that come to their minds.

From these images, infer all of the possible meanings of crossing.

Sandra Cisneros

BREAD

Sandra Cisneros was born in Chicago, and is of Mexican-American descent. She is the author of three books, including *Woman Hollering Creek*, from which this story is taken. She currently lives in San Antonio, Texas.

Short story, 1/2 page   p. 607

This is a good piece to illustrate the theme of the chapter. We find it useful to begin by asking students to group as many details as possible that describe each of the characters. Get them to read carefully in order to decipher the relationship between these two people. We use the Study Questions to direct the discussion.

At some point these characters were willing to cross certain boundaries which led to "pain between us." However, they have returned to where they came from, to past expectations, or at least the male character has and the female expresses disappointment at the realization of how things have changed. Ask your students to explore these points and to find indications of such conclusions in the text.

Suggested Assignments

Q.1. This story, in some ways, is about crossing borders. What are the borders in the story? What do the characters expect in the crossing? from the present encounter? Compare and contrast these. In your opinion, who has the most sincere expectation? Support your answers with examples from the text.

Q.2. The action revolves around two main characters. Search the story for dialogues and encounters between the two. Are they harmonious or discordant? Based upon your list decide whether the relationship between the two is a positive or a negative one. Be prepared to defend your decision.

Student Encounter Activity

Think of a person you recently met whom you had not seen for a long time. Were you surprised by the encounter? Did it feel like you had changed? Like he or she had changed? If so, explain how. Where you disappointed in any way? Write a brief essay that describes the experience and summarizes the answers to the previous questions.

Tobias Wolff

SAY YES

Born in 1945, Tobias Wolff is the author of several books, including *This Boy's Life: A Memoir*, his most recent. Formerly a reporter for the *Washington Post*, he currently teaches at Syracuse University.

Short story, 3 pages   p. 608

We usually begin the discussion of this story by having students look at the relationship between the two main characters. From there, we move on to the more general question of racism.

The greatest challenge in teaching this story is getting students to look beyond what's being said and to analyze the characters' underlying motivations and desires. We find that reviewing point of view and the reader's role in "reading between the lines" can be helpful here. We ask students to describe each of the characters and explore if they are being truly sincere in their own expectations. We also get students to discuss the wife's question and her insistence that the husband say yes. If they don't point it out, we like to remind them of the title. Is the real objective of her question to explore his racism, or is it perhaps his acceptance of her and his understanding of who she is? In discussing this topic, you may want to refer to the last paragraph of the story. Why is she a stranger to him? And why is it advantageous to him to keep her a stranger?

From this discussion, we jump into the issue of racism. In the same way that the husband keeps the wife a stranger, does he, and do whites in general, keep blacks an exotic mystery? You may want to ask your students to look for passages that might indicate such an interpretation of the text and ask them to pay close attention particularly to the ending. We find it challenging for our students to openly discuss the black-white issues alluded to in the story and often get them to write about their reactions to the story before we discuss it in class.

Suggested Assignments

Q.1. If two people love each other, regardless of any differences they may have, then why are there "lots of things to consider" (paragraph 36)? Answer the question within the context of the story.

Q.2. Compare the husband's actions to his wife's reactions. Are these people understanding each other? If he had said yes, would their relationship have changed? If so, how?

Student Encounter Activity

The last paragraph of the story can be described as sensual, and almost erotic. If the story is taken as a representation for black-white race issues, then the last paragraph is critical. For the stereotype of "black" as erotica for "white" is old, persistent, and deeply ingrained in the white culture. Given this, look for examples from popular culture (music, movies, television, etc.) that support this premise. Then decide if the last paragraph exposes or reinforces the stereotype. Write an essay with your findings.

Robbie Clipper Sethi

GRACE

Robbie Clipper Sethi is a fiction writer who teaches English at Rider College in New Jersey. Her stories have appeared in such magazines as the *Literary Review, Mademoiselle*, and the *Atlantic Monthly*.

Short story, 14 pages   p. 612

A marriage between individuals from different cultures can suffer as a result of external cultural pressures, especially from family members. You can use "Grace" to explore issues such as privacy, marital expectations, family commitments, communication, and compromise. The Study Questions are very comprehensive and will help you to orient most of the discussion.

We would suggest you spend a good amount of time exploring your students' perceptions towards the characters. We have found students' reactions to the various characters and their alternatives will vary tremendously. Some feel Grace is being reasonable in her demands and Inder uncompromising in his inability to find a solution that satisfies all. Others find Grace to be selfish, unyielding, and obsessed with her work.

Also, try to get your students to articulate a theme for this story. Is it about marriage? the clash of cultures? the absence of communication? Point out how little communication takes place between Inder and Grace even before the marriage. What do they know about each other's expectations and families before the marriage? Inder seems driven by a loyalty to his family that Grace was totally unaware of earlier on. Ask students to find evidence to support this observation. Grace too seems unable to make her demands stick. She complains, but ultimately gives in to everything until it's too late and she moves out. Indeed, this story seems to be about people crossing lines without the tools to cope on the other side. Each eventually crosses back to the safety of what is familiar to him or her.

Suggested Assignments

Q.1. In this story, it is obvious that Inder and his family have participated in a "crossing." How has this crossing affected their lives? Have their lives changed in any way? If so, how? Has Grace also participated in a crossing of her own? Explain your answer.

Q.2. When two people engage in a relationship, they must be willing to make compromises, especially in a culturally mixed marriage such as the one found in this story. Do you find evidence that shows whether Grace and Inder are willing to compromise? Support your answer with specific examples from the text.

Student Encounter Activity

Put yourself in either Grace's or Inder's place. Then write a new version of the story that would offer a more compromising resolution to the familial crisis. In other words, what advice would you give them to resolve the dilemma?

Paula Gunn Allen

POCAHONTAS TO HER ENGLISH
HUSBAND, JOHN ROLFE

Paula Gunn Allen was born in 1939 in New Mexico, from Sioux-Laguna and Lebanese-Jewish descent. A professor of English at the University of California, Los Angeles, she has published a novel, a collection of essays, several books of poetry, and an anthology of stories written by Native Americans.

Poem, 1 page   p. 628

We find this poem useful to emphasize the power of a specific image or event as a catalyst for the poet to open a window to a much greater reality or truth. In this case, the author uses the story of Pocahontas and her relationship to her husband to parallel that of Native

Americans to European settlers. You may want to explore the advantages and possible disadvantages of this technique.

We move from poetic technique to theme by asking students to scan the poem for evidence of the broader theme. For example, we ask them to find lines that reveal this much broader interpretation of the story, such as "my world through which you stumbled / as though blind." Ask them what is meant by "my world" and why "stumbled." This approach can be repeated with many of the passages.

You may also want to discuss the tone of the poem. After your students have determined the tone, ask them if this was the only possible one. Given the circumstances, would other tones have been possible? How would a difference in the tone have changed the poem and its broader meaning?

Finally, you may want to explore how your students view John Rolfe based on Pocahontas's words.

Suggested Assignments

Q.1. The title of the poem is expository—that is, informative—but at a deeper level of understanding, the title can be representative or symbolic. With this in mind, and based on your reading of the poem, what are the other possible meanings of the title?

Q.2. In what ways has the speaker "turned the tables" on John Rolfe? Indeed, on the whole white culture's view of Native-American history?

Student Encounter Activity

Crossing over to another culture can be seen as brave and liberating, or as foolish and dangerous. Research the life of Pocahontas, who moved to England. Based on your research, decide whether her crossing was a brave and liberating act or a foolish and dangerous one.

Wendy Rose
JULIA

Wendy Rose, of Hopi/Miwok descent, is a major force in Native-American culture. She is an editor, poet, anthropologist, and professor of Native-American studies at the University of California, Berkeley.

Poem, 1 page   p. 630

There is a strange and striking similarity between this poem and Paula Gunn Allen's Pocahontas poem. Besides the fact that both are written by Native-American women, both poems are spoken by women to a beloved husband who feels or felt superior to them, both women are dead, and in both poems the time of speaking and of the events spoken about are complicated. Do your students find these poems at all similar? The grotesquerie and powerful pathos of Rose's poem overwhelms many of our students so that it is difficult for them to find any other poem comparable.

You may discuss, as with the Pocahontas poem, the use of the specific image or event to explore a greater theme. Do your students think this poem could be paralleling the relationship between Native Americans and whites as the Pocahontas poem does? If so, what is the view of each? Often students have trouble accepting such a harsh view of both groups; you may want to remind them of Geronimo's fate, the chief of the Chiricahua Apaches who led his tribe in war for ten years in Arizona until his surrender in 1886. Eventually, he ended up working for a circus as an exhibit of the "Fierce Geronimo." It is said he died of a great depression. How would this story reinforce the view in "Julia" of Native Americans seen by whites as "freaks"? easily exploited?

Suggested Assignments

Q.1. At what two levels is this poem "a haunting"? Within those levels, who is being haunted? Use specific examples and interpretations from the text.

Q.2. Imagine the manager/husband of Julia, standing in front of her case listening to her words. How would he respond to her?

Student Encounter Activity

Julia, the Elephant Man, and even Geronimo, the Apache warrior, all ended up as circus acts. What is it about the "normal" culture that makes of these people monsters? Write a brief essay discussing your viewpoint.

Lynn Nelson

SEQUENCE

Lynn Nelson lives with her family in the northeast.

Poem, 4 pages   p. 632

This poem gives an insider's view of an interracial relationship and the difficulties of the experience. You may want to begin by characterizing each of the individuals involved and how the story unravels. The Study Questions in the anthology are very helpful in this regard.

We work to get our students to pay attention to the husband's mother and the speaker's father. What role do they play in the relationship? How do your students feel about them?

After you have clarified the events and circumstances in the poem, you can get students to discuss their own reactions. It may be interesting to begin by asking how many of them assumed the spouse was black when they read the line "nightmarish wife" or "her worst taboo." If they did, does this reveal anything about themselves? Also explore the section "Frogs." How do they feel about the abortion? What could have motivated the couple? Do your students agree the action was justified?

Ultimately, this poem lends itself to continuing the discussion of crossing in a marriage and how individuals cope in a society still reluctant to accept such an event.

Suggested Assignments

Q.1. Memories of a love are often fond ones. Yet, reality can intrude and affect these, either positively or negatively. It is in how these perceptions are balanced that truth is revealed. List the fond memories the speaker holds of her marriage. List the intrusions of reality upon these memories. In what ways does the speaker react to the intrusions? What truths has she finally accepted? Use specific passages from the text to support your answer.

Q.2. Reread line 40, "That's the thing I can't forgive." Describe the thing she is referring to. Why is she so hard on herself? In your opinion, does line 40 reveal a healthier or more harmful attitude toward herself? Explain your opinion.

Elizabeth Alexander

WEST INDIAN PRIMER

Elizabeth Alexander, of Jamaican heritage, has published a collection of poems and teaches literature and creative writing at the University of Chicago.

Poem, 1 page   p. 637

For our students, the challenge of this poem is figuring out the relationships between the individuals mentioned. We find it helpful to ask students to draw a family tree of the speaker's family. They will quickly decipher that the speaker's grandfather was of mixed descent: his father, a European Jew, his mother, a black Jamaican. The great-grandfather is the most perplexing figure who unfortunately falls in the fault of the great earthquake with his stories still untold.

After discussing the lineage, we move on to the last stanza, which includes the title. Ask students what is meant by this stanza. Why are the family stories like genie lamps?

You may also want to emphasize the theme of the chapter. This poem deals with two crossings. The first and more obvious one is that of the great-grandparents' interracial marriage. The second one deals with the speaker's crossing into her familial past. This poem, the "West Indian Primer," is her first step into the past about which she knows so little.

Suggested Assignments

Q.1. A common route toward accepting the past is to intellectualize it, to study a safe, nonemotional aspect of it—say, its politics, geography, or chronological history. Yet for many, the death of a family member pulls an emotional string in that intellectual instrument, and a different route opens. Keeping this in mind, describe the speaker's state of mind as she embarks on a new route toward her past.

Q.2. What possible hurdles has the speaker crossed in order to write this poem?

Student Encounter Activity

Look at old photographs of your family. Reflect upon them and describe the images captured; then describe the emotions you sense in these and your own reactions to them. What do your findings reveal about your relationship to your past? Is your relationship deep or imagistic? Explain your response in a brief essay.

Juliet Kono

SASHIMI

Born and reared in Hilo, Hawaii, Juliet Kono is a published poet.

Poem, 2 pages   p. 638

This is a sensual and moving poem that illustrates a successful crossing. We take time exploring the beauty of the images and the tone of the poem with our students, especially since many of the pieces in this chapter explore the more negative and difficult sides of crossing.

We have found that our students sometimes feel uncomfortable discussing the seductive and enticing nature of the poem; nevertheless, we find it worthwhile to discuss how a positive sexual experience serves here as an important bridge for the crossing of these two people in a loving relationship. The relationship is not devoid of misunderstandings, which are natural. Point out the first stanza of the poem as an example. In this case, the speaker is appealing to what seems to be a successful crossing in the sexual realm, as a reference for the "you" to be openminded about the new palatal experience. Some students may feel the speaker is overdoing it. Do yours? In what way?

Suggested Assignments

Q.1. List the verbs that follow the "I" pronoun in the poem. List the verbs that follow the pronoun "you." In terms of will, desire, experience, and need, what do these verbs reveal about each of the persons involved?

Q.2. "The way to a man's heart is through his stomach" is an old saying in the world of love. In the poem, how is food used to illustrate this old saying?

Student Encounter Activity

Imagine that this poem is about a man trying to seduce a woman. Would your feelings toward the poem change? If so, explain in what ways, and why they would change.

Yusef Komunyakaa

TU DO STREET

Yusef Komunyakaa is a poet of African-American descent. He served as a correspondent in Vietnam and was the editor of *The Southern Cross;* he now teaches literature at the University of California, Berkeley.

Poem, 1 page   p. 641

This is a powerful poem that deals with racism and its ironies.

You may want to begin by asking students to determine the setting in the present and contrast it to the setting of the memory it evokes in the speaker. What do the two settings have in common? After comparing the settings, ask students to explore the irony in the poem. You can help students by pointing out certain lines such as "We have played Judas / for each other out in the boonies / but only enemy machinegun fire / can bring us together again"; and "we fought / the brothers of these women / we now run to hold in our arms." Here you may also want to discuss the politics of the poem. Ask students to point out other lines that show the ironies inherent in the situation in the poem.

Finally, you may want to explore the role women play in the poem. Are any of your students offended by their depiction?

Suggested Assignments

Q.1. Line 15, "just for the hell of it," is the speaker's justification for entering the bar. But, given the entire poem, there seems to be more than that at play. Why does he enter that bar? What is he seeking? What does he find?

Q.2. How does the title relate to the speaker's action?

Gogisgi

SONG OF THE BREED

Gogisgi (Carroll Arnett) was born in Oklahoma City in 1927 and is of Cherokee descent. The author of ten volumes of poetry and the recipient of a National Endowment for the Arts Fellowship, he is a professor of English at Central Michigan University.

Poem, 1/2 page   p. 643

An inability to cross cultures is what this brief, yet forceful poem depicts. The speaker seems burdened by the expectations of both his Native-American ancestors and those of the whites, so much so that he is annihilated by them. We like to explore with our students what they think those expectations could be. We also discuss what the speaker's attitude reveals about his own sense of self-esteem.

You may also want to recall other poems students have read earlier that reflect a similar angst, such as Lorna Dee Cervantes's "Refugee Ship" and Gustavo Perez-Firmat's "Limen," both in chapter 4. What similarities and differences do your students see?

Suggested Assignments

Q.1. If you were a friend to this speaker, what suggestions would you offer him in order to avoid getting hit?

Q.2. Why is the speaker so concerned about offending others?

Cyn. Zarco

FLIPOCHINOS

Cyn. Zarco was born in Manila, Philippines, in 1950, raised in Miami from the age of nine, and now lives in California. She won the Before Columbus Foundation's American Book Award in 1986 for her book *Cir'cum-nav'i-ga'tion*.

Poem, 1/2 page   p. 643

This is another poem about interracial relationships or perhaps interracial identity. The poem relies on the metaphor of the chico and the banana mating and, like Juliet Kono's poem earlier in this chapter, it emphasizes the sensuality of the encounter. You may want to ask your students if it reminds them of any earlier poems before you remind them of the similarities with Kono's poem. Point out how both poems use food and sensuous images to depict crossing. Do your students see any differences in the tone of each poem? How do they interpret the tone and the meaning of the last line?

Suggested Assignments

Q.1. Given the background of the poet and the title of the poem, whom do you think the speaker is referring to when she speaks of the brown person and the yellow person?

Q.2. Compare and contrast Zarco's poem to Kono's. How do they each deal with crossing and its consequences?

Alice Bloch

SIX YEARS

Alice Bloch has written two books, a memoir and a novel. Her work has also appeared in *The Penguin Book of Homosexual Verse*.

Poem, 2 pages   p. 644

The difficulties in the relationship depicted in this poem arise from two sources. One is the couple's, or at least the speaker's, resentment of the fact that society refuses to accept and sanction the homosexual relationship. The other is common to most relationships, homosexual or not: the conflicts that arise when expectations and reality don't match. We take each of these points and explore them at length with our students.

For the first point, we ask students to identify the lines where we see societal intrusion on the relationship. They can begin with the first two lines and go on from there.

For the second conflict, expectation versus reality, we like to ask students to make a list of what each individual was looking for in her partner and what she found instead. In spite of the pain of the relationship, the speaker seems to feel positive about the relationship. Do your students agree? Ask them to explore the last two stanzas. What keeps the couple together?

You may also want to point out the visual structure of the poem. Note how many lines divide abruptly and separate the "I" from the "you." Furthermore, when the speaker uses "we," this abrupt division does not take place. Can your students explain how these features enhance the theme of the poem? Does the technique make the poem more effective?

Suggested Assignments

Q.1. What makes the crossing depicted in this poem particularly difficult? Explain your answer using examples from the poem.

Q.2. If the speaker were to write this poem twelve years later, what would she have to say? Would she still be together with her partner?

Michael Lassell

HOW TO WATCH YOUR BROTHER DIE

Michael Lassell was born in 1947 in New York City. He works as a writer, editor, and photographer. He has published books of poetry and fiction.

Poem, 3 pages   p. 647

Before assigning this poem, you may want to ask your students to free write for ten minutes how they would feel if they discovered that one of their siblings or a close friend were homosexual. Their reaction will help them to relate to this poem better since it deals with a man's reaction to his brother's death, presumably from AIDS.

The poem is a straightforward narrative and should be easy for students to follow. The most interesting aspect is the characterization of the speaker. Ask your students to describe him. Do they find him obsessed with the brother's homosexuality? What lines can they cite that reflect his curiosity about the "other" world?

This poem, like previous ones, deals with two crossings. The initial crossing is that of the brother into the homosexual experience and a change of lifestyle the speaker finds difficult to understand; the second one is that of the speaker's crossing into his brother's world at the moment of his death. How does the speaker feel about this crossing? How does he feel about going back across to his home? You may want to discuss the speaker's early flight home, his Scotch on the plane, and the memories of his brother as a child and his own children. What do these events have in common?

Finally, you may want to explore the tone of the poem. How would the poem be different if it was written by the speaker's brother instead of by him?

Suggested Assignments

Q.1. Given the speaker's discomfort with homosexuality, what could he have meant with the words in line 98, "This is no moment not to be strong"?

Q.2. Both Lassell and Bloch write about homosexual experiences from different perspectives. In what way does the brother's lover in Lassell's poem resemble one of the lovers in Bloch's poem? What differences exist? Support your answers with specific examples from the text.

Joseph Bruchac

ELLIS ISLAND

Joseph Bruchac was born in Saratoga Springs, New York, in 1942 of Slovakian and Abnaki (Native American) heritage. He is a publisher, poet, novelist, editor, and anthologist. He is the author of five collections of traditional Abenaki and Iroquois tales, two novels, fourteen collections of poetry, and two books of nonfiction.

Poem, 1 page   p. 650

Like "Song of the Breed" and "Flipochinos," this poem concerns the offspring of a mixed marriage. The focus in this poem is on the Slovak grandparents and their forebears for a "thousand years" and on the Native-American forebears back before Columbus arrived in America. One of the offspring is the speaker.

We begin by sorting out the details with our students. The first two paragraphs particularize the conventional version of the American dream: poor immigrants who come to this country to make something of themselves, and to own property, as line 13 seems to suggest. The second verse-paragraph reinforces and generalizes this dream: "nine decades the answerer / of dreams."

The shift comes in the final verse-paragraph. The speaker's other heritage is Native American, and theirs is not the American Dream, but the American Reality, a culture in which land was not owned and whose dream was invaded.

After the class has outlined the details of the poem, we move on to a more content-centered discussion. We have found the following questions can be helpful: Are the immigrants the invaders? Are the later immigrants accessories to the crimes committed by Cortez? by

Andrew Jackson against the Cherokee and the Seminoles? We find our students strongly divided on these issues. Depending on how the discussion progresses you can add questions such as do we "owe" something to the Native Americans? Should we sell Manhattan back to them? Settle somehow? How?

This issue can be expanded to include slavery and what white Americans owe to those who helped build the country while in bondage and did not profit from their toil. Or further expanded to take in properties the Nazis confiscated from the Jews, or Castro from the Cubans and Americans after the 1959 revolution. Where do you stop the "property rights"? Who lived in Palestine—in 1947, 1897, 33 A.D., 2000 B.C.?

Suggested Assignments

Q.1. Discuss the irony in the expectations of immigrants coming to America hoping to own property and the reality of an America where property was never owned by Native Americans. Can such an irony be reconciled? Was it reconciled? Explain your answers.

Q.2. Reread the poem trying to decide if the speaker has resolved the apparent conflict of his mixed heritage. Has he? If so, how? If not, why not? Support your decision with specific examples from the text.

Student Encounter Activity

Find someone who is the offspring of a mixed marriage (even if you are one yourself). Interview them and, as you do, look for examples of difficulties they may have encountered as a result of this condition. Share your findings with the class.

Alice Childress

WEDDING BAND

Playwright and novelist, Alice Childress was born in Charleston, South Carolina. Her 1955 play *Trouble in Mind* won an Obie, and her novel *A Hero Ain't Nothing but a Sandwich* was nominated for both the Newberry Medal and the National Book Award.

Play, 41 pages   p. 652

After students have read the first scene, you can ask them to return to the stage directions and the sentence, "The playing areas of the houses are raised platforms furnished according to the taste of each tenant," and try to design the set to fit that description. We have sometimes found that students have initial difficulty in keeping the characters straight who are in supporting roles—in this play and in others. So you may want to spend time going over or distinguishing them. Particularly, have them document Fanny's "middle class" values, her "four piece, silver-plated tea service" that is "the first and only one to be owned by a colored woman in the United States of America," and even her mother who was a "genuine, full-blooded, qualified, Seminole Indian." We sometimes ask them to follow up the characterization of Fanny throughout the play, and ask them to discuss how this characterization prepares them for the relative congeniality of Fanny's meeting with Herman's mother. We use Fanny to try to illuminate how much there is in this play about class, how it interacts with the clash of race, and how both define the "politics" of the play. Class, or the concept of class conflict, seems to be one of the underlying themes of this moving, personal, humane, but not apolitical play.

We usually have to call attention to the date—1918—and are occasionally astounded to find out, when we start drawing out the references to the war that students have a good deal of fuzziness about which world war was which. We also have to supply some background on miscegenation laws and miscegenation as a concept. You may want to check on what particular barriers to marriage between ethnic groups there were in your state or region, because in many states, we know, the laws did not prohibit just black and white marriages.

Before we get too deeply into the war and its pervasive atmosphere in the play, we use a stop-and-go reading technique. We ask students, before they get past the first scene, what they expect to happen between Nelson and Julia (see Study Question 6)—that is, the notion that Herman and Julia must separate because Herman cannot offer her "his name and his protection." Sometimes what we find is that a number of students anticipate that Nelson will be the hero and "rescue" Julia from her uncomfortable situation. It helps that he is a soldier, but sometimes, if we probe enough and in the right way, we can bring to the surface the fact that many (on both sides of the racial "fence") want the play to end that way; even this late in the twentieth century, they are as uneasy as the South Carolina lawmakers and public about interracial love and marriage. We can sometimes go on from here to talk about reader response in terms of the reader's repertoire and prejudices or preconceptions, and how we sometimes read into a work our hopes as expectations. This may be the point at which to talk about evaluation. What are the advantages and disadvantages of having our hopes fulfilled (even when expectations have been aroused that threaten a different ending)? What does it mean to have our hopes modified? radically changed? disappointed? We try not to disclose our romantic assumptions that a text should be "new," that it should change the reader's perceptions, but it is difficult to escape our own vantage point and limitations.

Since a great deal of the power of this play depends on our recognition and acceptance of the love between Julia and Herman as real and deep and lasting, it may be necessary to ask students to find all the details they can in the play to substantiate that love. (If there is some cogent opposition, that side should draw evidence from the play as well.) We often ask students to compare the celebration of Julia's and Herman's tenth "wedding anniversary" in act I, scene 2, with the powerful confrontation between them in act II, scene 2, and to use these two scenes to define the power of their love and the power of the forces arraigned against them.

We don't like to leave discussion of the play without considering, at least a little, Herman's mother and in particular his sister. We try to bring out how some of the forces that prevent the marriage of Julia and Herman and the friendly relationship between the races also limit their lives. Despite the mother's role as virtual villain and her sometimes ugly hostility toward Julia, it seems she is treated sympathetically, as the agent rather than as the origin of the racism of the time and place, and as the economic victim of the same powers that reinforce the racism. It is easier to see the economic/class victimization of the sister, so we usually start with her and then go on to Herman's mother.

Suggested Assignments

Q.1. Scan the play for evidence that class is just as significant a barrier as racism. Discuss your findings and cite specific examples.

Q.2. Choose one of the minor characters in the play. Discuss his or her characterization and function in the play. How does the character enhance the plot and theme of the play?

Student Encounter Activity

Research the laws in your state that prohibited interracial marriages. Then, in a brief essay, discuss your findings and your reactions to them.

Gary Soto

LIKE MEXICANS

Gary Soto was born in California in 1952, from Mexican-American descent. He writes fiction, nonfiction, and poetry, and has won numerous awards, including a Guggenheim Fellowship. He teaches Chicano Studies and English at the University of California, Berkeley.

Essay, 3 pages   p. 695

If you discussed Alice Childress's play and class relations, this short piece by Gary Soto will be a good companion.

 Since it is a short piece, you may want to read it in class. If so, you may want to stop after the first line and ask students to free write for five minutes what bad advice and good advice they think the grandmother gave the author. You may want to stop again after the speaker tells his friend that he will never marry an Okie. Ask them to discuss their reaction to this statement (and make sure they know what it refers to). Then see if they are surprised to discover that the speaker has married outside of his culture. This point is important since the author's theme seems to be that class distinctions can be more difficult to surmount than racial or cultural ones.

Are your students surprised by the advice to "marry poor"? Are any of them offended by the poverty/untidiness of the Mexican and Japanese poor? Do they find it a hostile stereotype?

Suggested Assignments

Q.1. This essay seems to be giving the advice that one should marry within one's class status. What evidence can you find to support this conclusion? Would you agree or disagree with the advice? Give reasons for your answer.

Q.2. Do you think the fact that Carolyn is Japanese American—that is, a member of another marginal group and bicultural—makes it easier for the speaker than if she were an Okie, poor or not? Explain your answer.

Student Encounter Activity

Have you ever gotten advice from a parent or grandparent that you have found difficult to follow? Did you go against the advice? What happened? Write your reactions to these events.

Julia Alvarez

HOLD THE MAYONNAISE

Julia Alvarez was born in the Dominican Republic and was raised in the United States. She has published a collection of poetry, as well as a novel, *How the Garcia Girls Lost Their Accents.*

Essay, 2 pages   p. 699

This autobiographical essay usually appeals to our students. They enjoy the use of the mayonnaise as a fun way to depict cultural differences. After the seriousness of many of the earlier works, they welcome this lighter approach to the topic of crossing in a culturally mixed marriage.

The essay also introduces a new topic that has nothing to do with culture—that is, the relationship of stepchildren to a stepmother or a stepfather. That in itself can be considered a crossing, for the new spouse has to cross into an existing world of established relationships and expectations. This can be a frightening and frustrating experience, as well as a rewarding one. If we add cultural differences, as in this case, then certainly, the hurdles must be even greater.

We like to spend some time asking students to characterize the speaker and the stepdaughters. The Study Questions in the anthology can be helpful in this regard. Ask your students to explore the speaker's expectations as a young person and how these affected her behavior as an adult. Get students to talk about the relationships and behaviors. Do they empathize with the speaker? Why?

You may also want to discuss the more subtle yet controversial aspect of this essay. The author is aware of its implications when she says toward the end of the essay that the "assimilation approach is highly suspect." Do your students understand her point? You may want to point out how in the earlier part of this century, sociologists and others promoted the theory of assimilation. According to this theory, immigrants should abandon their roots and their language in order to become more quickly "Americanized" and be participants in American institutions. These theories are no longer widely held. Sociologists now believe that participating in the institutions, even if the individual is still well-rooted in the culture of "home," is what eventually leads the newcomer to become more "Americanized."

After discussing the implications of the speaker's comments, get students to analyze why she feels the way she does. Do your students believe there is a difference between a stepfamily and a society as she states in the last paragraph? Or are the principles the same?

Suggested Assignments

Q.1. Do you think the speaker would have had the same difficulties becoming a stepmother if she had been a "tall, strapping, blond, mayonnaise-eating" woman like the stepdaughters? Support your answer with examples from the text.

Q.2. Reread the last paragraph of the essay. What would you do if you didn't like what someone brought to the potluck dinner? Would you still eat it? If the potluck dinner is a metaphor for a family and the family is a metaphor for society, what are the author's implications about handling cultural differences in our society? After discussing her position, discuss if you agree. Explain your answer.

Student Encounter Activity

Interview a friend who has a stepmother or stepfather. Keeping in mind the issues introduced in Alvarez's essay, determine the common sources of conflicts for these types of situations. Also inquire if the stepfather or stepmother is from the same culture as your friend. Does he or she feel that makes a difference? Do you? Write a brief essay summarizing your findings for the class.

Lynn Minton

IS IT OKAY TO DATE SOMEONE OF ANOTHER RACE?

This selection, taken from the December 15, 1991, issue of *Parade* magazine, reflects a series of actual conversations recorded by columnist Lynn Minton.

Interviews, 3 pages   p. 702

This is another favorite of our students simply because they can relate to the topic and particularly to the voices of the speakers. We find one activity particularly helpful. We divide the class into seven groups of three to five students, depending on the class size. Then we assign each group one of the speakers. The task for the group is to identify the speaker's background, summarize his or her point of view, and discuss their own point of view.

After about ten minutes, we ask each group to choose one person who introduces his or her speaker to the rest of the class. By the time the groups have finished, numerous topics will have emerged that can lead to lively discussions on the topic of interracial marriage.

Since by now we have done a lot of discussion on the topic, we use this piece to let students relax and indulge in their personal opinions and experiences.

Suggested Assignments

Q.1. Scan the piece to see if you can find similarities in opinions according to gender or race. Discuss your findings.

Q.2. Find one opinion you strongly disagree with. Summarize it and explain why you feel so strongly against it.

Student Encounter Activity

Organize into groups of five. One of the members of the group should bring a tape recorder. Answer the same question as the title of this piece, "Is It Okay to Date Someone of Another Race?" As the group discusses, tape the discussion. Then have one of the members transcribe the tape and make photocopies for each member of the group. Read the transcript and analyze the opinions of the members of the group as if they were strangers. Are you surprised by anything said? If so, explain what and why.

Robert Anthony Watts

NOT BLACK, NOT WHITE, BUT BIRACIAL

Robert Anthony Watts was born in 1962 and lives in Atlanta, Georgia. He is a journalist who has written extensively on race relations and civil rights.

Essay, 3 pages   p. 706

After discussing the difficulties of biracial marriages, this essay can be very interesting to explore the response of a biracial offspring. Many of the earlier pieces present the problems; few offer solutions. This essay discusses the introduction of a new category, that of biracial or mulatto, to re-determine the way we look at biracial children who in the past would be considered black. We recommend you begin by assigning the Study Questions in the anthology. The questions for this selection are particularly comprehensive and can help students outline the major premises of the essay.

After reviewing students' responses to the study questions, we usually discuss the differences in attitudes in other countries. Since many, if not most, of our students are multicultural and often biracial, we ask them how race is perceived in their country of origin. The term mulatto, for example, has been a commonly accepted term for centuries in numerous countries. In many Latin American countries, in particular, biracial individuals have maintained a separate identity from others. Nevertheless, even in these countries, mulattos and mestizos often emphasize their white ancestry and socialize with whites in their society because they find it socially and politically advantageous.

One of the main issues to be discussed here is if this new categorization will help or further confuse the problem of racial intolerance. We try to use our own students as resources for the topic, if we can create enough of a friendly and relaxed atmosphere. Even today, we often find biracial students hesitant to acknowledge their identity as such.

Suggested Assignments

Q.1. "Biracial people say that rejecting part of their heritage is emotionally damaging." Based on your reading of this essay, and other selections in this chapter, why would this be true? Be specific in your answer.

Q.2. Could there be any disadvantages to using the biracial categorization? Use information from the essay, as well as your own ideas, to support your answer.

Student Encounter Activity

Research the one-drop rule and the Jim Crow laws in general. In a brief essay, summarize your findings and discuss your reactions to them. Also discuss what evidence of the legacy of these laws exists in your own community. Be specific with your examples.

The Craft of Writing

THEME

p. 710

The Afterword in this chapter gives a comprehensive overview of the concept of theme as well as the differences between subject and theme. You will want to assign this section to your students, especially if you emphasize the interpretation of literature in your class. It is often difficult for students to understand the difference between the general subject of the piece and the theme. Since we emphasize the writing process in our classes, it helps if we refer to subject as the equivalent of the topic and focus one writes about, and theme more like the message of the piece.

We particularly like the analogy the editors make of a literary piece as a musical score. We find it is worth rereading this section with the class and clarifying this meaning. Our students sometimes do not understand that hearing a summary of the work has nothing to do with reading the actual work. It is as if one hummed a score and expected the student to get a sense of the piece. Likewise, our students often want to begin writing their score without listening to it first and perceiving its uniqueness. We often compare the writing process to learning how to play an instrument. If one doesn't do it on a regular basis, with patience and discipline, one will never reap the rewards of a masterful piece, whether it's a musical one or a literary one.

Many of the assignments in this chapter ask students to compare and contrast. You may want to prepare them by pointing out that in developing their own subject and theme, their focus and viewpoint, they must be sure to move beyond a description of differences and similarities. They should ask themselves what these differences and similarities reveal, show, or illustrate about the situation or condition being discussed.

Finally, you may also want to review two techniques for structuring comparison and contrast essays, block by block or point by point.

Comments on Student Writing

p. 716

Even though we emphasize essay writing in our classes, from time to time we ask students to write a poem about a specific topic discussed in class. We find it helps them if we use the Imitations and Parodies assignments at the end of each chapter. The students usually prefer following some guidelines.

Some of the students are very inhibited by the assignment. They soon discover that writing an effective poem is much harder than writing an effective essay. In some classes where this is a problem, we have collected the poems and read them aloud anonymously. The students enjoy them without embarrassment. We have found that even those most hesitant enjoy this activity, especially if it is not graded. It gives them an opportunity to deal with the topics in a personal way.

This student poem is a perfect example of what we want them to do. We use it to illustrate how they can write their own poems. It is simple and accessible, yet it also shows insight and creativity, especially in the use of synonyms in the second stanza and the play of colors.

┌ 8 ┐

AMERICANS

This chapter explores what it means to be an American. As the editors point out in the introduction, there is, of course, no such thing as a typical American; consequently, the selections explore a variety of interpretations and perspectives of the concept. This heterogeneity means that the selections tend to make substantial demands on readers to supply information from outside the text. Footnotes help, and they have been provided when absolutely necessary, but the really crucial points about referencing cannot be provided in a line or two explaining a particularity. Context is critical to understanding these selections; consequently, the Afterword of the chapter takes up, in some detail, questions about context.

In the introduction, the editors provide an extensive discussion of what the term "American" implies. They talk about how the perception of the term has changed, even though the reality has remained constant, as this is a nation of diversity and flux. "No single set of cultural assumptions . . . covers the geography from Alaska to Puerto Rico or the ethnography from Native American . . . to Cambodian." It is in these differences that the sameness appears, and in the perception of America as a meeting place where a variety of peoples can come together hopefully in a "neutral" place.

The pieces in this chapter illustrate some of the many varieties of American experiences that result when these peoples confront each other. These confrontations can be rewarding as well as filled with tension. Most of the stories approach America in a spirit of hopefulness that is not always fulfilled.

Pre-Reading Activity

Before assigning readings from this chapter, you may want to explore your students' preconceptions and notions about what it means to be an American.

You can use the question "What is an American?" to generate discussion. For an added challenge and fun, ask students to answer the question from three different perspectives such as: an American living in 1910, an American now, and an American in the year 2050.

You may want to arrange the class in small groups according to each perspective, then have them discuss the differences that emerge.

Toni Cade Bambara

THE LESSON

Toni Cade Bambara was born and educated in New York. She is a dancer, teacher, critic, editor, activist, and writer. She has published two collections of short stories and a novel.

Short story, 6 pages   p. 723

The three short stories in this chapter suggest the heterogeneity of the American experience by giving us characters from three different ethnic backgrounds, within three distinct contexts. Each story begins by establishing the context.

Bambara's story, as well as the following one by Gish Jen, uses dialogue as one of the main ways to capture the heart of a people. Both stories excel in capturing speech rhythms, in characterizing people through their use of language, and in expressing views of human nature, especially through a sense of humor.

One way to begin is by asking the students what they find funny in the story and why they find it so. We begin with a discussion of setting which we channel into a discussion of context by asking students what the Fifth Avenue setting represents—to Miss Moore, to her students, and to us, the readers.

You can also discuss how African Americans, though not immigrants like the Chinese and the Hindus in the following stories, are presented here almost as immigrants, detached from the Fifth Avenue mainstream. They may be seen as the "other." Seeing African Americans in this way, as a distinct group often suffering worse misunderstanding and intolerance than immigrants, may lead to a lively discussion by students.

Suggested Assignment

Q.1. At the end of the story, the narrator gets angry at her friend for answering Miss Moore's inquiries. Explain why she reacts in this way.

Q.2. Imagine yourself as one of these youngsters. How would you feel discovering this part of the world you did not know even existed? How do the characters in the story feel? What behaviors give you clues as to their attitudes?

Student Encounter Activity

In groups of three to five, plan a trip to the most expensive store in your area. Do you feel comfortable there or not? What does your reaction say about you and your world? Share your feelings with the other members of the group and then with the class.

Gish Jen

IN THE AMERICAN SOCIETY

Gish Jen was born in 1955 to Chinese immigrants. She grew up in New York and was educated at Harvard University and the Iowa Writers' Workshop. She is a short story writer, essayist, and has published a novel, *Typical American*.

Short story, 11 pages   p. 730

If you have discussed the other stories in this chapter, you can continue with some of the same issues. In any case, we recommend you begin with the setting which is simple, in a way, but gets complicated as the scene changes. Get your students to fill out the details of the party scene especially, but lead up to that through simple recounting of what the pancake house seems to look like.

A related way to move into the central issues of the story is through the material objects important to individual characters—for example, the suit to the father and the bottle to Jeremy, as well as other material symbols important to the narrator and to the mother. They merge with setting in the symbolism of the country club and in the way things go "swimmingly" there (as the narrator says). What things represent to individuals and what places mean to them are important to the conflict of values: you can get at almost everything in the story through setting and things. Dialogue is also important and highly effective in characterizing the people in the story.

This story avoids simplification of characters and issues and thus works well to tie in many of the topics discussed in earlier chapters, such as generational conflict, fences, and crossing. We often ask our students to recall stories or poems from earlier chapters that remind them of aspects of this one.

If you have time, you can bring up subtler issues here, such as sexism, attitudes toward workers, racism in country clubs, etc.

Suggested Assignments

Q.1. Compare and contrast the attitudes of the father and the mother. Use specific examples from the text to show how different, yet how similar, they are in their attitudes towards acceptance.

Q.2. Reread the story looking for clues that will help you to identify generational conflicts. Can you recall other selections in the anthology that address similar conflicts? Explain the similarities with specific examples from both the texts.

Student Encounter Activity

The story mentions immigration laws which state that it is against the law for illegal immigrants to work, but not against the law for them to be hired. Research this law to confirm its veracity. Then analyze the implications of such a law and what it reveals about double standards.

Bharati Mukherjee

HINDUS

Bharati Mukherjee was born in Calcutta in 1940 and currently teaches English at the University of California, Berkeley. She is the author of three novels, two volumes of short stories, and two nonfiction books which she coauthored with her husband, Clarke Blaise. She has received numerous awards.

Short story, 7 pages   p. 743

Detailing the new world/old world contrasts may be the best way to begin class discussion. Such a discussion of contrasts leads quickly to a discussion of the narrator—which we put off as long as possible because it can create a bit of dramatic structure for the class—and to a growing sense of complication among worlds.

Your students may feel they need to know more about Hinduism. This is a complex mixture of beliefs within a common social structure. The chief end is liberation from suffering and rebirth. Three other goals include duty, material success, and love. The society has a strict caste system from which individuals cannot move in this life. Background knowledge such as this will lead students to worry about contexts and what they need to know. You may want to point out how the author is aware that she must provide some context, which she does, particularly at the beginning of the story.

Ultimately, have the class discuss in some detail how they feel about the narrator. It is probably best to hold off until the last discussion of her values and where they come from; this discussion will take you back to the new world/old world distinctions.

Suggested Assignments

Q.1. At one point in the story, the narrator states: "All Indians in America . . . constitute a village." Keeping the story in mind, how would you interpret this statement? Support your answer with examples from the text.

Q.2. What evidence can you find of Leela becoming "Americanized"? Do you believe her attitudes would be different if she were less "Americanized"? Explain your answer.

Student Encounter Activity

Research classes and the caste system in India. Determine if these beliefs are as strong today as they used to be. Are there indications of any changes in the story? Write an essay discussing your findings.

Joan Murray

COMING OF AGE ON THE HARLEM

Joan Murray grew up in New York City and has won several awards for her poetry. She is currently an instructor for the New York State Literary Center.

Poem, 5 pages   p. 750

As the title indicates, this poem reveals the coming of age of the speaker. We find it helpful to begin by asking students to define the expression in general terms. It helps them in seeing the speaker's journey of understanding her past.

You may want to ask your students to write a narrative that tells the story of this poem in order to clarify the events and descriptions. For some, this may be their first close encounter with Harlem and the context is critical to understanding the poem fully.

We also like to spend some time discussing the relationship between the speaker and her father, as well as her relationship to Kathy. You may want to ask them to compare the way she sees her father to the way she sees Kathy and what that reveals about her.

You may also want to discuss the tone of the poem and what it reveals about the speaker's attitudes toward Harlem.

Suggested Assignments

Q.1. Scan the poem carefully looking for the characterization of the father. Describe him as the speaker "feels" him. Now answer her question, "What man would toss his child to that swill?" (line 12).

Q.2. Keeping in mind what the poem reveals about Kathy, imagine yourself being Kathy. Write a letter to your old friend, answering the last two questions of the poem. Compare your letter to others in the classroom.

Student Encounter Activity

Think of three episodes in your life that best illustrate the phrase "coming of age." Write a brief essay explaining how the episodes affected your life. Compare and contrast your response with that of your classmates.

Juan Felipe Herrera

REVOLUTION SKYSCRAPER

Juan Felipe Herrera was born in 1948 in Fowler, California. He has published three works of literature and currently teaches Ethnic Studies at Fresno State University.

Poem, 1 page   p. 756

You may want to begin the discussion of this piece by looking at its structure. Some students may not be familiar with the concept of a prose poem. When our students insist this is not a poem (as they often do) we point out the poet's use of rhythm and the free association of ideas among the various traits that allow this to be considered a poem.

After that's out of the way, you can help students to decipher this poem by asking them to list those things associated with the Chicano heritage and those associated with the "American" heritage. Then ask them to infer the viewpoint. Ask them where the speaker of the poem stands in relationship to his own heritage.

You might want them to read this poem aloud so they can pick up on the speed and what that reveals about the emotions of the speaker. It's interesting how in the end, the speaker quotes several lines from the Garcia Lorca poem, "Lament for the Death of Ignacio Sanchez Mejia." Garcia Lorca's poem deals with the death of a bullfighter and how the speaker deals with that loss. It is a dramatic poem that also works best read aloud.

Finally, note the line in the middle of the poem "I never thought I would tell you this." This line seems to indicate a change of heart of the speaker concerning his heritage.

Suggested Assignments

Q.1. List the emotions the speaker experiences from start to finish in this poem. Provide textual evidence to support your list. What do these emotions reveal about the speaker's state of mind? What is causing these emotions?

Q.2. Find the one sentence in the poem that reveals a change of heart in the speaker. Keeping in mind the theme of this chapter, what process is he going through?

Fran Winant

CHRISTOPHER ST. LIBERATION DAY, JUNE 28, 1970

Poet and anthologist, Fran Winant was born in Brooklyn, New York, in 1943. Her poems have appeared in several anthologies. She is also well-known for her paintings.

Poem, 2 pages   p. 758

You may use this poem to discuss the theme of this chapter in relationship to homosexuals. Can we say that a homosexual is accepted as
just "another American"? Ask your students how they feel about the
ideas expressed in the poem. Can they relate to this call for brother-
hood and sisterhood? Why or why not?

You may want to ask your students to compare this poem to other
pieces that explore the gay reality such as the "The Limitless Heart" in
chapter 2. Which do they find more effective?

Suggested Assignments

Q.1. There are two cultures described here. Identify each by the
particular characteristics given. What does each culture seek of the
other? According to the poem, is there a possibility for reconciliation?

Q.2. Often we make choices in life. These can result in rewards or
painful consequences for us. In the poem, the speaker has made
choices. Identify these and decide what are her rewards and/or consequences. In your opinion, did she make wise choices?

Linda Hogan

BLACK HILLS SURVIVAL GATHERING, 1980

Linda Hogan, a Chickasaw, was born in Denver in 1947. She has
published several books of poems and a novel, and currently teaches
creative writing at the University of Colorado.

Poem, 2 pages   p. 761

Beginning with the title has certain advantages for class discussion.
The place, "Black Hills," leads quickly to a consideration of geographical setting, and "1980" defines the temporal setting involving the
larger cultural situation behind the poem's occasion. Both the other
words of the title are important and resonant too, and much of the
poem can be gotten at through a discussion of their implications. Why
is "gathering" important and what does it imply (community, common
values, the bringing together of disparate individuals into a whole)?
What various senses of survival are important to the poem? The Study
Questions will help to set up the discussion for you.

Another feature of the poem worth class time involves its organization and narrative aspects. In several ways, the poem organizes itself

much as a short story would, with setting, exposition, characterization, and emerging conflict being important elements in its early arrangement. But unlike a story, it simply presents and doesn't resolve, leaving its emphasis on the situation and appropriate emotional responses to it.

You can get a good discussion going about what would have to happen next to make the "plot" here work as a story. You might even have your students "finish" the story as a story, and discuss how different endings lead to effects entirely different from those generated by the poem. You can also discuss themes concerning the potential destruction of family or community life.

Suggested Assignments

Q.1. Look at the title and decide whether the word "survival" applies to the Black Hills or the people gathering. Use examples from the text to support your decision.

Q.2. What is the tone of the poem? Choose specific images that reveal its tone and explain how these images contribute to your understanding of the poem's tone.

Pat Mora

IMMIGRANTS

Pat Mora was born in El Paso, Texas, and is from Mexican-American descent. She has published three books of poetry. She lives in Cincinnati.

Poem, 1/2 page   p. 764

One way to get at tone, perhaps the most complex issue to solve here, is to look at the fact that "American" is capitalized in the first line but not in the last two. Another element of contrast that may help your students understand the subtle way attitude is expressed involves the growing darkness in the poem; from happy, cheerful, mindless advice at the beginning, the speaker moves to whispers and dark fears from line 9 on. You may also be able to get at tone and attitude through a discussion of the speaker, though your students will need to have developed a certain sophistication and subtlety for this strategy to work in class.

Irony may be a better way of getting at the central issues than through the concept of the speaker. Get your students to explore the irony in the tone. Can they explain what allows us to speak of this poem as ironic?

You may also want to discuss the final question of the poem to see what attitude your students think it reveals toward assimilation and the "American" way.

Suggested Assignments

Q.1. What factors, in your opinion, motivate immigrant parents to "Americanize" their children? List the factors implied in the poem and list your own factors. Which are negative ones? Which are positive ones? Is the process of "Americanization" good or bad?

Q.2. This poem starts by detailing a list of characteristics generally attributed to being "American." Would you say these represent a fair characterization or a stereotype of the "typical American"? In a brief essay, explain your answer and support it with concrete examples of your own.

Student Encounter Activity

Interview a person whom you know to be an immigrant. Ask the person why he or she came to America, what was left behind, and what has been retained from the old country. Inquire about his or her views on "Americanization." Share your findings with the class.

Gregory Orfalea

ARAB AND JEW IN ALASKA

Gregory Orfalea is the author of two books and lives with his family in Washington, D.C.

Poem, 4 pages   p. 765

You may want to assign this poem in advance and suggest to your students that they read it several times. If they don't get too confused by the Biblical and historical allusions, they will appreciate the power of this poem. For example, the epigraph cites both Exodus and the Koran. Exodus is a Biblical book telling the story of the Israelites' flight from bondage when God liberated them from the Egyptians. The Koran is the sacred scripture of Islam.

We begin by asking our students to establish the context and setting. Who are the speakers and where are they? What brings them together? How are they different yet alike? The Study Questions will help in this regard.

Most of the selections so far have dealt with how diverse "Americans" cope with differences. In this poem, we are asked to explore the differences back home that possibly motivated the migration of the speakers' families to the United States. The historical antagonism that follows these two people from their ancestry seems to melt away in this new land that accepts as well as rejects them.

Depending on how much time you have in class, you may want to select certain passages and concentrate on the particulars of those sections.

Suggested Assignments

Q.1. Scan the poem for references to snow. List these and infer what function they may play in the development of the poem.

Q.2. What reason could the poet have for including two epigraphs, one from Exodus and the other from the Koran? Explain your answer.

Mitsuye Yamada

THE QUESTION OF LOYALTY

Mitsuye Yamada was born in Kyushu, Japan, and was raised in Seattle, Washington. She was interned with her family in a concentration camp in Idaho during World War II. She has written several books of poetry and now teaches creative writing and Asian-American literature in southern California.

Poem, 1 page   p. 770

This poem is useful to compare with Dwight Okita's poem about relocation centers, although its tone and methods are different. It can provide a good example for showing students how different kinds of poems can be made from similar materials and thematic interests. The speaker here is worth a good bit of classroom analysis, and the question of what students come to think of the speaker may be easiest to approach through a comparison with the speaker in the Okita poem.

You can also use the poem to return to the topic of generational conflict by comparing the attitude of the speaker to that of her mother.

You may want to ask your students to come up with names of other selections that illustrate generational conflicts such as this one. There are many: Yamauchi's "And the Soul Shall Dance," Muñoz's "Little Sister Born in This Land," Apple's "Trotsky's Bar Mitzvah," to name a few.

Suggested Assignments

Q.1. Analyze the mother's point of view. What are her fears and concerns? Then analyze the speaker's. How do they compare?

Q.2. What do you think the speaker means when she says she was poor at math? What does math have to do with "The Question of Loyalty"?

Richard Olivas

[I'M SITTING IN MY HISTORY CLASS]

No biographical information is available on this writer; however, we do know Olivas wrote this as a student.

Poem, 1 page   p. 771

We like to get students to talk fully about the speaker here: what we know, what we don't know, and how he is characterized. This can lead to a good discussion of why particular words are used, what levels of language and what kind of humor are employed, and even how the rhyme is used. Get them to discuss what is effective about the rhyme here and why it fits this particular speaker. Get them to talk about how the repetition works here, how method reinforces content and tone.

You can probably get a lively debate going on tone here, especially on how to read the smart-alecky last stanza (which, we think, has to be read in terms of the external respect for authority—"Dare I ask . . ." and the raising of the hand). Ask them to show how the tone moves the poem from the jest to a serious questioning of what American history consists of. Then get them to show how the gradual revelation of character leads to the same place.

Suggested Assignments

Q.1. Think of other poems or stories you have read that use humor as a vehicle to make a point. Can you cite any? Did you find the works effective? Why or why not? In your opinion, what do authors hope to achieve by using humor?

Q.2. What point does the speaker hope to achieve in this poem? In your opinion, has he achieved it effectively? Explain your answer.

Student Encounter Activity

Think of a time when you were surprised or disturbed by something you were told in a history class. Then write a humorous paragraph or poem that captures the moment and its effects in your life. Be ready to share it with the class.

Mari Evans

THE FRIDAY LADIES OF THE PAY ENVELOPE

Mari Evans was born in Toledo, Ohio, and now lives in Indianapolis. She has worked as a television writer, producer and director, as well as authored several plays, four collections of poetry, and several children's books. She is also the editor of *Black Women Writers 1950–89: A Critical Perspective* and the recipient of numerous awards.

Poem, 1 page   p. 772

With this poem you can recall earlier issues of setting and extend them to context. We would begin, however, with questions about how the "ladies" are characterized, and get students to detail how Evans uses language to control the reader's feelings toward the ladies. To get students to care about contextual issues, you might ask them what they would ideally like to know about when and why Evans wrote this poem.

If your students are artistically inclined, you might also ask them to draw the setting and the visual characterization of the ladies. Or use photographs that depict similar settings.

Finally, you may want to explore the tone of the poem. Ask them what effect the speaker hoped to achieve through this description.

Suggested Assignments

Q.1. In your opinion, is there enough evidence to infer what the "pay envelope" refers to? If so, support your conclusion with specific details from the text.

Q.2. Keeping in mind that the theme of this chapter is "Americans," why do you think the editors selected it for this chapter? Explain your answer.

Student Encounter Activity

Visit your local welfare center. Sit or stand for half an hour and discreetly observe the people in line and the setting. Then go home and write a brief essay that includes a description of the setting, a description of the people and their attitudes, and your reaction to what you saw.

Jimmy Santiago Baca
SO MEXICANS ARE TAKING JOBS FROM AMERICANS

Jimmy Santiago Baca was born in New Mexico in 1952. He wrote the poems in his collection *Immigrants in Our Own Land*, from which this poem is taken, while he was in prison. He has published two more collections of poetry and won the Before Columbus Foundation American Book Award for one of them. He now lives on a small farm outside Albuquerque.

Poem, 2 pages   p. 774

The Study Questions here will set your students up to discuss the way the poem creates a metaphor out of an idiomatic expression (but the questions just put the issue in terms of vividness; you can supply the notion of metaphor).

The questions also will set up a discussion of values which can get heated. You may feel the need to set up the context of this poem, depending on your students. You can talk about the long history of Mexican legal and illegal migration into the United States and how it has been encouraged or discouraged depending on the economic demand. You can also talk about the devastating economic and political conditions in the home country that are the main reasons behind most migrations. For example, a factory worker who makes $1.50 an hour in Juarez, Mexico, can cross into the neighboring community of El Paso, Texas, and make at least the minimum wage of $4.35 an hour.

Finally, you may want to enter into a discussion of the recent NAFTA open trade agreement and its potential consequences.

Suggested Assignments

Q.1. Discuss the tone of the poem starting with the title. Does the tone shift anywhere? Explain where and why.

Q.2. The speaker of the poem puts a lot of emphasis on the children. Who are these children he is referring to? Why does he mention them so much? Why are they dead already?

Student Encounter Activity

Research the relationship between the United States and Mexico, focusing in particular on the history of legal and illegal migration into the United States. Prepare a summary of your findings for the class.

Lee Ki Chuck

FROM KOREA TO HEAVEN COUNTRY

Born in Seoul, "Lee Ki Chuck" (a pseudonym) came to the United States with his family in 1973. They first settled in a Los Angeles suburb but later moved to the New York metropolitan area. The following "autobiography" is taken from an oral interview in 1975.

Essay, 2 pages   p. 776

This autobiographical essay is based on an actual interview; as such it offers students not only an insider's view but his actual words and means of expression. Get your students to discuss fully how they feel about Lee Ki Chuck. You will probably find a wide range of opinions of him. Our students find it hard to like him, and we usually end up taking his part, with minimal support from a few other defenders.

The key to teaching this surprisingly complex narrative successfully is, we think, to get students to tie their responses to the language in the piece. Ask just what attitudes bother them (or which they admire). What expressions embed themselves in memory? How do they feel about the way he repeats himself? Which representations are at least sympathetic? Do they look down on his difficulties with the language? What values do they associate with the ability to control language in self-presentation? Get them to reflect on how their reactions to this piece could be indicative of their reactions to someone who has limited English language skills.

You may also want to discuss the issue of immigrant expectations. For this you will want to use the title. Get students to discuss why the expectations were not fulfilled for this speaker. You can also look ahead and have them compare the meaning of "heaven" here with that in Cathy Song's poem "Heaven" in chapter 9. Get them to account for the differences, in terms of character, culture, belief, tradition, literary mode, etc.

Suggested Assignments

Q.1. How did you feel when you started to read this piece? Where you surprised at the language? Did you find it amusing? How does the language in this narrative affect your perception of the speaker? Explain your answer.

Q.2 This interview took place in 1975, only two years after the speaker arrived with his family. Do you think he would feel the same way after five more years? Find evidence in the narrative to support your answer. Furthermore, do you think a Korean immigrant interviewed in 1993 would have responded in the same way? Explain why or why not?

Student Encounter Activity

Interview a recent immigrant residing in your city. Ask him or her similar questions to the ones that must have been asked of Lee Ki Chuck? How does this person's opinions compare with those of Lee Li Chuck. Based on the similarities or differences, what can you say about how your city copes with immigrants in general?

Jesse G. Monteagudo
MIAMI, FLORIDA

Jesse Monteagudo is a Cuban-American writer living in Fort Lauderdale, Florida. He is a regular contributor to *The Community Voice* and to a variety of lesbian-gay and mainstream publications and anthologies.

Essay, 7 pages   p. 778

The author of this essay takes time to detail the context. Before he even gets to the issue of homosexuality, the writer gives a general overview of Miami's Cuban community. The assumption may be that his reader will be unfamiliar with this community and will not fully understand his point unless he or she is first acquainted with the context. This may or may not be true for your students. Since we live in Miami, our students are very familiar with the context and usually react strongly, in agreement or disagreement, with the many observations made by the writer.

Once we get over the students' reactions to the author's descriptions of the community, we get into the gay issue. The Study Questions can be helpful in this regard. Sometimes, we find students hesitant to express their reactions openly, so we ask them to first write them down for about fifteen minutes. Then we ask them to read them. Other times, we find students, especially the males in the class, to be very outspoken about the issue. This essay works particularly well for our students because they are so familiar with the context; nevertheless, many topics in this essay can transcend the specific context.

Some of the issues you can get your students to talk about in general include intolerance to gays, the gay lifestyle as depicted in the essay, family acceptance or rejection, cultural acceptance or rejection, and coming to terms with one's culture in spite of its intolerance. You may also want to talk about crossing. Ask your students in what ways the speaker has crossed over the fence and back, if only partially.

Suggested Assignments

Q.1. Discuss in what ways this essay reinforces or contradicts your expectations of the gay lifestyle. Be specific with your answer.

Q.2. Discuss how the attitude of Miami's Cuban community to the gay world in the early 1970s was similar or different from that of any other community at that time. Do you think attitudes have changed since then? If so, how? Be specific with your answer.

Student Encounter Activity

Interview a young person whom you know is gay. Ask him or her to share what his or her experiences have been growing up gay in the late 80s and early 90s. Then contrast his or her experiences to those of Jesse Monteagudo. What can you infer about changes or the lack of changes from the similarities or differences you have found? Write a brief essay with your observations and share it with the class.

Adrienne Rich

IF NOT WITH OTHERS, HOW? (1985)

Adrienne Rich was born in Baltimore, Maryland, in 1929. She is one of the best-known poets of this day. She is a prolific writer, having published 16 books, most of them collections of poems, and has won numerous awards. Her book *Diving into the Wreck* won the National Book Award in 1974. The following essay is taken from *Blood, Bread, and Poetry*.

Essay, 5 pages   p. 786

This is a powerful essay to end the chapter on Americans. Not only do we find it useful to explore the issues of sexism and anti-Semitism in American culture and worldwide, but we also find it useful to round out our discussion of heritage and ethnic pride in general.

Rich reaffirms the need and validity of allowing dissent within an ethnic group without that dissent being interpreted as a betrayal of a legacy. This piece, like others in this chapter, seems to question certain aspects of the speaker's cultural heritage without denying it or discarding it completely.

Rich not only does so in the case of her Jewish ancestry, but she does it for her American legacy as well. In many ways, she seems even more critical of that "Disneyland" legacy, still in denial about its flaws and frailties.

Depending on how much time you have for this essay, you may want to open up the class to a discussion of the Israeli-Palestinian issue. You may want to have some students, if not all, present an overview of the situation to the rest of the class, in order to clarify the context.

You can also use this essay to demonstrate effective argumentation strategies and a balanced tone.

Suggested Assignments

Q.1. From a Jewish Orthodox point of view, reread paragraph 10 and explain why its ideas would be considered offensive. Where do you stand on the Israeli-Palestine issue? Explain your answer.

Q.2. Given Adrienne Rich's diverse experiences with being a "victim," how do you explain the tone of the essay as one written from a position of strength?

Student Encounter Activity

Write an argumentative essay defending either the Israeli or the Palestinian interpretation of who is right. Use as many factual details as possible. Be ready to participate in an informal debate in class.

The Craft of Writing:

CONTEXTS

p. 792

The Afterword in this chapter discusses questions about context in some detail. As you have seen by now, the selections in the chapter make substantial demands on the reader to supply information. Some pieces provide more context than others. The Afterword reviews the importance of context. When the texts deal with cultures or historical moments unfamiliar to the reader, providing sufficient context becomes critical.

The Afterword also provides an overview of the demands made on the reader. In examining these, we like to emphasize that these demands are placed on the writer as well. These demands include knowledge of the language, the historical and cultural context, the literary form used, the authorial context, the setting, and the stereotypes applied. The more the reader knows, and the student writer provides, the better.

In preparing our students for the writing assignments, we ask them to ask themselves, keeping in mind the discussion of context in the Afterword, Have I provided sufficient information and background to establish a clear context for the reader? If the answer is no, we make it clear to them that they must continue to work on their piece until they can answer with an assertive yes. This may entail more research, observation, interviewing, or brainstorming. Context is particularly important for the type of writing our students do in class.

Comments on Student Writing

p. 797

We find this student essay useful in illustrating to students how to write an in-depth, documented essay that responds to literature. The student writer begins with the Mukherjee story included in the anthology and goes on to read the author's complete volume of stories *Dark-*

ness. From these, she discerns various points that lead her to the thesis of her essay. The student also researches some background information on the author's life that allows her to make further observations about the relationship between the fiction and the author.

We recommend you use the essay to review the organizational structure of an essay in general, highlighting the main divisions, the topic sentences, and the introductory and concluding techniques. The essay also uses transitions and examples effectively.

The most important aspect of this essay, we think, is that it demonstrates to students how to effectively thread direct quotes from the stories into the analysis. Our students often have trouble doing this. If yours do, we suggest you select several paragraphs and go over them in detail, discussing the language and transitions used by the student to weave in and out of the examples. The essay also illustrates the proper use of parenthetical citations, as well as the format for the Work Cited page at the end of the essay.

In summary, this would be a good sample piece to review with your students before assigning a similar, documented essay.

9

BELIEFS

In the introduction to this chapter, the editors add a new dimension to the study of new worlds of literature. This new dimension is in the realm of beliefs, as the chapter is aptly titled. The selections in the chapter explore the relationships of our peers to the "cosmic, the universal, the eternal, the supernatural."

Even though Western society has become increasingly more secularized, for many the relationship to a Higher Being or a spiritual entity is still prevalent. So much so that, since the end of World War II, as the editors point out, a trend of religious revival has been emerging.

The increasing interactions of world cultures—for example, the Western, Eastern, and Southern worlds—have introduced diverse spiritual possibilities within one's own cultural belief system. This is especially true in modern U.S. society, as it becomes increasingly multicultural. The texts in this chapter allow students to explore the different journeys toward or away from a spiritual heritage.

Pre-Reading Activity

As a way to introduce this final chapter on beliefs, you may want to approach the issue of the existence of a God or Higher Being head-on. We have found the following pre-reading activity very constructive, if not passionate.

You can write the following "simple" question on the board: Is there a God? Then ask students to free write an answer for at least fifteen minutes. When time is up, ask for volunteers to share their responses with the class. We often find it necessary to control the discussion by focusing on the philosophical issue and not the diverse religious practices in order to avoid a competition of whose religion is "better."

We have found that asking students to write a haiku (a three-line poem, the first and last lines consisting of 5 syllables, and the second of

7 syllables) from their free writing helps them to control the passion this subject ignites. It helps them to distill their beliefs and express them succinctly.

After they have shared their responses, introduce chapter 9 as a compilation of reflections on beliefs that they can use to compare and contrast to their own.

Toshio Mori

ABALONE, ABALONE, ABALONE

Toshio Mori was born in California in 1910, of Japanese ancestry. He is the author of a novel and is best known for his two volumes of short stories.

Short story, 2 pages   p. 807

Not all our students find this story as compelling or hypnotic (like polishing abalone shells?) as we do. What they say is that it's weird. Exactly, we say, meaning mysterious. We like to begin by making sure they know what abalone, or at least mother of pearl, looks like. Then we try to get them to describe just how the speaker gets hooked on abalone shells and what it is he sees in them (we try to get them back to paragraphs 9, 16, and 17).

Finally, we ask them to figure out why two or three of these beautiful shells are not enough. Why keep piling them up? They'll probably refer to the line that says that they are all alike yet different. This allows us to talk about nature and how each leaf, tree, fingerprint, snowflake, human is alike yet different.

We also like to get them talking about the "simplicity" of this task of collecting shells which somehow seems to fulfill the characters in a deeply meaningful way. Get them to talk about it and see if they can share their feelings about similarly simple tasks. We also like to mention how the simplicity of the story itself reinforces its theme.

Suggested Assignments

Q.1. Usually, elders are seen by younger people as either "out of place" or "wise seers." In this story, how does the speaker see Mr. Abe? Use excerpts from the story to support your view. With your view in mind, why does Mr. Abe refuse to tell the speaker the reason for his collection?

Q.2. The speaker writes, "I had a hard time taking the grime off the surface." Besides the actual act of cleaning a dirty shell, which other possible meanings could this sentence have? How did you discern this meaning?

Student Encounter Activity

Choose a task such as sea-shell polishing, whittling, planting, needlepoint, weaving, or some other activity usually associated with older people where your hands are busy at work. Perform this task for one to three hours. Write a journal entry describing your state of mind while performing the activity. Include in it your feelings toward the task before you started and after you finished. Be prepared to share your findings with the class.

Helena Maria Viramontes

THE MOTHS

Helena Maria Viramontes was born in East Los Angeles in 1954. She is frequently anthologized in Chicano/Chicana publications, and some of her stories have been collected in her 1985 volume *The Moths and Other Stories*.

Short story, 4 pages   p. 810

You might want to begin the discussion of this piece by addressing the fantastic elements in the story. Even though the story has much to discuss that does not depend on these, if your students are unfamiliar with Latin American literature and the use of the fantastic or magic realism, they may be too distracted to go beyond these elements.

We usually spend some time talking about magic realism as a technique that Latin American writers use to capture the mythical, supernatural, violent nature of the Latin American reality and landscape. We also mention writers some of our students are usually familiar with such as Gabriel Garcia Marquez, Isabel Allende, and Mario Vargas Llosa who use magic realism in their writing. Perhaps your students have seen the film *Like Water for Chocolate*, which can also provide many examples. We get these students to provide further examples of the technique.

Then we go back to the Viramontes story. The potato slices, the balm made of dry moths, and especially the moths fluttering out of the mouth of the dead grandmother are supposed to be accepted by the reader as reality. You may talk about the writer asking the reader to suspend disbelief in order to accept the magic of the moment, the spiritual, mythical component.

We don't like to concentrate solely on the magic realism traits in this story, because this piece has other important and interesting elements to grasp. We move on to lively discussions of the relationships between the main character and the other members of the family. We pay particular attention to the relationship with the mother and the grandmother. Ask the students to explore why, in the final scene, the main character calls out for Amá while she is holding Abuelita. Also get them to discuss what the grandmother means to the main character and especially what role she plays in fulfilling the main character's spiritual needs and desires.

Suggested Assignments

Q.1. Read the last two sentences of paragraph 5. In what ways do they characterize the speaker? In what ways do they characterize the grandmother? What do these lines reveal about their relationship? How would you characterize it? What is it based on? How do you know it?

Q.2. Who "died" in the story?

Student Encounter Activity

Magic realism is a literary concept often associated with well-known Latin American writers. Find out what the term means. Based on your findings, determine whether Viramonte's story illustrates this technique. Is magic realism a hard concept for you to comprehend? Explain why this may or may not be so in a brief essay.

Louise Erdrich

FLEUR

Louise Erdrich is of Chippewa and German-American descent. She is well known as a novelist, story writer, and poet. She grew up in North Dakota and resides now in New Hampshire.

Short story, 10 pages   p. 815

We usually begin the discussion of this story by asking students to review the plot. Our students sometimes get confused with the details, particularly toward the end when the action moves very quickly. You may find it helpful to point out the significance of the scene between Lily and the sow in relation to the men's intention toward Fleur. You can also explore the question of how the men got trapped in the meat locker.

We move on to a discussion of Fleur. You can ask your students to characterize her and the features that single her out. We see her at the beginning and the end of the story by the water. Nature and its mystical powers are central to the story and to this character in particular. Fleur is obviously an outcast, being a Chippewa, a seer, and a woman. Get your students to discuss how these elements are depicted in the story and how they come together.

After discussing Fleur extensively, we turn to the narrator. We get our students to describe her and particularly her relationship to Fleur. We then get them to analyze how her encounter with Fleur may represent an awakening, and the ways in which she has awakened. You may want to remind the students that the narrator's mother also came from the reservation. In many ways, the narrator seems to gain spiritual, cultural, and personal strength as a result of her encounter with Fleur. Get your students to define how this is so.

Finally, you may want to explore the "belief" aspect of this story. What elements of the story do your students find perplexing or difficult to grasp? What belief system must they accept in order for them to grasp the story's full potential? You may want to discuss here the initial story of Misshepeshu and the birth of the child to Fleur in the end.

Suggested Assignments

Q.1. In what ways are Fleur and Pauline outsiders? Even though outsiders, they seem to have more insight than the insiders themselves. How is this paradox possible?

Q.2. What lesson were the men "teaching" Fleur? What lesson were they "teaching" Pauline? Was Pauline justified in causing the death of the three men? Explain your answer.

Student Encounter Activity

Compare the motivations and intentions of the men in relation to Fleur and Pauline to those of men accused of date rape. What are the similarities? What does the story and your understanding of date rape reveal to you about the actions and attitudes of certain men?

Barry Targan

DOMINION

Barry Targan was born in Atlantic City, New Jersey. He is the author of three collections of short stories, two collections of poetry, and two novels. He currently teaches creative writing at the State University of New York at Binghamton.

Short story, 17 pages   p. 826

This story can thrust the class back into a familiar discussion of generational conflict. In this case, the conflict revolves around a religious conversion that is unacceptable to the elder. Our students react differently to the father and his interference in the life of his son. Some students center the argument on the son's ability to choose his own life, his own beliefs. Other students are familiar with the power of some cults and defend the parents' right to be concerned and fearful. The recent events in Waco, Texas, with the Branch Dividian cult, helps these students to support their arguments.

We basically let our students have their say when it comes to discussing the Society of the Holy Word. Generally they have had more experience with such groups—being recruited or involved—than we have and know what to look for and how to read this portion of the story. There are some who find Poverman blasphemous, but we can usually rely on the rest of the class to judge the Society fairly accurately, or at least to see what Poverman finds and fears.

When this has been thrashed out, we turn to paragraph 195 and what follows. We have them read the paragraph sentence by sentence, covering as much as we can of the "business" imagery, the colloquial language ("scram") next to the more formal or Biblical ("vaunt"), and inferring the determination Poverman has made. We draw their attention to the parenthesis in paragraph 202 "(cotton/polyester—60/40, not silk)" and ask why it is there—it doesn't take long for its relation to Poverman's business and its implication of inelegance, impurity, maybe even tackiness to transfer from the robe to the Society.

Most students are usually touched, as we are, by Robert's actions: he breaks in when his father is abasing himself, calling himself "a bad man and stained with sin." You may suggest that what we learn about Poverman from the inside and from his actions makes us reluctant to have him confess to being "bad."

You may want to contrast Poverman's reaction to his bankruptcy in the first part of the essay to his reaction to the potential loss of his son in the second part. How are his reactions different, and what do they say about his attitude to money and his son?

We ask about the imagery in the final paragraphs to try to get students to suggest that it is religious. We hope they argue that the father's attack is not upon religion or God, but upon what he thinks of as a false or feeble religious cult, destructive of his son's earthly life without saving his immortal soul. Fighting for his son, indeed, is not without glory, no matter how uneasily we might at first have thought the word sat on poor Poverman's head.

Suggested Assignment

Q.1. Is the term "dominion" a positive or negative one for you? How do you visualize it? Describe the images that come to your mind. How do your images compare with the association of the title to the story?

Q.2. In Jewish culture, childhood has traditionally been an important time of life. The care, education, and respect given to children are the underpinnings of a parent's mission to ensure the well-being of the child and of the culture. Keeping this in mind, reflect on how Poverman and Robert would each react to this idea. Decide who has the "better" interpretation of the view. Defend his position using examples from the text. Who do you most agree with?

Student Encounter Activity

Apart from intimate love, no other cultural elements solicit a more emotionally charged passion than that of religious beliefs, especially opposing ones. Think of your own experiences, or those of people you know, who have held religious beliefs in conflict with the expectations of those around them. Describe the actions and reactions of those involved. Emotionally, how would you characterize these? What motivated these emotions? Discuss your answers in a brief essay.

N. Scott Momaday

THE EAGLE-FEATHER FAN

N. Scott Momaday was born in Lawton, Oklahoma, in 1934 of Kiowa parents. He is a poet, editor, novelist, and adapter of Indian tales. His first novel, *House Made of Dawn*, won the Pulitzer Prize for fiction. He currently lives in Tucson, Arizona, and teaches at the University of Arizona.

Poem, 1/2 page   p. 845

We like to begin the discussion of this piece by asking students to describe what the speaker says is happening in the poem (he is probably dancing to the music, the singing, and the drums, and is certainly holding a fan made of eagle feathers. He says the fan is actually an eagle which takes off with his hand that has become part of the eagle-fan and soars in the heavens over the mountains).

From here, we try to get our students to explore the possibility of looking at the universe and reality in a different way. We point out that they don't have to believe in the other reality to appreciate someone else's perspective. This seems to us an important aesthetic and ethical/moral principle to discuss.

Finally, you may want to recall other pieces by Native Americans in the anthology that explore the role of nature in their belief system and their spiritual sense of life and the universe.

Suggested Assignments

Q.1. Given the resurgence of Native-American cultures in the late twentieth century, how would you characterize this poem: nostalgia or reaffirmation?

Q.2. To have "fine / and hollow" bones is a genetic disease by modern medical reality, yet in the poem the condition is viewed differently. Can these interpretations be reconciled?

Student Encounter Activity

What is the significance of the eagle to some Native-American cultures? Compare this to the significance of the eagle to the U.S. government. For each culture, what does the eagle symbolize? If, in your opinion, this simultaneous use of the eagle, by different and distinct cultures, bears a strong dose of irony, explain what accounts for the irony. You may need to do some research to answer these questions.

Stephen Shu-Ning Liu

MY FATHER'S MARTIAL ART

Stephen Shu-Ning Liu was born in Fu-Ling, China, in 1930, and emigrated to America in 1952. His poetry has appeared in over 200 literary magazines and in a bilingual collection of poems. He has won many awards and teaches at Community College of Southern Nevada in Las Vegas.

Poem, 1 page   p. 846

This poem explores the emotions of a son who seems to feel abandoned. The father has left him alone in the "real" world of oncoming traffic to find spiritual refuge in the cliffs. There is a tension between admiration for this father who has performed incredible feats and taught the son tricks, and disappointment, even perhaps a bit of mockery, in the mother's words "he looked / like a monk and stank of green fungus." We like to ask our students to list the details that illustrate the two poles.

These seeming contradictions also exist in the descriptions. For example, we like to point out, if the students haven't already, the contrast between the busy streets and "brood over high cliffs," as well as the smog/smoke dichotomy. You can ask them to explore how these images that contradict or transcend the physical and realistic make them feel. Get them to infer from them about the son's/speaker's feelings.

You may also want to refer to Li-Young Lee's "The Gift" or Toshio Mori's "Abalone, Abalone, Abalone." Ask your students to contrast the elder and youth relationship in those selections to this one.

Suggested Assignments

Q.1. If each man were on a journey, describe where each would be headed. Could these men share their experiences along the way? With this in mind, what is the son seeking with the father? What is the father giving the son?

Q.2. On a scale of "feet on the ground to head in the clouds," where is each man's heart in the poem? Who has the more realistic grip on life? Use excerpts from the text to support your answer.

Ishmael Reed

I AM A COWBOY IN THE BOAT OF RA

Ishmael Reed was born in Chattanooga, Tennessee, in 1938. He is the author of numerous novels, collections of essays, poetry volumes, and anthologies; he is also a songwriter, publisher, and playwright. He is the founder of the Before Columbus Foundation. He teaches at the University of California at Berkeley.

Poem, 2 pages   p. 847

We see this poem not only as a celebration of blackness and its demand for equal status with myths of the American West, but also as an emblem of the mixed heritage of the *African*-American/African-*American* people in this country.

You may want to go through this elaborate work line by line. Students have trouble with humor, especially in poetry, so you may need to point out some of the playfulness in this work. You can let Study Questions 1 and 2 do some of the work and get the students set for the final verse-paragraph.

Even though this is a playful poem, it deals with serious issues you can explore more thoroughly, such as the role and veracity of world history.

Suggested Assignments

Q.1. In what specific ways does the epigraph relate to the poem? Use excerpts from the poem in answering the following questions: Who is the devil, what must be revealed, and why must these be burned?

Q.2. Does this poem question the writing of history as fact? If so, what evidence can you provide to prove the point?

Student Encounter Activity

Find out the racial characteristics of the ancient Egyptians. Given these, why do European-American scholars and African-American

scholars still hold different interpretations regarding this dead civilization's race? Explain your answer in a brief essay.

Olive Senior

ANCESTRAL POEM

Olive Senior was born in Jamaica and educated there and in Can-
ada. She is both a poet and story writer and the author of *A–Z of
Jamaican Heritage*.

Poem, 2 pages   p. 850

This poem can recall earlier discussions on heritage, generational
conflict, and the search for home. You may want to ask students in
what ways does this poem remind them of other works in the anthology such as Neil Bissoondath's "There Are a Lot of Ways to Die," in
chapter 5. We like to get our students to compare and contrast the sentiments in each of these pieces since they deal with similar settings.
    Or you can compare this with Stephen Shu-Ning Liu's "My
Father's Martial Art," which conveys similar conflicting emotions. You
can ask your students to explore how the speaker feels about her parents and, by association, her home and heritage.

Suggested Assignments
    Q.1. What are the speaker's beliefs as revealed in the poem? Are
these in harmony or in conflict with her ancestors?
    Q.2. In most literature, sunlight is seen as enlightenment. Yet here
it is betrayal. Why does the speaker view sunlight in this way?

Cathy Song

HEAVEN

Cathy Song was born in 1955, in Hawaii. A poet and anthologist,
her books include *Picture Bride*, in which the title poem tells the story
of her Korean grandmother who was a mail-order bride.

Poem, 2 page   p. 852

Because poetry often seems difficult and alien to inexperienced readers, one way of discussing a poem like this one is to get your students, at first, to talk about the narrative elements. Here are three characters—the "dreamer" son, the speaker, and the grandfather pictured primarily as a boy—plus two vivid settings and a plot connected over three generations.

In reality there is no story, only conclusions and feelings. You can probe your students with questions such as these: What are the people like? How are the connections between them made with little or nothing "happening" in the poem? How are the interests here different from those in a story? How are the elements of character, setting, and plot handled differently?

If you have not talked about Chinese migration to the western United States in the nineteenth century when Chinese railroad workers were brought over supposedly on a temporary basis, you may want to discuss it now. You may also want to discuss other themes alluded to in the poem such as returning, mixed heritage, childhood dreams, regrets, etc.

Suggested Assignments

Q.1. In second-generation immigrant families, conscious and unconscious cultural feelings are passed on to the offspring. Based on examples from the poem, what feelings is the boy revealing about the cultural adjustment going on within this family?

Q.2. If the mother views her son as a "dreamer," how does she view herself?

Student Encounter Activity

Have you, or someone you know, lived another's dream? Why does this occur? Interview a campus counselor for a professional opinion on the matter. In your opinion, is this a positive or negative course for someone to take? Discuss your reactions in a brief essay and share it with the class.

Walter K. Lew

LEAVING SEOUL: 1953

Walter K. Lew was born and raised in Baltimore, and is of Korean descent. He is a poet, a performance artist, a scholar, and a television producer. He has won numerous awards for his writings and performances.

Poem, 1 page   p. 854

This poem is intensely interesting and moving in some way, even though it is puzzling as well. We suggest you begin by exploring with your students the details of the story line. What is happening here? It is Seoul, 1953, and this family is leaving. The father is at the airport while the mother is rushing to bury the urns. Why they have to bury the urns and what it is the father doesn't get seem to be linked to the last two lines. Yet these last two lines are puzzling in themselves. Get your students to try their hand at interpreting what they mean.

You may also want to use the title to guide the discussion. Is the speaker perhaps playing on the words Seoul and Soul? Are the souls of the ancestors being left behind, protected in their burial ground? If so, does the need to revere parents and forebears give them power (dominion) over us?

Suggested Assignments

Q.1. Is the title a play on the word "soul"? If so, how would this affect your understanding of the poem?

Q.2. Why does the speaker seem obsessed with urns? Why hasn't he buried the ones he taps?

Student Encounter Activity

Pair up with a classmate and ask each other the following questions: How often do you visit the burial grounds of a deceased ancestor? When was the last time? Compare your findings to the other members of the class. What general statements can you make concerning the relationship between your peers and the deceased? What do your findings say about modern American culture and its view toward buried ancestors?

Mary Stewart Hammond

CANAAN

Mary Stewart Hammond is a poet, a print and broadcast journalist, and a critic. She lives in New York City.

Poem, 2 pages   p. 856

In this poem, the speaker uses Biblical allusions to thread the story of her upbringing in a rural mountain setting. You may want to begin discussion by asking your students to talk about the tone of the poem. How does the speaker feel about her family and her childhood? Can they support their opinions with details from the poem? The setting is important to this poem and you can make references to some of your earlier discussions of context. The Study Questions can be helpful in this regard.

We also like to relate this poem to the general theme of the chapter. What belief systems are revealed here by the father, the mother, the speaker? Are they in conflict? If so, in what way? Finally, you may probe your students to see if any can relate similar experiences of their upbringing and their reaction to it now that they are in college.

Suggested Assignments

Q.1. The speaker has an astute command of the Old Testament. Based on this observation, to what purpose does she utilize her religious knowledge?

Q.2. If Papa could speak to her daughter now, what would he say to her? Answer within the context of the poem.

Pat Mora

GENTLE COMMUNION

Pat Mora was born in El Paso, Texas, and is of Mexican-American descent. She has published several books of poems and currently lives in Cincinnati.

Poem, 1 page   p. 859

This is a touching poem about the speaker's relationship to her dead Mamande (the grandmother we assume?), a relationship so real that the speaker senses her alongside her at all times. Some students will take the speaker at face value and accept this powerful presence as real; others will have trouble with the spiritual, supernatural elements of the poem.

In any case, the most important aspect here is the way the speaker views Mamande. The dead woman plays a spiritual role for the speaker that nurtures her in a religious way. Point out to the students, if they don't come up with it first, the comparison of the grapes, "I know not to bite or chew," to a Catholic communion.

Suggested Assignments

Q.1. In a communion, each participant gives something to the other. In this poem, what are Mamande and the speaker giving to each other?

Q.2. This poem illustrates one aspect of the power of the dead over the living and of the living over the dead. Give examples from the poem that support each facet of this statement. Do you foresee a time when the living and the dead will leave each other alone? If so, when and why?

Rafael Jesús González

SESTINA: SANTA PRISCA

Rafael Jesús González was born in El Paso, Texas, in 1935. He has authored a collection of poems and teaches creative writing and literature at Laney College.

Poem, 1 page   p. 860

We find that this poem is challenging for students and that they need help in understanding what is going on. We would suggest you begin by reviewing how a sestina works. The first Study Question can help you begin. Then ask your students to visualize the images here, and encourage them to look up the words they are unfamiliar with. You may even ask them to draw the saints and as much of the church as possible. Help them to see how intricately the words and the images are intertwined. For example, ask them to list the words that are recurrent in the verse endings, particularly iron and floor. Why choose these two particular words?

Finally, getting your students to establish where the tension comes in the poem will usually help clarify things for them. There seems to be a shift in the poem that begins to emerge in the fifth stanza with the intrusion of the bougainvillaea climbing from the floor. We like to get our students to contrast the life, color, and passion of the plant to the stone saints. What might this contrast be saying about traditional religion which relies on these gesticulating saints? Here you may want to point out, if the students haven't done so yet, lines 22–23 where the speaker refers to "dead theologies." How do these lines help us to clarify the direction of the poem?

Suggested Assignments

Q.1. Describe the interactions between the stones and the flowers in the poem. Would you characterize it as competitive, cooperative, or subjugative? Explain your answer with textual interpretations.

Q.2. In terms of beliefs, characterize the tension taking place in the poem. Do you agree with the speaker's conclusions? Why or why not?

Student Encounter Activity

Distill each stanza of this sestina into a haiku form using the words stone, iron, floor, and wood. Which form do you find most effective?

Alice Walker

REVOLUTIONARY PETUNIAS

Alice Walker was born in Georgia in 1944, and now lives in San Francisco. She has published four volumes of poetry and two novels. She is probably best known for her novel *The Color Purple*, for which she won the Pulitzer Prize.

Poem, 1 page   p. 862

You may want to begin the discussion of this poem by asking students to review the narrative. Once they understand what is "happening" in the poem, you can get them to discuss the implications. Who is Sammy Lou and why is she labeled militant? Is this how she sees herself? Have them contrast the title to the last lines of the poem where Sammy Lou asks for her purple petunias to be watered. Are these purple because of the association of purple with pain and suffering in Christian tradition?

You can move on from there to the historical allusions to George, Martha, Jackie, and Kennedy. What is the speaker saying about the role of this backwoods woman and the history of this country? Whom does she represent? In general, you can use this poem to engage in discussions about the role of African-American women in this society and the burdens they have carried.

Suggested Assignments

Q.1. What does the speaker mean by saying that Sammy Lou "raised a George, / a Martha, a Jackie and a Kennedy"?

Q.2. In what ways are Sammy Lou's petunias revolutionary?

Estela Portillo

THE DAY OF THE SWALLOWS

Estela Portillo is a playwright, novelist, and story writer, born in El Paso, Texas, in 1936. She has taught in high school, conducted a television talk show, and helped found a bilingual theater. She is director of the arts in El Paso Community College.

Play, 30 pages   p. 864

Stage Directions and Scene 1

We find it worthwhile the day before assigning *The Day of the Swallows* to spend fifteen minutes or so having the introductory paragraphs read aloud, one by one, in class, asking mostly about tone and expectations. How does the first paragraph end? The second? "Here it [the lake] drinks the sun in madness" and "No one dares ask for life" don't seem to promise comedy or romance (despite the romantic setting). If we have time left, we go on with the two paragraphs setting up scene 1. The contrast of the first scene with what precedes it should raise some questions. (Our more perceptive students seem to expect this beautiful room to somehow be threatened by the barrio—the conquered conquering the conquerors. Which only goes to prove that perceptive readers get more out of a text but do not necessarily guess the outcome correctly.) Most of our students, trained by television and movies, "know" that what Alysea is doing is washing blood out of the carpet. This is a good place to leave them; they're almost sure now to read on.

We suggest, however, that when they finish the first scene students pause and think back and project forward before going on. We often have them keep a reading journal with each entry dated and timed. A fair number, we find, catch on to such red herrings as Alysea looking at her hands when Clemencia is there; it is perfectly natural in the light of what she is doing, but it does cast suspicion on her as the spiller of blood (and our students feel that where there's blood, there's a murder). At the end of the scene, we ask them whether they believe Alysea or Josefa about David's fate and future. We also ask them about the last line of the scene, "Anything . . . anything is worth this!" What's "this"? What do they think "anything" portends?

Our students are suspicious of Josefa right away. She's too good to be true and they are leery of people who talk about patterning "our lives for one beautiful moment," though they are quick to pick up the simile—"like this lace . . . little bits and pieces come together . . . "— and write SYMBOL in the margin. So we have to defend Josefa and stress her beauty and sensitivity; after all, the play would lack passion if we didn't care what happened to her.

By the time they have read the first scene students should have noticed the symbolic insistence on lace and light and will probably have some idea of what they mean to Josefa and the play.

Act I, Scene 2

We don't usually like to carry on the stop-and-go reading technique we use to talk about expectations. However, the scene with Eduardo raises many possibilities, especially that he and Josefa might have a relationship. He also introduces elements other than plot that raise expectations, such as calling the room a room for women, suggesting that Josefa will not like his taking Alysea away as his "squaw," and setting up a binary opposition between the room and "the open." We ask students what associations they have with inside and outside here, and, since this chapter, after all, deals with myth, symbol, and religion, we call students' attention to Father Prado's approval of the "holier temple" among the pines. We also ask them to focus on the conversation between Josefa and Eduardo when they are alone and gloss the implied meanings of sea and lake, whirlwind, barrio, desert, and, especially when Alysea returns, the magicians. Sometimes we ask a couple of students to read the parts.

We get mixed responses to Josefa's description of her mystical experience. Those who find her language pretentious find this somewhat silly; those who accept her as sensitive and mysterious find this passage moving. It is an especially good passage to have performed, preferably repeatedly performed, by different students to wring all the possible tones and meanings out of it.

If we give two class periods to the play—and we usually do—the first assignment ends with the second scene. It is therefore another good place to test expectations, especially since Tomás has returned with David's horse. Moreover, the fact that Josefa crippled the man who was chasing Alysea and left David's drunken father to die darkens the picture of her and makes the mystery of what happened to David even more ominous. And Tomás? What role will he play later?

Act I, Scene 3

Clara, the aging beauty put aside by her lover for a younger woman and turning to drink, is something of a stock figure, though it takes us a while to get that out of a class. We then try to turn the tables a bit and challenge them "as actresses" to breathe new life or depth or individuality into the part by their reading. What comes out, when it comes, usually has to do with her relationship to her rival, Alysea, though once we got a new angle from a student who had Clara read "My downfall? [*In a whisper.*] My life?" in such a way as to suggest a certain amount of fear of, along with admiration for, Josefa.

This is also a good scene with which to play the expectation game. We usually end the first assignment with scene 2, but you might prefer the division Portillo herself made and divide the assignment by acts so that this would be the point at which to pause, take stock, and project. (A theater audience would have to pause here for intermission rather than after scene 2. Come to think of it, maybe we should make the division here next time.)

Act II

In the previous scene and in the early lines of this act, more and more is being said about the magicians. We sometimes have students as they go through the play collect references to the magicians sequentially and try to frame descriptions or definitions after each set or group of appearances of the term. We suggest that this framing of a definition, a configuration, is wholly analogous to framing expectation, making some kind of shape or whole out of the fragments we gather as we read. The projected definitions of the magicians get particularly interesting when Don Esquinas reports that Clara said Josefa's magicians have no faces. We have had some success as well asking students to keep similar configurations of Josefa's character—that is, periodically stopping and trying to define just what kind of a person she is. That exercise too gets particularly intriguing in the early stages of the final act when Tomás suggests he knows about Josefa and Alysea, for example, or when Don Esquinas says Josefa has done enough harm to Clara already, supplying her with liquor and "lies" (and all this after the tender scene with the injured bird).

A few of our students have had some difficulty relating "putting ugliness away" and "atonement," so you might want to get that connection on the table early in discussing the scene.

The scene with Don Esquinas, besides his accusations about Josefa's harming Clara, may be a good point at which to review the gender issue, starting with Josefa's frequent attacks on men and their ways. If you have assigned the first act as the first day's assignment, before your students read the final act you may want to have this scene read aloud in class. Review the treatment of gender in the play at this point before the denouement, and even before Tomás's revelations later in the scene.

What do your students make of Josefa's final speech in act II? What is the new birth of light? Who or what is Josefa's lover? The moon? magicians? (It is not until well into act III that we learn she means the lake.)

Act III

We sometimes use the exchange between Josefa and Father Prado on the festival to reopen the discussion on ritual (which we have usually generated earlier). In the exchange, he asks if it isn't true that the festival for her is "just ritual," and she responds that for the barrio people it is rebirth. Father Prado clearly means ritual, repeated ceremony divorced from its religious meaning. Josefa gives it new religious meaning, rebirth into life and joy and belief, perhaps. We review with the class the polishing of the abalone, the burial of urns, the dance with the eagle-feather fan, the sacrifice of the goat and bullock, even the anti-ritual of the Brethren coming up, in a kind of overview of the chapter.

If you dare, before your students have read this final act, you might have them read the beginning of Josefa's confession. Go through the longish speech that begins "Last night . . . last night . . . ," or even down to Josefa's "I told her . . . go with me when the moon comes out . . . ," and have them recount what they think Josefa did to David. Do you think this red herring, as it were, is intended; that we are supposed to think that Josefa, a man-hater we know by now, castrated him? If so, how do you read the real event?

You might want to ask your students how they understand Father Prado's feelings of guilt at not understanding that underneath Josefa's calm exterior there were "twisted fears." How do they understand the final thirty lines or so in which Father Prado sees much God in her and she says instead she is the "high priestess" of the light her magicians gave her? We are not sure we could paraphrase all this and certainly not all its implications, but it can make for a good class period, a cooperative exploration.

Final Scene

Father Prado reportedly said Josefa is like a cathedral, like the silence of the cathedral, the stained-glass windows her soul. She says her magicians will let her come back as light and the final stage direction dictates choir voices, church bells, birds in full life, and light that is almost unearthly. All this seems to celebrate Josefa's suicide and virtually authorize or underwrite her vision, her belief in "magicians," and so on. How does your class respond to that? (How do you?) We don't know whether you want to get into this, but so many independent or unconventional women in fiction (including drama) end up committing suicide—Emma Bovary by poison, Anna Karenina under the train—and not only those created by male authors. Kate Chopin's Edna Pontellier, like Portillo's here, drowns herself (a gentler and symbolically more "feminine" ending, perhaps). Is this the measure of the hopelessness of female freedom in a patriarchal society? or, analogously, the only ending imaginable for the writer writing in such a society (since it is difficult for him or her to imagine a wholly happy ending for such a "misfit")?

Suggested Assignments

Q.1. How would you characterize Josefa's and Father Prado's communication? What scenes in the play illustrate their forms of communicating with each other? In your opinion, are they both just two sides of the same coin? or are they different coins?

Q.2. How do you feel about Josefa's suicide?

Student Encounter Activity

Research the rising number of teenage suicides in the nation. Outline the main causes attributed to the problem. Do you find any similarities between these and the causes leading to Josefa's suicide or that of other literary characters you may be familiar with who also commit suicide? Write a brief essay discussing your findings.

Leonard Begay
BEYOND SACRED MOUNTAINS

Leonard Begay, a member of the Navajo Nation, wrote the following essay soon after he entered Northern Arizona University.

Essay, 9 pages   p. 897

In some ways, this essay sums up most of the issues discussed throughout the anthology. The narrator is trying to reconcile his going "Beyond Sacred Mountains" by attending college, with his deep love and belief in the traditions of his people, the Navajo. You may want to see how your students feel about his search and if they think he has succeeded in reconciling both worlds.

The story itself should be easy for them to grasp. You may want to use the Study Questions to guide a discussion of the structure and focus of the piece. Again, the structure can remind them of the power of storytelling in relating myths, values, and histories from one generation to the other. This is particularly true in certain cultures steeped in the oral tradition, such as that of Native Americans. For these cultures, the elders are very important as teachers. By now, students should appreciate that perspective.

You may want to focus on the relationship between the grandparents and the speaker as a boy and a young man. Explore with your students the different expectations the grandparents had of him. Try these questions: What are the grandparents' goals for the boy? Are they narrow-minded and possessive or considerate of the boy's special place in the family? How does the grandfather suggest to the boy that he accept his new education? Is this a valid reason for exposing a young member of the family to a different and sometime hostile culture?

Your students may find it curious that the parents left the early years of upbringing to the grandparents. Allow your students to explore the parents' intentions. Some of the students may wonder about the younger sister as well, and the differences in upbringing. This may open up the discussion into gender issues and cultural differences.

Suggested Assignments

Q.1. Reread paragraph 17 recounting the "cruising" story. Keeping in mind the importance the grandparents place on education, how do you think his grandparents would react to this event?

Q.2. What evidence is there in the essay that the concept of time is changing for Begay? Once beyond Sacred Mountains, do you think he will return as his grandfather wished? Explain your answer.

Student Encounter Activity

To Begay's grandfather, education was important to survive in the white man's world. If you flip the reasoning and imagine Begay as a white boy having a grandfather sending him to a Native-American reservation for his schooling, would you say that the reasoning still holds? What would he learn at the reservation that he wouldn't learn otherwise? Write a brief essay summarizing your ideas.

Garrison Keillor

PROTESTANT

Garrison Keillor was born in Minnesota, in 1942. He is best known for his weekly radio program, "The Prairie Home Companion." This piece is from his bestseller *Lake Wobegon Days*.

Essay, 8 pages   p. 908

You may feel it necessary to deal with the third Study Question first: religion and humor do not mix very well in American public life at times. If your class is particularly sensitive, you may want to turn the abstraction lever up a notch and guide the discussion into the frequent tendency of highly principled organizations—religious, political, or social—to splinter on narrower and narrower grounds. We do not do this in American public life: the Democratic and Republican parties, for example, are very broad and overlapping. (Some would say too much.) Would it be better, however, to have more parties with firmer, if narrower principles?

You may prefer to start the class a different way. You can begin by discussing the humor in the piece. It's very difficult to explain why something is funny, but it does seem necessary to advise the solemn youth in class that a piece actually read for an assignment can be funny.

Keillor can be very subtle or quiet, so sometimes you may need to turn up the volume. The beginning of paragraph 3 both raises the blasphemy issue and illustrates Keillor's humorous twists: "Jesus said, 'Where two or three are gathered together in my name, there am I in the midst of them,' and the Brethren believed that was enough." Christ's words are not being made fun of, but the Brethren's demand that only those whose beliefs were "pure" (that is, identical) doomed them to very small congregations and they thought that was enough, perhaps even proof of their purity. Even that belief is not being made fun of; it is the result, the tiny congregation, that is shown as somehow ludicrous (at gatherings). There is no overt scoffing at the purist positions described in the paragraph, but the five sentences beginning with "No" give the impression that the Brethren's purity was more a matter of negation and denial than of positive and joyous belief. Perhaps the total seriousness, the spare, severe rigors of their faith, and the absence of joy are what seem to require some humor or joy in their description to balance the picture.

What may make this seem difficult to understand for our students is our generally hedonistic culture; the Brethren might seem to them "kooks" or masochists. The almost wistful respect for such honest self-denial in Keillor's tone that must be appreciated to make the whole piece both funny and moving may be lost. It's up to us to make sure it isn't.

Suggested Assignments

Q.1. The central question to answer seems to be how does a Protestant protest his family's religious beliefs. Write a brief essay summarizing Keillor's view on religion. Do you favor his views? Use examples from the text to support your ideas.

Q.2. Read paragraph 32, where the family leaves the restroom. Do you view this episode as quaint and inflexible or as courageous and worthy of respect? Where would you draw the line between coexisting with or compromising your religious beliefs?

Student Encounter Activity

Compare how members of the following religions publicly display their beliefs: Fundamentalists, Muslims, Protestants, Buddhists, Catholics, Jews, and Krishnas. Then debate the following question with your classmates: How far should individuals go with their public displays of religious beliefs?

Martin Luther King, Jr.
I HAVE A DREAM

Martin Luther King, Jr., was born in Atlanta, Georgia, the son and grandson of ministers. He received his doctorate from Boston University and eventually became minister of the same congregation led by his father.

Essay, 3 pages   p. 917

This is a legendary speech your students will probably be familiar with—if not with its entirety, then at least with parts. This is a powerful speech meant to be heard. For this reason, we like to read it aloud to the class or, if you prefer, you can ask for volunteers to give a dynamic reading of the speech. The oratorical quality of the words, the hypnotizing repetition, and the power of the images usually overwhelm the students. We have found that these words truly touch our students and that little explanation is necessary.

We recommend using the Study Questions to review the structure of the essay at home while using the class to allow students to react emotionally to the words. How do they feel about King's message almost thirty years later? Are his words only meaningful to African Americans or can all humans be touched by them? Would he be disappointed or content with changes in the United States since his death? Get them to lead the discussion in whatever ways they want.

Then I would ask the students to discuss why they think the editors ended this anthology titled *New Worlds of Literature* with this piece.

A final note to the kind readers from the authors of this manual. Martin Luther King, Jr.'s words are so simple yet so profoundly moving that we felt it best to let the text be. We equate understanding this speech with the episode in Mori's selection, "Abalone, Abalone, Abalone," of the young man who picked up an abalone shell. Like the shell in the story, King's words must be discovered and polished by one's own hands.

The Craft of Writing
MYTH AND SYMBOL

p. 921

In reading the selections in this chapter, students will encounter myths, rituals, the supernatural, and symbols that are both religious and literary. The Afterword of this chapter defines each of these terms clearly and succinctly. We suggest you review these definitions with your students and make sure they understand them. The editors have provided excellent examples from the pieces in the chapter to illustrate the terms. It will help students not only in comprehending the selections but also in being able to talk or write about them in a knowledgeable and articulate way.

We find it particularly helpful to ask our students to use examples from their own religious backgrounds to illustrate the distinctions between the terms. For example, we ask them to narrate a myth that is used by their religion to articulate a certain truth about the universe, to describe a specific religious ritual they've participated in, and to cite examples of symbols used in religious or spiritual ways. Myths, rituals, and symbols have traditionally been associated with religious and spiritual experiences; however, they have also become part of the literary realm. Knowledge of them in one realm will facilitate their use in the other.

Comments on Student Writing

p. 925

This piece is a response to the "Imitations and Parodies" assignment. The student has chosen to write a parody of Mori's story "Abalone, Abalone, Abalone." The student writer, by equating the macaroni with the abalone, successfully reveals her point of view regarding Mori's story. This student example is a technically correct parody using the macaroni as a parallel to the abalone shell. The student effectively weaves direct images and phrases from the original into her own story. However, the piece does not transcend into its own world.

With this in mind, you may want to point out to the students that authentic parody transcends the object of its imitation. In this student example, the preoccupation with parallelism is too strong. The student's own voice does not come through fully. Point out to your students how parody can sometimes be one of the hardest forms of literary expression. This is so because there are many competing voices: the original work, the original reader's interpretation, the author's parody, and the new reader's interpretation. An effective parody creates a world of its own from these varied seeds. You can get your students' feedback on these points in relation to the student piece.

COMMENTS ON WRITING
ABOUT LITERATURE

p. 929

The editors of *New Worlds of Literature* have added this new section, Writing about Literature, which works as a mini-rhetoric for students and teachers. It is an important component of the book that supplements the anthologized texts and corresponding writing assignments.

The purpose of this section is to provide guidelines, approaches, and techniques that will help students write more effectively about literature. As the editors point out, writing about literature should be easier than writing about anything else; however, this is only true if the student knows how to read effectively, and if the student possesses the language skills necessary to convey his or her ideas in writing. These skills include a good working vocabulary, and a sense of organization, of how to link ideas and determine what to include or leave out. Writing about Literature will provide your students with some of these basic principles of writing.

The editors have divided this portion into six major sections. In the first section, Representing the Literary Text, they define and provide examples of some of the terms commonly used in depicting literature: copying, paraphrase, and summary.

In the second section, Replying to the Text, the editors explain what is meant by more complex terms such as imitation, parody, re-creation, and reply. These are used to react to a piece emotionally, intellectually, or psychologically. This section will be particularly important for the student assignments at the end of each chapter.

If students are asked to explain a text, then they need to read over carefully the third section, Explaining the Text. Here the editors review three techniques often used to explain a text: description, analysis, and interpretation. The summary on interpretation is rather comprehensive and discusses issues such as how to determine the themes,

225

opinions, and ideas expressed in the text. Ample examples are provided.

Once the student feels comfortable with the text and capable of describing, analyzing, and interpreting the themes and ideas, he or she must decide what to say about the piece. Sometimes this is the hardest part. The section Deciding What to Write About, gives students helpful suggestions for coming up with something to say.

Once the student begins to write, he or she should examine with care the section, From Topic to Rough Draft. It is an extensive section that will take students through the entire writing process, including how to gather evidence, how to organize notes, how to develop an argument, and how to write the first draft. This section is followed by the final segment on revision and rewriting. We find the checklist here particularly precise and useful. At the end of both of these sections, students will also find a helpful, step-by-step summary of the process. We recommend you review this in class with your students after you have assigned the longer segment to read.

In summary, we feel you will find this portion of the book a necessary complement to the anthology and recommend you have your students read it before assigning the writing assignments. You may want to divide it into its natural parts, and assign and discuss these separately as the course develops.

SAMPLE COURSE SYLLABI

On the following pages we present sample syllabi for a fifteen-week course in writing and another for a ten-week course. These will give you further ideas on how to use New Worlds of Literature.

We usually include two types of written assignments. The journal entries are informal pieces, and are not graded. Their purpose is to get students thinking and writing without the pressure of a grade. We have included suggestions for these from the Writing about Reading sections at the end of each chapter in the anthology. In addition to these exercises, we also have formal graded essays. The purpose of these is to have the students practice certain skills normally associated with the various rhetorical modes such as description or comparison and contrast. We usually allow our students to choose their own topics as long as they apply the formal techniques. You may want to assign specific topics from the chapter themes.

For the readings, we use the thematic organization established by the editors of the anthology. Since there are more selections in each chapter than any instructor could possibly cover in one course, we have included our own suggestions of readings based on personal preference, as well as on the anticipated interest and relevance to our students. Of course, you can substitute others that you prefer. You may even choose to highlight only one cultural group or gender depending on the objective of your course.

Sample Fifteen-Week Course Syllabus

Course Outline

REQUIRED TEXTS:
* Norton's *New Worlds of Literature*, Second Edition
* A grammar handbook

COURSE REQUIREMENTS: To complete this course with a passing grade, you must satisfactorily complete the tasks listed below.

1. Attend class and conscientiously participate in class activities and discussions.
2. Complete the scheduled reading assignments before they are discussed in class.
3. Write five 600-word essays for 50 percent of your grade.
4. Complete various assignments including a journal, in-class writing assignments, revisions, quizzes, group projects, homework, grammar exercises, etc. for 25 percent.
5. Read a novel or a collection of poems or stories selected from the suggested reading list and satisfactorily write a final essay about the work for 25 percent of your grade. You must pass the in-class final with a C to pass the class.
6. Purchase a file folder in which to turn in essays.

ATTENDANCE POLICY: Undocumented 4–5 absences, one grade reduction; 6+ automatic failure.

ESSAY FORMAT: Some of your essays will be typewritten. These should be typewritten on standard 8 1/2-by-11-inch white paper. Leave margins of 1 inch and always double space. Unless otherwise indicated, essays should be 600 words in length. They must be turned in on due dates, stapled and without a cover page.

ESSAY STYLE: We will practice what rhetoricians call the plain style, which means you ought to aim for the simplest, most direct, unadorned, and unaffected style possible. As a guide, you should think in terms of sentences averaging twenty words or so, combining shorter or longer ones from time to time. Your paragraphs should have a clear topic, with every subsequent sentence growing naturally from your intentions regarding its development. These paragraphs should average five to eight sentences and should be coherent with a clear structured plan. Always aim for clarity of expression, without jargon, cliches, or slang.

Week 1: Introductions

Reading Assignment:
Introduction; from Writing about Literature: Introduction, Representing the Literary Text, and Replying to the Text

Written Assignment: Diagnostic sample

Week 2: Discussion of Planning and Drafting; The Thesis

Reading Assignment:
Chapter 1
Anthony, *Sandra Street*
Howard, *Escape the Ghettos of New York*
Cervantes, *Freeway 280*
Revard, *Driving in Oklahoma*

Written Assignment: Journal entry from Personal Essays and Narrative at the end of chapter 1

Week 3: Discussion of Paragraphing

Reading Assignment:
Tan, *A Pair of Tickets*
Muñoz, *Returning*
Ali *Postcard from Kashmir*
Sheffield, *The "Gentle Wholeness" of Home*

Written Assignment: Revision of diagnostic for a grade

Week 4: Discussion of Description and Setting

Reading Assignment:
Afterword in chapter 1
Chapter 2
Woo, *Letter to Ma* and student response

Written Assignment: Journal entry from Personal Essays and Narratives at the end of chapter 2

Week 5: Discussion of Sentences and Revisions

Reading Assignment:
from Writing about the Reading (continue with Explaining the Text)
Lee, *The Gift*
Muñoz, *Little Sister Born in This Land*
Ortiz, *My Father's Song*
Ortiz, *Speaking*
Johnson, *The Limitless Heart*

Written Assignment: Personal essay due, to be graded

Week 6: Discussion of Organization and Language

Reading Assignment:
Chapter 3

Kingston, *No Name Woman*
Angelou, *Africa*
Young Bear, *in the first place of my life*

Written Assignment: Journal entry from Personal Essays and Narratives at the end of chapter 3

Week 7: Discussion of Sentence Variety and Diction

Reading Assignment:
Afterword in chapter 3
Engle, *Digging for Roots*
Cofer, *More Room*

Written Assignment: Narration essay due, to be graded

Week 8: Discussion of Guidelines for Cause and Effect

Reading Assignment:
Chapter 4
Rodriguez, *Aria: A Memoir of a Bilingual Childhood*
Lee, *Persimmons*
Pau-Llosa, *Foreign Language*

Written Assignment: Journal entry from Imitations and Parodies at the end of chapter 4

Week 9: Introduce Research Assignment on Independent Reading

Reading Assignment:
Naylor, *"Mommy, What Does 'Nigger' Mean?"*
Chelminski, *Next to Brzezinski, Chelminski's a Cinch*
Afterword in chapter 4

Written Assignment: Cause and effect essay due, to be graded

Week 10: Discussion of Guidelines for Comparison and Contrast

Reading Assignment:
Chapter 5
Bisoondath, *There Are a Lot of Ways to Die*
Shaheen, *The Media's Image of Arabs*
Birtha, *Johnnieruth*

Written Assignment: Journal entry from Comparison and Contrast at the end of chapter 5

Week 11: Discussion of Definition and Group Work

Reading Assignments:
Chapter 6
Seilsopour, *I Forgot the Words to the National Anthem*
Thomas, *Next Life, I'll Be White*
Afterword in chapter 6

Written Assignment: Essay on independent reading due (P/F)

Week 12: Continue Group Work

Reading Assignment:
Chapter 7
Alvarez, *Hold the Mayonnaise*
Soto, *Like Mexicans*
Minton, *Is It Okay to Date Someone of Another Race?*

Written Assignment: Group work due

Week 13: Discussion of Revision and Research

Reading Assignment:
Chapter 8
Mukherjee, *Hindus*
Student essay
Monteagudo, *Miami, Florida*

Written Assignment: Journal entry from Analytical Papers at the end of chapter 8

Week 14: Discussion of Documentation

Reading Assignment:
Chapter 9
Mori, *Abalone, Abalone, Abalone*
Begay, *Beyond Sacred Mountains*

Written Assignment: Thesis and outline for final essay due

Week 15: Final Discussions

Reading Assignment:
King, *I Have a Dream*

Written Assignment: Final research essay due

Sample Ten-Week Course Syllabus

Week 1: Introductions and Diagnostic Sample and Revision
Reading Assignment: Introduction and Writing about Literature
Written Assignment: Revision of diagnostic sample

Week 2: Discussion of Planning, Drafting, and Paragraphing
Reading Assignment:
Anthony, *Sandra Street*
Tan, *A Pair of Tickets*
Howard, *Escape the Ghettos of New York*
Cervantes, *Freeway 280*
Revard, *Driving in Oklahoma*
Sheffield, *The "Gentle Wholeness" of Home*
Written Assignment: Journal entry from Personal Essays and Narratives at the end of chapter 1

Week 3: Discussion of Description and Setting
Reading Assignment: Afterword in chapter 1
Woo, *Letter to Ma* and student response
Lee, *The Gift*
Muñoz, *Little Sister Born in This Land*
Ortiz, *My Father's Song*
Johnson, *The Limitless Heart*
Written Assignment: Description essay due, to be graded

Week 4: Discussion of Language and Sentence Structure
Reading Assignment:
Kingston, *No Name Woman*
Angelou, *Africa*
Young Bear, *in the first place of my life*
Engle, *Digging for Roots*
Written Assignment: Journal entry from Imitations and Parodies at the end of chapter 3

Week 5: Discussion of Organization and Point of View
Reading Assignment:
Cofer, *More Room*
Rodriguez, *Aria: A Memoir of a Bilingual Childhood*
Lee, *Persimmons*
Written Assignment: Narration essay due, to be graded

Week 6: Discussion of Guidelines for Cause and Effect
Reading Assignment:
Pau-Llosa, *Foreign Language*
Naylor, *"Mommy, What Does 'Nigger' Mean?"*
Chelminski, *Next to Brzezinski, Chelminski's a Cinch*
Afterword in chapter 4
Written Assignment: Essay on independent reading due (P/F)

Week 7: Introduction of Research Essay and Discussion of Definition
Reading Assignment:
Bisoondath, *There Are a Lot of Ways to Die*
Shaheen, *The Media's Image of Arabs*
Birtha, *Johnnieruth*
Written Assignment: Cause and effect essay due, to be graded

Week 8: Discussion of Guidelines for Comparison and Contrast
Reading Assignment:
Scilsopour, *I Forgot the Words to the National Anthem*
Thomas, *Next Life, I'll Be White*
Soto, *Like Mexicans*
Alvarez, *Hold the Mayonnaise*
Written Assignment: Comparison and contrast essay due

Week 9: Discussion of Revision and Documentation
Reading Assignment:
Mukherjee, *Hindus*
Student essay
Monteagudo, *Miami, Florida*
Mori, *Abalone, Abalone, Abalone*
Written Assignment: Thesis and Outline for final essay due

Week 10: Final Discussions
Reading Assignment:
Begay, *Beyond Sacred Mountains*
King, *I Have a Dream*
Written Assignment: Final research essay due

List of Suggested Readings for Final Research Essays

(Students may read other novels or collections of poems or stories by authors included in the anthology with approval from the instructor.)

Adrienne Rich, *Diving into the Wreck* (poetry)
Gish Jen, *A Typical American* (fiction)
Amy Tan, *The Kitchen God's Wife* (fiction)
Tobias Wolff, *This Boy's Life: A Memoir* (nonfiction)
Li-Young Lee, *The City in Which I Love You* (poetry)
Gary Soto, *Who Will Know Us? New Poems* (poetry)
Gustavo Perez Firmat, *Do the Americas Have a Common Literature*
      (nonfiction)
Alice Walker, *The Color Purple* (fiction)
Maxine Hong Kingston, *The Woman Warrior* (fiction)
Rudolfo Anaya, *Bless Me Ultima* (fiction)
Richard Rodriguez, *Hunger of Memory* or *Days of Obligation* (nonfiction)
Yvonne Sapia, *Valentino's Hair* (poetry)
Gloria Naylor, *Women of Brewster Place* (fiction)
Maya Angelou, *I Know Why the Caged Bird Sings* (fiction)
Sandra Cisneros, *The House on Mango Street* (fiction)
Margarita Engle, *Singing of Cuba* (fiction)
Toni Morrison, *Beloved* or *Jazz* or *Song of Solomon* (fiction)
Judith Ortiz Cofer, *Silent Dancing: A Partial Remembrance of a*
      Puerto Rican Childhood (poetry and nonfiction)
Carolina Hospital, *Cuban American Writers: Los Atrevidos*
      (poetry and fiction)
Luise Erdrich, *Love Medicine* (fiction)
Ricardo Pau-Llosa, *Cuba* (poetry)
Julia Alvarez, *How the Garcia Girls Lost their Accents* (fiction)
Michael Anthony, *Green Days by the River* (fiction)
Cathy Song, *Sister Stew: Fiction and Poetry by Women*
Lorna Dee Cervantes, *Emplumada* (poetry)
Simon Ortiz, *Earth Power: Short Fiction in Native American Literature*
Helena Maria Viramontes, *Moths and Other Stories* (fiction)
Pablo Medina, *Exiled Memories: A Cuban Childhood* (nonfiction)
Armando Valladares, *Against All Odds* (Prison Memoirs nonfiction)
Oscar Hijuelos, *Our House in the Last World* (fiction)
Roberto Fernandez, *Raining Backwards* (fiction)

This section is designed to help you build a syllabus more specific to your needs by providing lists of selections grouped by the ethnicity of the author, or by an issue that relates to a specific group, even if the author is not of that cultural group. For example, Sharon Olds's poem, "On the Subway," is written in the voice of a Caucasian woman who is thinking about an African-American boy on the subway. Its subject matter prompted us to include it in the African-American writers and/ or cultural issues list. These groupings are not meant to be exhaustive; you may find other selections that fit.

The groupings are African-American writers and/or cultural issues, Caribbean writers and/or cultural issues, Asian-American writers and/or cultural issues, Middle-Eastern writers and/or cultural issues, Native-American writers and/or cultural issues, Latino writers and/or cultural issues, and selections that address gender, gay, or lesbian issues.

Selections by African-American writers and/or about African or African-American culture and issues:

Chapter 1
Vanessa Howard, Escape the Ghettos of New York (poem)
Lucille Clifton, in the inner city (poem)
Elise Sprunt Sheffield, The "Gentle Wholeness" of Home (essay)

Chapter 2
John Edgar Wideman, Little Brother (story)
Sherley Williams, Say Hello to John (poem)
Naomi Long Madgett, Offspring (poem)

Chapter 3
Maya Angelou, Africa (poem)

Chapter 4
James Alan McPherson, I Am an American (story)
Rita Dove, Parsley (poem)
Derek Walcott, A Far Cry from Africa (poem)
Gloria Naylor, "Mommy, What Does 'Nigger' Mean?" (essay)

Chapter 5
Becky Birtha, Johnnieruth (story)
Sharon Olds, On the Subway (poem)
Etheridge Knight, Hard Rock Returns to Prison from the Hospital for the Criminal Insane (poem)
Maya Angelou, My Brother Bailey and Kay Francis (autobiographical narrative)

Chapter 6
Toni Morrison, "Recitatif" (story)
August Wilson, Fences (play)
Laurence Thomas, Next Life, I'll Be White (essay)

Chapter 7
Tobias Wolff, Say Yes (story)

Lynn Nelson, Sequence (poem)
Yusef Komunyakaa, Tu Do Street (poem)
Alice Childress, Wedding Band (play)
Lynn Minton, Is It Okay to Date Someone of Another Race? (interview)
Robert Anthony Watts, Not Black, Not White, but Biracial (essay)

Chapter 8
Toni Cade Bambara, The Lesson (story)
Joan Murray, Coming of Age on the Harlem (poem)
Mari Evans, The Friday Ladies of the Pay Envelope (poem)

Chapter 9
Ishmael Reed, I Am a Cowboy in the Boat of Ra (poem)
Alice Walker, Revolutionary Petunias (poem)
Martin Luther King, Jr., I Have a Dream (speech)

Selections by Caribbean writers and/or about Caribbean culture and issues:

Chapter 1
Michael Anthony, Sandra Street (story)
Audre Lorde, Home (poem)

Chapter 3
Yvonne Sapia, Grandmother, a Caribbean Indian, Described by My Father
(poem)
Dennis Scott, Grampa (poem)

Chapter 4
Derek Walcott, A Far Cry from Africa (poem)

Chapter 5
Neil Bissoondath, There Are a Lot of Ways to Die (story)
Grace Nichols, We New World Blacks (poem)

Chapter 6
Madeline Coopsammy, In the Dungeon of My Skin (poem)
Michelle Cliff, If I Could Write This in Fire I Would Write This in Fire
(essay)

Chapter 7
Elizabeth Alexander, West Indian Primer (poem)

Chapter 9
Olive Senior, Ancestral Poem (poem)

Selections by Asian-American writers and/or about Asian culture and issues. Includes writers of Filipino and Indian descent:

Chapter 1
Amy Tan, A Pair of Tickets (story)
Luis Calbaquinto, Hometown (poem)
Agha Shahid Ali, Postcard from Kashmir (poem)
Wakako Yamauchi, And the Soul Shall Dance (play)
Bao Gia Tran, My Home (student poem)

Chapter 2
Cynthia Kadohata, Charlie-O (story)
Eric Chock, Chinese Fireworks Banned in Hawaii (poem)
Li-Young Lee, The Gift (poem)
Merle Woo, Letter to Ma (essay)
Marie G. Lee, My Two Dads (essay)

Chapter 3
Maxine Hong Kingston, No Name Woman (story)
David Mura, Listening (poem)
Agha Shahid Ali, Snowmen (poem)
Virginia Cerenio, [we who carry the endless seasons] (poem)
Gail Y. Miyasaki, Obachan (essay)

Chapter 4
James Alan McPherson, I Am an American (story)
G. S. Sharat Chandra, Still Kicking in America (poem)
Li-Young Lee, Persimmons (poem)
Israel Horovitz, The Indian Wants the Bronx (play)

Chapter 5
Margaret Atwood, The Man from Mars (story)
Mitsuye Yamada, Looking Out (poem)
James Fallows, The Japanese Are Different from You and Me (essay)
Mark Salzman, Teacher Wei

Chapter 6
Cathy Song, Lost Sister (poem)
Dwight Okita, In Response to Executive Order 9066: ALL AMERICANS OF JAPANESE DESCENT MUST REPORT TO RELOCATION CENTERS (poem)

Chapter 7
Robbie Clipper Sethi, Grace (story)

Juliet Kono, Sashimi (poem)
Yusef Komunyakaa, Tu Do Street (poem)
Cyn. Zarco, Flipochinos (poem)
Gary Soto, Like Mexicans (essay)
Juli Nishimuta, A Lavender Life (student poem)

Chapter 8
Gish Jen, In the American Society (story)
Bharati Mukherjee, Hindus (story)
Mitsuye Yamada, The Question of Loyalty (poem)
Lee Ki Chuck, From Korea to Heaven County (interview)

Chapter 9
Toshio Mori, Abalone, Abalone, Abalone (story)
Stephen Shu-Ning Liu, My Father's Martial Art (poem)
Cathy Song, Heaven (poem)
Walter K. Lew, Leaving Seoul: 1953 (poem)

Selections by writers from the Middle East writing about Arab, Israeli, or Jewish issues:

Chapter 1
Edward Said, Reflections on Exile (essay)

Chapter 3
Muriel Rukeyser, To Be a Jew in the Twentieth Century (from *Letter to the Front*) (poem)
Max Apple, Trotsky's Bar Mitzvah

Chapter 5
Jack G. Shaheen, The Media's Image of Arabs (essay)

Chapter 6
James Seilsopour, I Forgot the Words to the National Anthem (essay)

Chapter 8
Gregory Orfalea, Arab and Jew in Alaska (poem)
Adrienne Rich, If Not with Others, How? (1985) (speech)

Selections by Latino writers and/or about Latino culture and issues:

Chapter 1
Richard Dokey, Sánchez (story)

Lorna Dee Cervantes, Freeway 280 (poem)
Elías Miguel Muñoz, Returning (poem)
Elena Padilla, Migrants: Transients or Settlers? (essay)

Chapter 2
Simon J. Ortiz, My Father's Song (poem)
Jimmy Santiago Baca, Ancestor (poem)
Elías Miguel Muñoz, Little Sister Born in This Land (poem)
Simon J. Ortiz, Speaking (poem)

Chapter 3
Lorna Dee Cervantes, Heritage (poem)
Pat Mora, Borders (poem)
Yvonne Sapia, Grandmother, a Caribbean Indian, Described by My Father (poem)
Alberto Alvaro Ríos, Mi Abuelo (poem)
Magarita M. Engle, Digging for Roots (essay)
Judith Ortiz Cofer, More Room (essay)

Chapter 4
Hugo Martinez-Serros, "Learn! Learn!" (story)
Gustavo Perez-Firmat, Limen (poem)
Lorna Dee Cervantes, Refugee Ship (poem)
Ricardo Pau-Llosa, Foreign Language (poem)
Richard Rodriguez, Aria: A Memoir of a Bilingual Childhood (essay)

Chapter 5
Marcela Christine Lucero-Trujillo, Roseville, Minn., U.S.A. (poem)

Chapter 6
Pat Mora, Sonrisas (poem)
Ricardo Pau-Llosa, Sorting Metaphors (poem)

Chapter 7
Sandra Cisneros, Bread (story)
Gary Soto, Like Mexicans (essay)
Julia Alvarez, Hold the Mayonnaise (essay)
Lynn Minton, Is It Okay to Date Someone of Another Race? (interview)

Chapter 8
Juan Felipe Herrera, Revolution Skyscraper (poem)
Pat Mora, Immigrants (poem)
Richard Olivas, [I'm sitting in my history class] (poem)
Jimmy Santiago Baca, So Mexicans Are Taking Jobs from Americans (poem)
Jesse G. Monteagudo, Miami, Florida (essay)

Chapter 9
Helena Maria Viramontes, The Moths (story)
Pat Mora, Gentle Communion (poem)
Rafael Jesús González, Sestina: Santa Prisca (poem)
Estela Portillo, The Day of the Swallows (play)

Selections by Native North American writers and/or about Native North American culture and issues:

Chapter 1
Maurice Kenny, Going Home (poem)
Carter Revard, Driving in Oklahoma (poem)

Chapter 3
Leslie Marmon Silko, Private Property (story)
Linda Hogan, Heritage (poem)
Ray A. Young Bear, in the first place of my life (poem)

Chapter 4
Salli Benedict, Tahotahontanekentseratkerontakwenhakie (story)
Louise Erdrich, Jacklight (poem)
Nora Dauenhauer, Tlingit Concrete Poem (poem)
Linda Hogan, Song for My Name (poem)

Chapter 5
Leslie Marmon Silko, [Long Time Ago] (poem)
Carter Revard, Discovery of the New World (poem)

Chapter 6
Wayne D. Johnson, What Happened to Red Deer (story)
nila northSun, up & out (poem)
R. T. Smith, Red Anger (poem)

Chapter 7
Paul Gunn Allen, Pocahontas to Her English Husband, John Rolfe (poem)
Wendy Rose, Julia (poem)
Gogisgi, Song of the Breed (poem)
Joseph Bruchac, Ellis Island (poem)
Lynn Minton, Is It Okay to Date Someone of Another Race? (interview)

Chapter 8
Linda Hogan, Black Hills Survival Gathering, 1980 (poem)

Chapter 9
Louise Erdrich, Fleur (story)
N. Scott Momaday, The Eagle-Feather Fan (poem)
Leonard Begay, Beyond the Sacred Mountains (essay)

Selections that address gender, gay, or lesbian issues:

Chapter 1
Audre Lorde, Home (poem)
Elena Padilla, Migrants: Transients or Settlers? (essay)

Chapter 2
Tony Ardizzone, My Mother's Stories (story)
Cynthia Kadohata, Charlie-O (story)
Sherley Williams, Say Hello to John (poem)
Merle Woo, Letter to Ma (essay)
Fenton Johnson, The Limitless Heart (essay)

Chapter 3
Maxine Hong Kingston, No Name Woman (story)
Virginia Cerenio, [we who carry the endless seasons] (poem)
Yvonne Sapia, Grandmother, a Caribbean Indian, Described by My Father
(poem)
Judith Ortiz Cofer, More Room (essay)

Chapter 5
Margaret Atwood, The Man from Mars (story)
Becky Birtha, Johnnieruth (story)
Perry Brass, I Think the New Teacher's a Queer (poem)
Sharon Olds, On the Subway (poem)

Chapter 6
David Leavitt, A Place I've Never Been (story)
Cathy Song, Lost Sister (poem)
Rita Mae Brown, Sappho's Reply (poem)
Laurence Thomas, Next Life, I'll Be White (essay)
Michelle Cliff, If I Could Write This in Fire I Would Write This in Fire
(essay)

Chapter 7
Sandra Cisneros, Bread (story)
Tobias Wolff, Say Yes (story)
Robbie Clipper Sethxi, Grace (story)
Paula Gunn Allen, Pocahontas to Her English Husband, John Rolfe (poem)

Wendy Rose, Julia (poem)
Lynn Nelson, Sequence (poem)
Alice Bloch, Six Years (poem)
Michael Lassell, How to Watch Your Brother Die (poem)
Alice Childress, Wedding Band (play)
Lynn Minton, Is It Okay to Date Someone of Another Race? (interview)

Chapter 8
Joan Murray, Coming of Age on the Harlem (poem)
Fran Winant, Christopher St. Liberation Day, June 28, 1970 (poem)
Jesse G. Monteagudo, Miami, Florida (essay)
Adrienne Rich, If Not with Others, How? (1985) (essay)

Chapter 9
Louise Erdrich, Fleur (story)

SELECTED BIBLIOGRAPHIES

Note: Many of the biographical sketches which precede each piece include a complete list of publications for the author. They are not repeated here.

Paula Gunn Allen
Poetry
The Blind Lion (1974)
Coyote's Daylight Trip (1981)
A Cannon Between My Knees (1981)

Nonfiction
Studies in American Indian Literature: Critical Essays and Course Designs (1983)

Maya Angelou
Autobiography
I Know Why the Caged Bird Sings (1970)
Gather Together in My Name (1974)
Singin' and Swingin' and Gettin' Merry Like Christmas (1976)
The Heart of a Woman (1981)
All God's Children Need Traveling Shoes (1986)
Wouldn't Take Nothin' for My Journey Now (1993)

Poetry
Just Give Me a Cool Drink of Water 'fore I Diiie (1971)
Oh Pray My Wings Are Gonna Fit Me Well (1975)
And Still I Rise (1978)
Shaker, Why Don't You Sing? (1983)
Now Sheba Sings the Song (1987)
I Shall Not be Moved (1990)
On the Pulse of Morning: The Inaugural Poem (1992)

Drama
Cabaret for Freedom (1960)

The Least of These (1966)
Ajax (adaptation of Sophocles's Ajax) (1974)
And Still I Rise (1976)
Moon on a Rainbow Shawl (1988)

Screenplays
Blacks, Blues, Black (1968)
Georgia, Georgia (1972)
All Day Long (1974)

Children's books
Mrs. Flowers: A Moment of Friendship (1986)

Michael Anthony
Fiction
The Games Were Coming (1963)
The Year in San Fernando (1965)
Green Days by the River (1967)
Cricket in the Road (1973)
Sandra Street and Other Stories (1973)
King of Masquerade (1974)
Streets of Conflict (1976)
Folk Talkes and Fantasies (1976)
All That Glitters (1982)
Bright Road to El Dorado (1982)
A Better and Brighter Day (1987)

Nonfiction
Glimpses of Trinidad and Tobago (1974)
Profile Trinidad: A Historical Survey from the Discovery to 1900 (1975)
David Frost Introduces Trinidad and Tobago (editor, with Andrew Carr) (1975)
The Making of the Port of Spain 1757-1939 (1978)
Port of Spain in a World at War (1983)
First in Trinidad (1985)
Heroes of the People of Trinidad and Tobago (1986)
Towns and Villages of Trinidad and Tobago (1988)
Parade of the Carnivals of Trinidad, 1839-1989 (1989)

Margaret Atwood
Novels
The Edible Woman (1969)

Surfacing (1972)
Lady Oracle (1976)
Life Before Man (1979)
Bodily Harm (1981)
The Handmaid's Tale (1985)
Cat's Eye (1988)
The Robber Bride (1993)

Short fiction
Dancing Girls (1977)
Encounters with the Elephant Man (1982)
Bluebeard's Egg (1983)
Murder in the Dark (1983)
Unearthing Suite (1983)
Wilderness Tips (1991)
Good Bones (1992)

Poetry
Double Persephone (1961)
The Circle Game (1966)
The Animals in That Country (1968)
Poems for Voices (1970)
The Journals of Susanna Moodie (1970)
Procedures for Underground (1970)
Power Politics (1971)
You Are Happy (1974)
Selected Poetry (1976)
Two-Headed Poems (1978)
True Stories (1981)
Interlunar (1984)
Selected Poems II (1986)

Nonfiction
Survival: A Thematic Guide to Canadian Literature (1972)
Second Words: Selected Critical Prose (1982)

Children's books
Up in the Tree (1978)
Anna's Pet (1980)
For the Birds (1990)

Toni Cade Bambara
Fiction
Gorilla, My Love (1981)

Salt Eaters (1981)
The Sea Birds Are Still Alive (1982)

Nonfiction
Southern Black Utterances Today (editor, with Leah Wise) (1975)

Joseph Bruchac
Fiction
The Last Stop (1974)
There are No Trees in Prison (1978)
The Good Message of Handsome Lake (1979)
The Light from Another Country: Poetry from American Prisons (1984)
Iroquois Stories: Heroes & Heroines (1985)
The Wind Eagle and Other Abenaki Folk Stories (1985)
North Country: Writing from the Upper Hudson Valley and the Adirondacks (editor, with others) (1986)
New Voices from the Longhouse: An Anothology of Modern Iroquois Literature (1988)
Keepers of the Earth: Native American Stories and Environmental Activities for Children (with Michael Caduto) (1988)
The Faithful Hunter: Abenaki Stories (1989)
The Return of the Sun: Native American Tales from the Northeast Woodlands (1989)
Survival This Way: Interviews with American Indian Poets (1990)
Keepers of the Animals: Native American Stories and Wildlife Activities (with Michael Caduto) (1991)
Native American Stories (1991)
Raven Tells Stories: An Anthology of Alaska Native Writing (1991)
Thirteen Moons on Turtle's Back: A Native American Year of Moons (editor, with Jonathan London) (1992)
Turtle Meat & Other Stories (1992)
Native American Animal Stories (1992)
Dawn Land (1993)
Fox Song (1993)
The First Strawberries: A Cherokee Story (retold) (1993)
Flying with Eagle, Racing the Great Bear: Stories from Native America (as told by Bruchac) (1993)

Virginia Cerenio
Fiction
Trespassing Innocence (1989)

Alice Childress
Novels
Like One of the Family: Conversations from a Domestic's Life (1956)
Black Scenes (editor) (1971)
A Hero Ain't Nothing But a Sandwich (1973)
A Short Walk (1979)
Rainbow Jordan (1981)
Many Closets (1987)
Those Other People (1989)

Drama and short fiction
Florence (1949)
Just a Little Simple (1950)
Gold Through the Trees (1952)
Trouble in Mind (1955)
Wedding Band (1966)
The World on a Hill (1968)
Wine in the Wilderness (1969)
String (1969)
Martin Luther King at Montgomery, Alabama (1969)
A Man Bearing a Pitcher (1969)
Young Martin Luther King (1969-71)
Mojo: A Black Love Story (1970)
The African Garden (1971)
When the Rattlesnake Sounds (1975)
Let's Hear it for the Queen (1976)
Sea Island Song (1979)
Gullah (1984)
Moms (1986)

Screenplays
A Hero Ain't Nothing But a Sandwich (1978)

Lucille Clifton
Poetry
Good Times: Poems (1969)
Good News about the Earth (1972)
An Ordinary Woman (1974)
Two-Headed Woman (1980)
Good Woman: Poems and a Memoir 1969-1980 (1987)
Next: New Poems (1987)
Ten Oxherding Pictures (1988)
Quilting Poems 1987-1990 (1991)

Nonfiction
Generations: A Memoir (1976)

Children's books
The Black BCs (1970)
Some of the Days of Everett Anderson (1970)
Everett Anderson's Christmas Coming (1971)
Everett Anderson's Year (1971)
All Us Come Cross the Water 1973
The Boy Who Didn't Believe in Spring 1973
Don't You Remember? (1973)
Good, Says Jerome (1973)
Three Wishes (1974)
My Brother Fine with Me (1975)
Everett Anderson's Friend (1976)
Amifika (1977)
Everett Anderson's 1-2-3 (1977)
Everett Anderson's Nine Month Long (1978)
The Lucky Stone (1986)
My Friend Jacob (1980)
Sonora Beautiful (1981)
Edward Anderson's Goodbye (1988)

Rita Dove
Fiction
Through the Ivory Gate (novel) (1992)
Fifth Sunday (1985)

Poetry
The Yellow House on the Corner (1980)
Museum (1983)
Thomas and Beulah (1986)
Grace Notes (1989)

Verse drama
The Darker Face of the Earth (1994)

Louise Erdrich
Fiction
Love Medicine (1984)
The Beet Queen (1986)
Tracks (1988)
The Crown of Columbus (with husband, Michael Dorris) (1992)

Poetry
Jacklight (1984)
Baptism of Desire (1989)

Essays
Route Two and Back (with husband, Michael Dorris) (1991)

Linda Hogan
Poetry
Seeing Through the Sun (1985)
Savings (1988)
Mean Spirit (1990)
Red Clay (1991)
The Book of Medicines (1993)
The Native Americans: Indian Country (with N. Scott Momaday)
(1993)

Israel Horovitz
Fiction
Cuppela (1973)
Nobody Loves Me (1975)

Drama
The Comeback (1958)
The Death of Bernard the Believer (1960)
This Play is About Me (1961)
The Hanging of Emanuel (1962)
Jump (1962)
Hop and Skip (1963)
The Killer Dove (1963)
The Indian Wants the Bronx (1964-66)
It's Called the Sugar Plum (1965)
Line (1967)
Rats (1967)
The Honest-to-God Schnozzola (1968)
Morning (or Chiaroscuro) (1968)
The World's Greatest Play (1968)
First Season (collection of plays) (1968)
Leader (1969)
Morning, Noon and Night (with others) (1969)
Acrobats (1971)
Play for Germs (TV) (1972)

Dr. Hero (1972)
Shooting Gallery (1972)
The Primary English Class (1975)
Uncle Snake (1975)
The Bottom (1975-76)
The Wakefield Plays (seven cycle play including Hopscotch, The 75th, Alfred the Great, Our, Father's, Failing, Alfred Dies, Stage Directions, and Spared (1977-79)
Mackeral (1977)
The Former One-On-One Basketball Champion (1977)
Saulte Ste. Marie Trilogy
Today, I Am a Fountain Pen (1977)
The Chopin Playoffs (1978)
A Rosen By Any Other Name (1979)
The Good Parts (1979)
The Great Labor Classic (1979)
Sunday Runners in the Rain (1979-80)
Park Your Car in Harvard Yard (1980-83)
Firebird at Dogtown (1984-85)
Henry Lumper (1984-87)
Year of the Duck (1984-87)
North Shore Fish (1985-87)
The Widow's Blind Date (1985-88)
Faith (1988)
Strong-Man's Weak Child (1988-90)
Fighting Over Beverly (1988-93)
Unexpected Tenderness (1993)

Screenplays
The Deuce (or The Glouster Waterfront)
Payofski's Discovery
The Pan
Barbers in Love
Letters to Iris
Strong-Man
The Strawberry Statement
Believe in Me
Author! Author!
A Man in Love
Damon

Maurice Kenny
Fiction
Dead Letters Sent (1959)
Blackrobe (1982)
The Mama Poems (1984)
Between Two Rivers: Selected Poems (1987)
Rain and Other Fictions (1990)
Tekonwatonti: Molly Brant (1992)
Wounds Beneath the Flesh (editor) (1986)

Maxine Hong Kingston
Fiction
The Woman Warrior (1976)
China Men (1980)
Hawaii: One Summer (1987)
Through the Black Curtain (1988)
Tripmaster Monkey: His Fake Book (1989)

Etheridge Knight
Poetry
Black Voices from Prison (1971)
The Essential Etheridge Knight (1986)

Tato Laviera
Poetry
La Carreta Made a U-Turn (1979)
Enclave (1981)
AmeRican (1985)
Mainstream Ethics (1989)
Continental (1991)

Drama
Pinones (1989)
La Chefa (1981)
Becoming Garcia (1984)
Here We Come (1985)
Am e Rican (1986)
Base of Soul in Heaven's Cafe (1988)

Naomi Long Madgett
Poetry
Songs to a Phantom Nightingale (1941)

252 / Instructor's Guide

One and Many (1956)
Star by Star (1965)
Pink Ladies in the Afternoon: New Poems, 1965-1971 (1972)
Exits and Entrances: New Poems (1978)
Phantom Nightingale: Juvenilia (1981)
Octavia and Other Poems (1988)
Remembrances of Spring: Collected Early Poems (1993)

Nonfiction
Success in Language and Literature B (with Ethel Tincher and Henry
B. Maloney) (1967)
Deep Rivers, A Portfolio: Twenty contemporary Black American Poets
(1978)
A Student's Guide to Creative Writing (1980)
A Milestone Sampler: 15th Anniversary Anthology (editor) (1988)
Adam of Ife: Black Women in Praise of Black Men (1992)

Pat Mora
Children's books
A Birthday Basket for Tia (1992)
Pablo's Tree (1993)
Tomas and the Library Lady (1993)

Bharati Mukherjee
Novels
The Tiger's Daughter (1972)
Wife (1975)
Jasmine (1989)
The Holder of the World (1993)

Short fiction
Darkness (1985)
The Middleman and Other Stories (1988)

Nonfiction
Days and Nights in Calcutta (with Clark Blaise) (1977)
Kautilay's Concept of Diplomacy: A New Interpretation (1976)
The Sorrow and the Terror: The Haunting Legacy of the Air India
Tragedy (with Clark Blaise) (1987)
Political Culture and Leadership in India (1991)
Regionalism in Indian Perspective (1992)

Sharon Olds
Poetry
The Matter of This World (1987)
The Sign of Saturn (1991)

Simon J. Ortiz
Fiction
Blue and Red (1981)
The Importance of Childhood (1982)
The People Shall Continue (1988)
Woven Stone (1992)

Adrienne Rich
Fiction
The Will to Change, Poems 1968-1970 (1971)
Diving into the Wreck (1973)
Of Woman Born (1976, 1986)
On Lies, Secrets, and Silence: Selected Prose, 1966-1978 (1980)
A Wild Patience Has Taken Me This Far: Poems 1978-1981 (1981)
Blood, Bread, and Poetry: Selected Prose 1979-1985 (1986)
Your Native Land, Your Life: Poems (1986)
Time's Power: Poems 1985-1988 (1989)
An Atlas of the Difficult World: Poems 1988-1991 (1991)
Adrienne Rich's Poetry and Prose (Norton Critical Edition) (1993)
Collected Early Poems 1950-1970 (1993)
The Dream of a Common Language: Poems 1974-1977 (1993)
The Fact of a Doorframe: Poems 1950-1984 (1984, 1993)
What Is Found There: Notebooks on Poetry and Politics (1993)

Muriel Rukeyser
Fiction
Willard Girls (1942)
The Life of Poetry (1949)
One Life (poetry and prose) (1957)
The Orgy (1965)
The Traces of Thomas Hariot (1971)
The Muriel Rukeyser Reader (1994)

Poetry
Theory of Flight (1935)
U.S. 1 (1938)
A Turning Wind (1930)

Wake Island (1942)
Beast in View (1944)
The Green Wave (1948)
Elegies (1949)
Orpheus (1949)
Selected Poems (1951)
Body of Waking (1958)
Waterlily Fire: Poems 1935-1962 (1962)
The Outer Banks (1967)
The Speed of Darkness (1968)
29 Poems (1972)
Breaking Open (1973)
The Gates (1976)
The Collected Poems of Muriel Rukeyser (1978)

Drama
The Middle of the Air (1945)
The Colors of the Day (1961)
Houdini (1973)

Screenplays
All the Same Way Home (1958)

Translations
Octavio Paz: Selected Poems and Sunstone (1963)
Gunnar Ekel"f: Selected Poems (with Leif Sj"berg) (1967)

Children's books
Come Back, Paul (1955)
I Go Out (1961)
Bubbles (1967)
Mazes (1970)
Uncle Eddie's Mustache (poems for children by Bertolt Brecht, translated by Muriel Rukeyser) (1974)

Leslie Marmon Silko
Fiction
Laguna Woman: Poems (1974)
Ceremony (novel) (1977)
Storyteller (poetry and short fiction) (1981)
With the Delicacy and Strength of Lace: Letters (1986)
Almanac of the Dead (1991)

R. T. Smith
Fiction
Banish Misfortune (1988)
The Cardinal Heart (1991)
From the High Dive (edited by Charles Fishman) (1983)

Gary Soto
Fiction
Entrance: Four Chicano Poets (1976)
The Elements of San Joaquin (1977)
The Tale of Sunlight (1978)
Father is a Pillow Tied to a Broom (1980)
Where Sparrows Work Hard (1981)
Black Hair (1985)
California Childhood: Recollections and Stories of the Golden State
(editor) (1988)
Who Will Know Us? (1990)
Fire in My Hands: A Book of Poems (1990)
Home Course in Religion (1991)
The Shirt (1992)
Pacific Crossing (1992)
Taking Sides (1992)
Local News (1993)
The Pool Party (1993)
Too Many Tamales (1993)
Pieces of the Heart: New Chicano Fiction (editor) (1993)

Essays
Living Up the Street: Narrative Recollection (1985)
Small Faces (1986)
Lesser Evils: Ten Quartets (1988)
A Summer Life (1990)

Childrens' books
The Cat's Meow (1987)

Derek Walcott
Poetry
Selected Poems (1964)
In a Green Night: Poems, 1948-1960 (1964)
The Castaway and Other Poems (1965)
The Gulf and Other Poems (1969)

Another Life (1973)
Sea Grapes (1976)
The Star-Apple Kingdom (1980)
The Fortunate Traveler (1982)
Midsummer (1984)
Collected Poems 1948-1984 (1986)
The Arkansas Testament (1988)
Omeros (1991)
Selected Poetry (1993)

Drama
Henry Christophe: A Chronicle (1950)
Henry Dernier (1951)
Ione (1957)
Three Plays: The Last Carnival; Beef, No Chicken; A Branch of the Blue Nile (1986)
Dream on Monkey Mountain & Other Plays (1971)
Antilles: Fragments of Epic Memory (1993)
Odyssey: A Stage Version (1993)

John Edgar Wideman
Novels
A Glance Away (1967)
Hurry Home (1970)
The Lynchers (1973)
Hiding Place (1981)
Sent for You Yesterday (1983)
Reuben (1987)
Philadelphia Fire (1990)

Short fiction
Damballah (1981)
Fever (1989)
The Stories of John Edgar Wideman (1992)

Nonfiction
Brothers and Keepers (1984)

New Worlds of Literature Student Essay Contest

Rules:
1. Essays must be written on a work included in *New Worlds of Literature*, Second Edition. Essays may be any length.
2. Each entry must be accompanied by a copy of this form, which may be photocopied.
3. Each instructor may submit two essays for each section taught.
4. Instructors may submit essays from May 1, 1994 to December 31, 1995.

Winning essays will be published in the Third Edition of *New Worlds of Literature*. An honorarium will be offered to the student winners and their sponsoring instructors.

Student Information

Name
_____

Home Address (very important for gaining permission)
_____

City   State/Prov.   Zip/PC
_____

College/University
_____

Semester student was enrolled in your course
_____

Course number   Section number
_____

Course name
_____

Instructor Information

Name
_____

Address
_____

City   State/Prov.   Zip/PC
_____

College/Univ.
_____

Telephone
_____

Send nominations to Carol Hollar-Zwick, Associate Editor
W. W. Norton & Company, 500 Fifth Avenue, New York, NY 10110.